WordPress

ABSOLUTE
BEGINNER'S
GUIDE

Tris Hussey

800 East 96th Street,
Indianapolis, Indiana 46240

WordPress Absolute Beginner's Guide

ISBN-13: 978-0-7897-5290-1

ISBN-10: 0-7897-5290-5

Library of Congress Control Number: 2014935805

Printed in the United States of America

First Printing March 2014

Trademarks

Warning and Disclaimer

Special Sales

For information about buying this title in bulk quantities, or for special sales opportunities (which may include electronic versions; custom cover designs; and content particular to your business, training goals, marketing focus, or branding interests), please contact our corporate sales department at corpsales@pearsoned.com or (800) 382-3419.

For government sales inquiries, please contact governmentsales@pearsoned.com.

For questions about sales outside the U.S., please contact international@pearsoned.com.

Associate Publisher
Greg Wiegand

Acquisitions Editor
Michelle Newcomb

Development Editor
Brandon Cackowski-Schnell

Managing Editor
Sandra Schroeder

Project Editor
Seth Kerney

Copy Editor
Barbara Hacha

Indexer
Erika Millen

Proofreader
Sarah Kearns

Technical Editor
Christian Kenyeres

Publishing Coordinator
Cindy Teeters

Book Designer
Anne Jones

Compositor
Studio Galou, LLC

Contents at a Glance

Table of Contents

About the Author

Tris Hussey was Canada's first professional blogger, and along the way he became a freelance writer, best-selling author, technologist, and lecturer. He has written several best-selling books on social media and technology, including *Create Your Own Blog* (1st and 2nd editions), *Using WordPress*, *Sams Teach Yourself Foursquare in 10 Minutes*, and *WordPress Essentials* (video). You can read Tris' posts on TrisHussey.com and other sites around the Internet.

Tris lives and works in beautiful Vancouver, British Columbia.

Dedication

For Mom.

Acknowledgments

This book couldn't have happened without the help, direction, and prodding of many, many people.

Most importantly, my beloved Sheila for supporting me and believing in me through this whole process. And putting up with a lot of days and nights with me glued to my computer.

We Want to Hear from You!

As the reader of this book, *you* are our most important critic and commentator. We value your opinion and want to know what we're doing right, what we could do better, what areas you'd like to see us publish in, and any other words of wisdom you're willing to pass our way.

You can email or write us directly to let us know what you did or didn't like about this book—as well as what we can do to make our books stronger.

Please note that we cannot help you with technical problems related to the topic of this book.

When you write, please be sure to include this book's title and author as well as your name and phone or email address. We will carefully review your comments and share them with the author and editors who worked on the book.

Email: consumer@samspublishing.com

Mail: Sams Publishing
800 East 96th Street
Indianapolis, IN 46240 USA

Reader Services

Visit our website and register this book at informit.com/register for convenient access to any updates, downloads, or errata that might be available for this book.

INTRODUCTION

Welcome to the *Absolute Beginner's Guide to WordPress*. Before we dive into the book, I want to make sure we're all on the same page about who the book is for, how it's organized, and how I deal with the inevitable updates to WordPress after this book goes to press.

Who This Book Is For

First, who is this book for? Almost everyone. I've written the book to be accessible for the novice user but helpful as a reference book for the intermediate user. Advanced users? This isn't the book for you, unless you're giving it as a gift to someone you'd like to see jump onto the WordPress bandwagon. I've been using WordPress for seven years; I've written two books on it, taught hundreds of people how to use WordPress, and given talks at WordCamps all over North America. I'm approaching this book differently than most other introduction to WordPress books. I'm looking at the process of learning about WordPress from the perspective of the average computer user who just wants to make a website or blog and wants to make sure they do it "right." I go through the steps in the order that I think make sense for people to follow.

How This Book Is Organized

All the above said, this book is written and organized to be flipped through. Think of it as a quick reference to WordPress (which makes it handy for intermediate users). Jump to the section you need right now to solve the problem at hand. So if you get through Chapter 5, "Installing WordPress Themes," and want to jump right to Chapter 7, "Setting Up Your WordPress Site the Right Way: SEO, Social Media, and More," no problem! You can circle back to "How WordPress Themes Work" (Chapter 9) and "All About Jetpack Settings" (Chapter 8) when you're ready. The book is organized like this so you can (if you want) read it start to finish, cover to cover, and have a complete understanding of WordPress. If you're already pretty familiar with WordPress and need a book to look up something quickly, that works, too.

The Only Constant Is Change...and WordPress Updates

Let's talk about WordPress updates. At the time of writing this book (fall of 2013), WordPress has just celebrated its 10th anniversary, and WordPress 3.6 has just come out. Ten years is a long time in the software world, and I can honestly say WordPress just gets better and better with each new version. Speaking of versions, I'm starting this book just after WordPress 3.6 (Oscar) has been released and expecting WordPress 3.7 to be released in October and WordPress 3.8 a couple months after that. This means that while writing this book, I'm planning for at least three versions of WordPress that will come out while this book is in production. Challenging? Yeah, you could say that. However, I am going to take the same approach here that I did with *Using WordPress*, which is to write and cover all the features and facets of WordPress as version agnostic as I can. There are some things that I don't expect to change in WordPress anytime soon, and some things I know will be changing in coming versions. By the time you read this book, chances are that there will be new versions of WordPress available, so screenshots, steps, and features may look different here versus what you're seeing in real life. Don't sweat it. Between the built-in help within WordPress, this book, and updates that I'll post on my own website (http://trishussey.com), you should be good to go.

Now that those details are out of the way, let's talk about what this book is really about: Freedom.

This book is all about learning to use one of the best (and easiest) website and blogging platforms around. About 20% of the world's websites run WordPress, and a good number of the biggest websites in the world (like CNN and The New York Times) use WordPress, making this free, open source tool a great choice for sites large and small. Most importantly, to me, WordPress represents the ability for regular people to be able to install, manage, and customize their own blogs and websites without needing professionals to help them. WordPress is about the freedom to create, build, compose, and publish to the world. You can start out completely free on WordPress.com and move all the way up to a completely customized website like the big players have, all using the same tools and software. Throughout this book, there are tips, tricks, interesting facts, techniques, and tools to help you get the most out of your WordPress-powered website.

A Note About Browsers and Such

I'm a Mac guy, so all the screenshots in the book use Chrome (or Safari) for Mac and Chrome or Safari for iOS (for iPad- and iPhone-related discussions). This *doesn't* mean that I'm ignoring all the Windows (or Linux) users out there; it just means that this is what I use, so that's what I have for examples. Great pains have been taken to double (and triple) check that what you see on a Mac screen is *pretty darn close* to what you see on a PC screen. Does this mean that there aren't going to be *slight* differences? Nope. Buttons and menus might look a little different, but that's going to be about it. Because WordPress is designed to work within a web browser, it doesn't matter what operating system (OS) you use. Whether it's on Mac, PC, or Linux, WordPress itself works the same in all three. As I mentioned previously, I've written the book to be as "future proof" as possible. The goal is that the book won't be worthless to you in six months or a year. I've written this book so that you can get years of use out of it before you think, "Wow, things are really different now."

Conventions Used in This Book

The Absolute Beginner's Guide to WordPress uses a number of conventions to provide you with special information. These include the following elements:

 TIPS   offer suggestions for making things easier or provide alternative ways to perform a particular task.

 NOTES   provide additional, more detailed information about a specific WordPress feature.

 CAUTIONS   warn you about potential problems that might occur and offer advice on how to avoid these problems.

Sidebars interspersed throughout the chapters cover things that are related to the topic at hand, but go into more detail than the flow of the chapter allows for.

IN THIS CHAPTER

- Learn about domain names
- Pick a domain name
- Choose a host for your website

1

HOW WEBSITES WORK

I know you're dying to get into the meat of learning about WordPress, but after teaching WordPress for five years, I've learned that a lot of people have some misunderstandings about how the Internet, websites, web hosts, and domain names work, so bear with me as I briefly (I promise) explain a few things about domains and web hosts. In this chapter, you'll learn about picking a domain name, choosing a host for your website, and how to get everything set up and ready to install WordPress.

All About Domain Names and DNS

What's in a name? Well, a rose by any other name would still smell as sweet, but websites without (domain) names are rather hard to find. The Internet is based on connectivity, and I don't mean just you to your favorite site—I mean all the computers on the Internet to each other. If you imagine for a moment how many computers might be online at any given time, how do we manage to keep things sorted out and all the computers and people going to the right places? It's all thanks to domain names and the Domain Name System (DNS). When you type "www.google.com" into your web browser of choice, you're kicking off a series of really amazing things in the background so you can do a search for the best WordPress books on the Internet (like mine!). Every domain name on the Internet matches to a string of numbers called an Internet Protocol (IP) address or number. In Google's case, one of its IP addresses (it has many that all point to the same place) is 24.244.19.177. That would be really hard to remember if you had to type it in every time you needed to search for something, so we have domain names instead. Before we get into the magic of how www.google.com matches to 24.244.19.177 and you can do your search, let's talk about the *parts* of a domain name.

A typical domain is made up of three parts: the top-level domain (or TLD), the name, and the subdomain. The TLD for google.com is .com, and you've seen a lot of different TLDs as you surf around the Internet. Each country has its own TLD (.ca is Canada, .us is the United States, .uk is the United Kingdom) and ones like .net, .org, .edu, and .gov serve different purposes. U.S. government websites are the only ones that can use .gov, and only schools can use .edu. In the past, .net was limited to companies who provided Internet network services (such as your Internet service provider), but that restriction has since been lifted. Likewise, .org used to be only for nonprofit organizations, but it can now be used by anyone with a few bucks. TLDs are managed by an international body called ICANN, so no one "owns" them, per se. You can't just start using .artstudio if you want to (although the rules about how many TLDs are available are changing and there are *hundreds* of new TLDs becoming available); that's not one of the approved TLDs. You could, however, have artstudio.com if you wanted. Which brings me to explaining domain names.

Keeping with www.google.com as the example, "google" is the domain name. Now we typically think of google.com as the domain name, but because you can go to google.ca or google.co.uk as well, what's the part that is really controlled by Google? Right, "google". When you want to get a domain name, you go to a domain name registrar who, in concert with thousands of similar companies, allows you to search and see what words (or names) are available and which ones have already been taken by someone else. Here's an example of a quick search for "absolutebeginnersguidetowp.com" on my registrar of choice, Namecheap.com (see Figure 1.1).

FIGURE 1.1

Search for absolutebeginnersguidetwp.com on Namecheap.

So what are you getting for that $10? That would let me use absolutebeginnersguidetowp.com for one year. You don't "buy" a domain name and keep it forever; you rent or lease the name for up to five years at a time. To keep using the name, you have to keep paying for the name. This isn't a scam, nor is it intended to be. This system allows people to secure and use a name for a while, and if they decide in the future they don't need it, it lets someone else use the name instead. However, if you forget to pay the renewal fee, someone else could start using your domain name out from under you. Don't worry—most registrars start bugging you to renew months ahead of time to make sure that doesn't happen.

That's the name, now what about this subdomain stuff? A subdomain is anything in front of your domain name. So the "www." in front of "www.google.com" is a subdomain. You can create as many subdomains as you want or need for free. You might have seen names like mail.google.com or smtp.shaw.ca or imap.zoho.com as you've used different services and applications online; all those are subdomains. We use subdomains in lots of ways. The preceding examples all have to do with email. Having subdomains allows you to have different applications—or websites—using your domain name at the same time. For example, I have facebook.trishussey.com, linkedin.trishussey.com, and twitter.trishussey.com pointing to my profiles on those social networks. I also have my website at www.trishussey.com, but if you type in just **trishussey.com**, you'll get to my website as well. All these subdomains are independent from each other, and all are managed by the next piece of tech magic: DNS.

DNS stands for the Domain Name System (or Domain Name Server, which is the computer that does the actual work), which is like a phone book because it matches domain names (for example, www.google.com) to (IP) addresses like 24.244.19.177 (which happens to be the IP number that matches, or resolves to, www.google.com) or URLS (like my facebook.trishussey.com example). DNS was built so we could use easy-to-remember names (domain names) instead of having to remember the IP addresses of websites. For us geeky types, DNS allows us to tell the Internet where a website "lives" and what other services or sites that domain is connected to on the Internet. For the most part, you'll only need to worry about your DNS settings for your domain when you first buy your domain and set it up with your web host. Every domain needs to have a master DNS address (like a master phone book entry) that the rest of the Internet will refer to and defer to for changes and updates. You set your master DNS record when you first buy your domain and then update or change it with information your web host provides so you can use the domain with that host for your web site.

What makes DNS interesting is that there isn't just one DNS server on the Internet, but thousands of them, and each server holds the records for not only the domains its responsible for, but many other domains as well. Why this duplication? It saves a vast amount of time. When you go to your browser and type in **www.google.com**, your computer asks a DNS server where it should go; if that DNS server doesn't know, it asks another one, and so on until an answer is found. The whole process is a lot faster if you get the answer from the first server, so the data is replicated around the Internet to speed things up for everyone. Your computer also stores (or *caches*) the DNS information for sites you visit often to speed things up even more. This cache isn't kept very long on your computer, so don't worry that you're seeing old websites.

Choosing a Good Domain Name

Before I move on to picking a web host (or just host) for your site, I'm going to touch on another question I'm frequently asked: How do you pick a good domain name? It's actually pretty simple. Start with the word or words that describe your site (try to stick with no more than three short words), search for that at a registrar like Namecheap, and see what comes up. Sometimes you'll get lucky and find the perfect name on the first try; other times, it might take a while—and some creativity—to find the right name. While you're looking, keep these points in mind:

- Easy to remember

- Easy to spell

- When you read the domain name, it's easy to associate with the website it matches with

- Has search engine-friendly keywords (for example, your company's name, or product or service)

So, the example I've been using (absolutebeginnersguidetowp.com) is available and certainly has all the right words in it, but it is terrible to try to type (and type correctly). Sure, it might also be easy to remember, but I'll still probably take a pass on it because the name is just too long for my liking.

 CAUTION These are some of the most famous (or infamous) domain blunders around. Some of the sites still exist; others don't, but the point is to make sure that before you buy the domain (or if you bought the name, before you publicize it), you've triple-checked that you haven't spelled (or misspelled) something you'll regret later:

Pen Island—www.penisland.net

Italian Power Generator—www.powergenitalia.com

www.ipanywhere.com

www.speedofart.com

Now that we've covered the name portion of your website, let's talk about where that site is going to *live*—your web host.

Choosing a Web Host

The first step in picking a good web host is striking a balance between cost and features. In general, the more you pay, the more features you get in return. All the hosts recommended by WordPress.org (see the following note) give a basic standard of service. The price differences among them center on extra features, stability, and redundancy. Most of us—myself included—are going to be happy with standard, shared hosting. This means that lots of websites are stored and run from one physical machine (a server). Shared hosting isn't bad. Servers today are more than powerful enough to handle the load of lots of "basic" websites at the same time. Big and popular websites are often upgraded to dedicated servers or virtual private servers (VPS) so the site has more server resources available for it to load quickly and not affect other sites, either.

In the end, a web host is going to give you the resources you need to run a website. Because WordPress is so popular, almost every host today has all the components needed for WordPress to run correctly and efficiently. Many hosts even offer easy one-click installs to get you up and running fast.

We'll talk more about that in Chapter 3, "Installing WordPress."

WORDPRESS.ORG RECOMMENDED HOSTS

Because the WordPress community and Automattic (http://automattic.com/) have worked with so many hosts, there are a few hosts recommended on WordPress.org. The recommended hosts are the following:

- BlueHost
- DreamHost
- LaughingSquid

I've used several of the ones listed and have found them to be good, reliable hosts. Rest assured, you will find people who have had bad experiences with all these hosts (I've had bad experiences with a couple), but that is true for all hosts. If you go to http://wordpress.org/hosting/ and choose one of the recommended hosts, WordPress.org receives a referral commission from the host. So by going that route, you can choose a host that you know will work well with WordPress out of the box and support the WordPress community overall. Not a bad deal.

Details on the server requirements to install WordPress are covered in Chapter 3. If hosts provide details on their core server package, look for PHP version 5.2.4 or later and MySQL version 5.0 or later to ensure that you can install WordPress. If in doubt, ask before you sign up for a package.

If you are already using a host for other websites (or converting a "regular" website to WordPress), don't worry—most hosts can generally handle WordPress. When looking at a host other than the ones previously listed, compare their features to the one you're considering. If they match up (and the price is right), you're probably going to be just fine. The thing to keep in mind about hosts is that they all suck and they are all awesome. Take any given host and you'll find people who've had good and bad experiences with them.

WHAT IS A SERVER?

Imagine a metal pizza box with flashing lights, a fan inside, and connected to the Internet. That's a server. Essentially, a server is a computer with a larger hard drive than you'd have at home (and probably several of them), more RAM than you have (lots more), and faster processors (and probably several of those, too) that is designed to run many programs really, really quickly for lots of people. You've probably seen pictures of server rooms on TV or the movies (yeah, they usually do look like that) with rows and rows of cabinets full of blinking lights. That's pretty much it. Servers are really only cool to geeks like me; to most other people, they look like really boring computers.

TIPS ON GETTING HELP FROM YOUR HOST

- If you received an email from your host that you don't understand, reply to it (unless it says "Don't reply to this message...") or call the host's technical support to have them explain it.

- Although it's common sense, be cheerful and polite in emails and on the phone. Honestly, nothing greases the wheels of tech support better than a simple "please."

- If you receive an error message, try to copy it down exactly. This is important. Take a screenshot or copy and paste the error message into a document or email. If you email support saying, "I got this error message—I don't know what it said, but now my site doesn't work...," they are only going to email back to try to get more information from you.

- Speaking of information, provide as much information as you can about the problem you are having. Include your operating system, what web browser you use, what you were doing at the time, your name, your user id, and your contact information. I don't recommend giving your password. Tech support *shouldn't* need it to check out your account or site for issues.

- Be as patient as you can with tech support's questions back to you. They are in a position where they are trying to figure out the problem, maybe without being able to see it or re-create it. Yes, they might take some shots in the dark to try to figure it out and ask you to do some obvious (to you) things. Bear with them.

- Finally, if you feel like you aren't being helped at all, ask to be bumped up to a supervisor. Supervisors might have more years of experience under their belts and might also be able to give you compensation, like a free month if your site is down for an extended period of time because of their error.

The last thing that ties together this whole domain name, DNS, and web host discussion is getting your domain to work with your host. For your host to use your domain for your website, the host (usually) needs to be the DNS source of record (the master record) for your domain and have the domain entered into its system as one of the domains it hosts websites for.

This sounds really complicated, but it's actually a very simple process of filling in a few web forms, clicking some buttons, and *reading directions*. When you sign up for a web host, most of them ask at the start of the process what domain you'll be using with them. If this is a new web host for you and a new domain, you'll use your new domain. If you're moving to a new host and have existing domains and websites to move—this isn't the book for you. That is a horse of a different color and it can be really complicated to walk people through. If you already have a host and are adding a domain to the account, that's probably the easiest of all, because you've probably already gone through these steps and kind of know what's going on (even if you need to refresh your memory a tad).

Whether it's a new host and new domain or just a new domain, the steps are going to be something like the ones that follow:

 NOTE Some hosts will offer a free domain name with sign up. If you took them up on that offer and registered your domain through them, you can skip all this—you're ready to go! Also, if you are using WordPress.com and selected the option that you didn't have a domain already and registered a domain through them, you're good to go as well!

1. Log in to your control panel of your web host and find the option to add a domain name. Go through the steps (usually a simple form) and finish. If you're setting up a new host and a new domain to go with it, this step is usually handled during your sign-up process.

2. In the welcome email from your host, there should be a section of the email that says something like this:

    If you are using your own domain name, please update your domain name servers to: Ns1.yournewwebhost.com Ns2.yournewwebhost.com.

    This is the information you are going to need for step 3.

3. Log in to your domain registrar and find the place where you can update the DNS settings for your domain. Mine looks something like Figure 1.2.

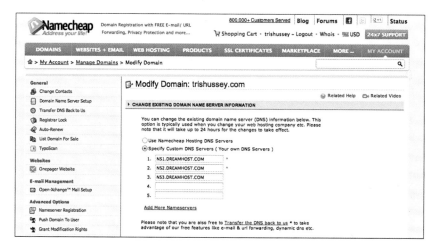

FIGURE 1.2

Example of updating a domain's DNS settings on a domain registrar.

4. Click the button to submit the changes.

5. Wait.

Updating the DNS settings for a domain takes as little as a couple of hours to as many as 48. There is no way to know how long it will take, but there are easy ways to find out when the change has been made. While you're waiting, there isn't too much you can do, except for reading more of this book and probably looking around for WordPress themes you'd like to try out. (Jump to Chapter 5, "Installing WordPress Themes," if you'd like to start browsing now.) The way to know when the switchover is complete (we call it propagating) is to visit your domain through your web browser to see what you get. Truthfully, you should do this before you make the switch so you know what the default "This is a brand-new domain" page looks like from your domain registrar; then you can check to see if it's different later. If you didn't do this, that's okay because all hosts create a placeholder page for you, so you can see if your site is "working" or not. When you see the page has changed, you're ready to go. If things seem to be taking a little longer than you'd like, there are some cool (and not too geeky) websites you can visit to check how the process is going.

Go to www.network-tools.com or www.who.is (yes .is is the TLD, not .com), enter your domain name, and choose a "whois" look up. This will give you what servers on the Internet at large say your master DNS name servers are. These sites check the major name servers that stay updated and update frequently, so if you see the correct information there but not when you visit yourself, your ISP might be the laggard in the process. Be a little more patient, and things will work themselves out in short order.

 TIP   To avoid the hassles of your ISP not updating its DNS frequently enough, try a service like OpenDNS (www.opendns.com). OpenDNS maintains a large number of DNS servers around the world and updates them frequently. You can set your computer or router at home to use OpenDNS instead of your ISP's default DNS settings. This little trick might save you hours of waiting to get a site ready as your ISP takes its sweet time updating its DNS.

This has been a pretty short and high-level intro to the world of domains, DNS, servers, and web hosts, but I hope it's been enough to get you ready for the *really* cool stuff: learning about WordPress! Starting with Chapter 2, "What WordPress Is and How it Works," we'll be rolling up our sleeves and getting down to the business of using and learning WordPress. Buckle up, it's going to be fun.

Conclusion

This intro chapter hasn't really gotten into the nuts and bolts of WordPress yet, but given the number of questions I field about domains, hosts, and servers when I teach my Intro to WordPress classes, I know these are things people need to know and are often confused by. The world of domains and web hosts hasn't really changed much over the past nearly 20 years that I've been developing websites. The servers are faster, it's easier to get a domain name, and hosting packages certainly give you more bang for your buck, but how they work hasn't fundamentally changed.

As you work through the book and learn more about WordPress and creating a site with it, the more the things talked about in this chapter will start making sense.

2

WHAT WORDPRESS IS AND HOW IT WORKS

Now that we know a little about domain names, how websites work, and how to pick a host for your site, let's get into the real topic of the book—WordPress. This chapter gets into what WordPress is—and isn't—and how WordPress works (in general, we'll get to the details throughout the rest of the book). We'll also work through one of the most confusing parts of the WordPress community: WordPress.org versus WordPress.com. Let's kick things off with the most basic question of all: Just what is WordPress?

What Is WordPress?

The summer of 2013 was the 10th anniversary of the first public release of WordPress (WordPress 0.7). WordPress has come a long time since then (by the time you're reading this book, WordPress will be at least version 3.8, probably 3.9) and has evolved from "just a tool for running a blog" to a powerful tool for creating blogs, websites, and all manner of web-based tools. So, is WordPress for blogs? Yes. Websites? Yes. Big websites? Certainly. Really huge websites? Is *The New York Times* big enough? Can I build an online shopping site on WordPress? Sure, lots of folks do. Is there anything WordPress can't do? It can't jump to warp speed or alter the space-time continuum, but they're working on that.

In all seriousness, WordPress is a powerful, easy to use, free, open-source Content Management System, or CMS. Which means that WordPress is great at letting people publish words and pictures on the Internet and wrapping a great layout around it—for free. As open-source software, WordPress is free to download and use—and even modify yourself—by anyone. There is no charge for downloading and using WordPress, even for commercial groups. WordPress.com is a little different, and we'll get to that in a moment.

WHO OWNS WORDPRESS?

So, just who owns WordPress? Everyone and no one. All the people who have contributed code to the core of WordPress hold the copyright to that code. Because so many hundreds of people have contributed code to WordPress over the years, it would be virtually impossible for any one person, group, or company to "take over" WordPress and change the rules (like requiring a license fee). Essentially, this mass ownership makes WordPress a safe, long-term bet for any site to run on.

Yes, there are some things that WordPress isn't great at (like very complex websites with lots of rules about what users can see and do based on their roles), but there are tools like Drupal that pick up where WordPress leaves off (and are harder to use, too). Roughly 20% of the websites on the Internet run on WordPress (that's more than 60 million sites, by the way), and the majority of major websites use WordPress as well. So, it's safe to say that if you're choosing WordPress for your blog or website, you're not only in good company, but it's a choice that millions of other people have made as well.

GETTING INVOLVED

One of the best parts of WordPress is the community of people who love and support it. Beyond the forums and websites dedicated to WordPress, there are meetups about WordPress, and in cities around the world, you'll find WordCamps taking place. WordCamps are mini-conventions of WordPress users who get together to learn about WordPress, talk about WordPress, and get help with WordPress questions. I've spoken at a number of WordCamps and always find them exciting conferences full of new ideas and great opportunities to learn. You can find a WordCamp near you at WordCamp central (http://central.wordcamp.org/), and a quick search for WordPress at Meetup.com will probably give you even more events in your city to attend to learn more about WordPress. Believe me once you start getting into WordPress, you'll get hooked on the community as much as the software!

How WordPress Works

So how does WordPress make all this magic happen? It's not magic—okay, it seems like magic sometimes—just a clever combination of code and a database that interactively pulls pieces and parts to get to make a "website" appear on the Internet. First, WordPress is a content management system, or CMS, which (generally) means that the content for a website and the settings are stored in a database, and the code to make the website appear and the look and feel of the site (called a theme or template) are stored separately as individual files on the server. What this means in practical terms is that your content is divorced from the look and feel of the website. So changing the website's theme doesn't break or alter the content (and generally, vice versa). This also means that if you change how the website looks, you don't have to retype all the content or touch every page of the site for the change to take effect across the site. Changes to a site's theme or template aren't only global, but instantaneous as well.

In the case of WordPress, the database used is the open source database MySQL, and the "engine" that pulls information in the database together with other files to make the website is the scripting language PHP. For the scope of this book, you're not going to have to worry too much about MySQL or PHP, but we'll talk about them both a little bit throughout the book (just enough so you know what's going on).

All the content and settings for a WordPress-based website are stored in a MySQL database that is created when you first install WordPress (we'll cover this in Chapter 3, "Installing WordPress"). Your database is the most important part of your WordPress website, and one of the first things we'll do after setting up the website is install tools to back up and maintain the database automatically. If your WordPress database becomes corrupted, you can conceivably lose your entire website. We don't want this to happen, so we'll make plans to avoid that situation.

All that information stored in the database is useless if you can't get to it. That's where PHP comes in. PHP is a scripting language like JavaScript that is great at pulling information from databases, combining it with templates that have both HTML and PHP code in them, and making a website appear. It's really that simple. When you visit a WordPress-powered website, PHP scripts run to query the database for information (what content should I show here and how should it look) and then puts everything together to display the website. It happens really, really fast (milliseconds for some of the queries), and most people don't even consider how amazing it is that the web page you're looking at was just displayed nearly instantaneously for you just when you asked for it. The page *doesn't really exist until you want to see it*. For efficiency's sake, many sites use programs to cache or save the most popular pages as static files that change only if the content of the page is changed. This lets the server spend time serving the less-popular pages and allows the popular ones to appear faster to more users.

The same PHP-MySQL interaction goes on not just for the part of the website your visitors see, but the section of the website that you use to administer the site—and all at the same time. So while you're administering the site, people can still visit and read your content without knowing that you're working behind the scenes writing new content or making changes.

WordPress uses themes to make your site look how you like it. Themes are a collection of PHP, HTML, images, and style sheet (CSS) files that come together to define the layout of the site and how content is presented. WordPress also uses little sets of mini scripts called *plugins* (which we'll cover in more depth in Chapter 4, "Installing WordPress Plugins") that add additional features to a website. Features like contact forms, slideshows, security, search engine optimization (SEO) tools, and more. It's the combination of plugins and themes that *really* makes WordPress a powerful CMS that can meet almost any website need.

Over the past 10 years, WordPress has gotten more powerful, easier to use (which is rare in software), faster, and more feature rich. Although many of the pieces and parts of WordPress use newer and newer technologies to work better (like HTML 5 and advanced JavaScript code for special features), at its core, it's still PHP and MySQL that are doing a lot of the work to make your website appear to the world.

WordPress.org Versus WordPress.com

If there is one thing about WordPress that is confusing, it's the relationship between WordPress.org (Figure 2.1) and WordPress.com (Figure 2.2). It can get a little confusing, especially when you need to talk about both of them at the same time. The bottom line is that they are very similar, but also different. They serve different needs and niches, but also run on (nearly) the same code. Learning WordPress on a website running on WordPress.com is a great way to start, and you can make the transition to WordPress.org in no time. So, what are the differences? Here we go.

FIGURE 2.1

The WordPress.org home page.

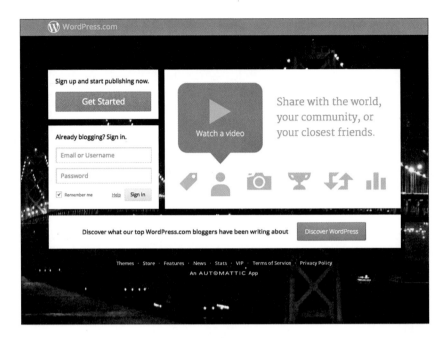

FIGURE 2.2

WordPress.com home page.

Essentially, WordPress comes in two "flavors"—the install-it-yourself version found at WordPress.org and a hosted solution run by Automattic (the company that also supports the WordPress community) at WordPress.com. The install-it-yourself (do-it-yourself/DIY) flavor is how WordPress was originally released 10 years ago, and WordPress.org is the heart and soul of the WordPress community. Most of us within the WordPress community started using WordPress by installing through WordPress.org. WordPress.com is a freemium, hosted blog service (like Google's Blogger or Tumblr). WordPress.com runs a nearly identical version of WordPress as you can download from WordPress.org. In fact, you can start your own hosted service running on WordPress starting with the version you download from WordPress.org (just like WordPress.com). Automattic is the company that owns and runs WordPress.com (and many other website tools). Matt Mullenweg, one of the original creators of WordPress, started Automattic so there could be a business of WordPress (first WordPress.com and then many other solutions and services as well). Automattic doesn't own WordPress.org, but it supports the non-profit WordPress Foundation, which holds the master copyright to the code, logo, and intellectual property of WordPress.

NOTE A *freemium* is a service that is free but also allows you the option of paying for extra features.

When we talk about the DIY version of WordPress from WordPress.org, and we talk about "installing" it yourself, we're not talking about installing a program on your computer at home—WordPress isn't that kind of application. To work, WordPress needs a web server, database server, and other applications normally only found on servers. WordPress is something you install on a server. In this case, we're talking about a web server run by your web host, as we discussed in Chapter 1, "How Websites Work." When WordPress is installed on a web host, you have a lot of control over WordPress, and a lot of responsibility, too. Out-of-the-box WordPress comes with three basic (but very nice) themes and can be a very serviceable website just like that. However, the reason people install WordPress themselves is for control and flexibility. Using WordPress.org, you can install any theme you'd like so that you can make your site look exactly how you want it; you can add features such as newsletters, social media tools, and slideshows using plugins (which we'll talk about more in Chapter 4). However, it's also your responsibility to keep WordPress and all the other components of your site (such as the plugins and themes you install) updated with the latest versions and releases. Updates to WordPress, plugins, and themes aren't just to add new features—these updates also fix bugs and close security holes. It's essential that you keep your installation of WordPress up to date to reduce the chances that your site will be vulnerable to hackers. How much of this updating is automatic? Starting with WordPress 3.7, you can choose how much of WordPress you'd like to have updated automatically. The most essential part of WordPress to keep up to date is WordPress itself. Between major releases (like 3.6, 3.7, and 3.8), there are "point releases," such as 3.6.1, which primarily fix bugs and security holes. Major WordPress releases (like 3.6, 3.7, and 3.8) fix bugs and tend to introduce new features and improvements (such as automatic updates for point releases coming in WordPress 3.7).

Why all the fuss about updating? Because WordPress is open source, the source code for the entire system is freely available to download and peruse yourself. So, when an update to WordPress is released, especially if it's deemed an urgent security fix, all the bad guys have to do is compare the code between the two versions to understand how to hack *any site still running the older versions of WordPress.* Get it? Good.

On the other hand, WordPress.com is a hosted version of WordPress very much like Google's Blogger. The folks at Automattic have many servers all around the world running WordPress.com. Although WordPress.com and WordPress.org essentially are the same code, because WordPress.com is a hosted service, there are limits placed on the things you can do within WordPress.com. You can still do all the basic things on WordPress.com that you can with WordPress.org (posting content, uploading images, quickly changing themes, and other personal touches), but you are limited to the number of themes available (roughly 290 themes), and you can't install a plugin to add a feature that you need (if it isn't available on WordPress.com). This means that the features and themes you see offered on WordPress.com are what you get; you can't add more for love or money. But with roughly 290 themes available (most are free, but there are a few paid ones) and enough features to satisfy all but power WordPress users, it's hard to argue with the price—free. Yes, on WordPress.com, you can have a blog or website for free. If you want to pay extra, you can use your own domain name with your site as well as pay for other add-ons that do give you more flexibility with your site. The other thing about WordPress.com that you should know is that it almost never goes down. Like all most hosted website services, Automattic puts a huge priority on ensuring that WordPress.com and all the sites on it are available 99.99% of the time.

These are the top-line differences between DIY and WordPress.com, so the question you're probably asking yourself is how you choose between one and the other. Let me help you with that decision.

Which WordPress Is Right for You?

I often liken DIY to living in a condo and WordPress.com to living in a dorm. In a condo, you own the property and are responsible for a lot of things; however, often there are rules you have to follow, and the condo association takes care of some maintenance for you. This is what a web host is like. You're responsible for the upkeep of your site, and you have to play by some rules, but the host will make sure the servers stay running and connected to the Internet. On the other hand, WordPress.com—and just about all other hosted systems—is like a dorm room. You get some space and you can do a lot within that space, but there are more rules and less flexibility. In a dorm room, you can put up posters, but not install a bay window. In a condo, you can install the bay window yourself, but if it falls out and damages the building, you're in trouble.

One potential gotcha with WordPress.com is that it does not allow third-party ads of any sort. So if you'd like your website to be supported with Adsense or other advertising, that's a no go from the start. If you make things (for example, for sale on Etsy) or write books (like me!), you can link to the places for people to buy your stuff. The problems come when you have ads for other people and other people's stuff (pretty much all the ads you see online). The next decision sits entirely with you: Do you need a custom look or custom features in your site? If you are creating a website that needs to match a certain look and feel and branding, chances are WordPress.com isn't for you.

Here's what it comes down to:

- WordPress.org gives control and flexibility.
- WordPress.com gives simplicity and reliability.

Using WordPress.org, you have complete control and flexibility over your site. You can do pretty much whatever you'd like with WordPress (including modifying how WordPress itself works), the theme, and the features. This option always means you will need a web hosting account of some kind (as well as a domain name).

Using WordPress.com, you have a simple and fast way to launch a website for free. We'll talk about the paid add-ons in WordPress.com in Chapter 14, "All About WordPress.com"—go ahead and jump forward if you'd like—as well as ways you can make WordPress.com your own. However, the simplicity of just clicking and launching a website with no fuss or muss comes at a cost of being able to control every aspect of the site. You do get a very reliable host, but the three web hosts that are recommended by WordPress.org are also very reliable as well.

 NOTE Automattic is offering more and more "business and enterprise" plans that do allow some custom themes and additional features not found on "regular" WordPress.com. However, these business and enterprise plans run from hundreds of dollars a year to hundreds of dollars a month.

My advice? Tinker with WordPress.com a bit. A WordPress.com account is pretty handy for many features of WordPress.org-based sites as well, so it can't hurt. Kick the tires and see if WordPress.com will do the trick for you. Throughout the remainder of the book, we'll be using a WordPress.org-based site for examples and reference, but if there is something that is different under WordPress.com, I'll point you to Chapter 14 for the details.

Conclusion

If you started thinking WordPress was just a simple tool for running a blog, I hope you now see that it's much, much more than that. WordPress is a powerful tool for building websites that is supported by thousands of people around the world. The WordPress community is one of the best things about using WordPress. There are people in just about every place in the world who can help you with your WordPress website—and they are more than happy to do it. Now it's time to dig into WordPress and get that new site of yours ready.

INSTALLING WORDPRESS

On WordPress.org, they brag about WordPress's "famous five-minute install," which is *technically* true—many people can install WordPress in just a minute or two with little or no effort. Although installing WordPress has never been *really* hard, it's safe to say that for a lot of novices, using FTP to upload files, creating a MySQL database, and editing a text-based configuration file was daunting.

The answer for many hosts was simple: create an easy install method—something that just about anyone could point, click, type, and be done with in a moment. Easy installs on hosts have gotten easier and easier (and better at giving novice users more plugins and themes preinstalled for them), so it's without hesitation that I tell you now to use the easy install option on your host if you can. Yes, WordPress can still be installed manually, and it's good to know how that process works (for troubleshooting, if nothing else), but most of you are going to gloss over it and that's okay. I'm including the information to be complete. (You can thank me later.)

Using One-Click or Easy Installs

As the name implies, this is the "easy" way to get WordPress running on your website. Getting this far assumes that you've signed up with a web host and gotten your domain name working with your web host (see Chapter 1, "How Websites Work"). Because WordPress is very popular, many hosts (like DreamHost and Media Temple) offer special "WordPress hosting" packages or features. On DreamHost, it's called DreamPress and is an additional monthly cost *on top of* your hosting fee. On Media Temple, it's called WordPress PowerPack (again, an extra fee applies). If you're just starting out and have a simple site, you probably don't need this level of boosted WordPress performance. Your host will *happily* help you spend more money with them at a later date if you need that kind of oomph down the road.

Easy installers are web forms that tell scripts on your host to install software for you on the server. Remember, this software is not running on your computer; it's on a server on the Internet. Easy installers aren't used only for WordPress. Hosts use them to install a myriad of other tools that website owners might find useful, like a forum, shopping cart, wiki (just like what Wikipedia runs on), and others.

What the easy install or one-click install is called or looks like depends on your host. Following are screenshots from DreamHost (Figure 3.1) and Rackspace (Figure 3.2). Regardless of what the start looks like, the behind-the-scenes progress is essentially the same.

FIGURE 3.1

Easy install on DreamHost (found under Goodies, One-Click Installs).

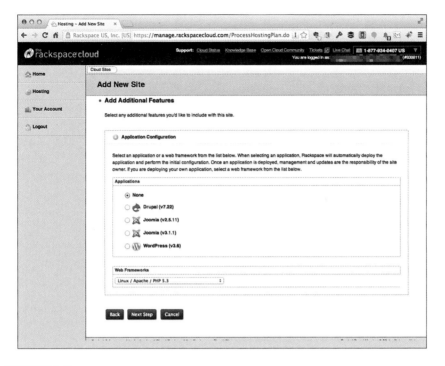

FIGURE 3.2

Rackspace one-click installs are automatically offered when you create a new website.

Here's what's generally happening:

- A fresh copy of WordPress (the latest released version) is decompressed and copied to the directory on the server where your website will live.

- A MySQL database is created with a username and a password.

- The configuration file for WordPress is edited to include location, name, username, and password of the database.

- The WordPress installer is run to create the first user and password and make the site live.

That's it really, just four steps. Because hosts all tend to do things a little differently as part of the easy install, you might need to fill in more or less information in the web form. Sometimes the host assigns a database name, username, and password for you; others give you the opportunity to do that. Some hosts let you set the username and password of the first WordPress user before the install; others (like DreamHost) let you do that as the final part of setting up WordPress on your site.

For example, Figure 3.3 shows what the form looks like for me on DreamHost.

FIGURE 3.3

The WordPress easy install form on DreamHost. It creates the database, but after it's completed, I'll be directed to a screen to finish the install.

DATABASE NAMES, USERNAMES, AND PASSWORDS

The heart and soul, and most critical part of your WordPress website, is its database. If the database becomes corrupted or is hacked, your site may crash or send out spam or other dastardly things. Hosts try to protect access to your database as much as they can, but you need to do your part by setting a strong password for your database user. For hosts that let you set the database name (and there are rules about what you can call a database in MySQL), my suggestion is to pick a name that makes sense to you, like mysite_db and then set the username to be mysite_usr (usr being shorthand for user). For the password, if you can, let the host set a random one for you. This isn't a password you'll need to know or use on a regular basis, and it's best if the password is as random as it can be to help prevent hackers from getting into the database directly. If you ever need that username or password (or the database name for that matter), they are safely stored in your configuration file.

PICKING YOUR WORDPRESS USERNAME AND PASSWORD

As with your database username and password—and maybe more so—you need to use a good password for WordPress. WordPress *can* set one automatically for you, and if you can handle a random password, do it. For the username, the first username doesn't have to be "admin" anymore. We used to recommend setting up WordPress using the admin username, then creating a new user with administrative privileges (and a different name), logging in with the new username, and finally deleting or disabling the original admin account. We had to go through this rigmarole because hackers *knew* that the first username created was "admin" and they could use that as a starting point and keep trying passwords until they got into the site. Not good. These days, because you can start off with the first user having any name you want, what you pick is up to you. Just don't pick admin.

After everything is all set and done—many hosts will send you an email when the site is up and running or whatever the next step is for your host—you should be able to log in to your WordPress Dashboard. Jump down to Figure 3.19 to see it.

Installing WordPress Manually

If installing WordPress with a one-click or easy install is so quick and painless, why would you do it any other way? Why bother with a manual install? Because sometimes hosts don't offer an easy install, the install doesn't work, or you need to fix something broken in WordPress and only *reinstalling* it will fix things. To reinstall WordPress, it helps to know how it was installed in the first place and what all the pieces and parts are. After you know how simple it is to manually install WordPress, if something goes sideways on your website, you'll feel that much more confident about fixing it.

Installing WordPress manually isn't hard. If you can download something from the Internet, unzip a compressed file, drag folders from one window to another, and edit files, you're pretty much good to go. Yeah, there are a couple sneaky details I've left out, but we'll get there in a moment.

Before You Get Started

Before we start this whole process of awesomeness, we need to download a program so we can transfer (upload) the files we're *downloading* from your computer to your web host. You're going to need an FTP client and learn one of the oldest and most fundamental parts of the Internet that very few people use regularly but that is *essential* to how everything on the Internet works. FTP stands for File Transfer Protocol, and is one of the original "programs" on the Internet and its design and purpose is very simple: FTP contains the instructions and tools to move files from one computer to another. These days, only a few people use FTP on a regular basis (lots of developers and people who work with large files— like book chapters!). These are the same developers who make websites and all the other amazing things we do online (like Google, Facebook, and so on), so although most Internet users have never heard of FTP and will never use it—it's still essential to how things work day to day.

An FTP client is just a nice, pretty program that makes it easy for you to copy files from your computer to your web host's server. Today, FTP clients are easy enough to use that if you can drag folders from one window to another, you're good to go. There are two FTP clients that I recommend to people: Cyberduck (http:// cyberduck.ch/) (Figure 3.4) and FileZilla (https://filezilla-project.org/) (Figure 3.5). Both are free, and either will do just fine. Personally I like Cyberduck for new users because it looks more "normal" and modern than FileZilla, but in the end both work just dandy. First, you need to pick one, download, and install it on your computer. Yes, this is a regular install on your computer type of program. It's designed to communicate with your server that's off somewhere on the Internet.

FIGURE 3.4

Cyberduck home page.

FIGURE 3.5

FileZilla home page.

When you launch the application, you're going to need to tell it where to connect to upload files—where your server is, what your username is, and what your
password is. Figure 3.6 shows you what this looks like for Cyberduck on a Mac.
The good thing is that most web hosts include this connectivity information in
the welcome email you receive when you first sign up for the service. Find that
email and you should have all the information you need. If you run into trouble,
don't worry. Connecting to a web host by FTP is such a common task that getting
help from your web host should be no problem. Before you move on to installing
WordPress, you need to have your FTP client all set up and ready to use.

FIGURE 3.6

Opening a connection with Cyberduck.

You already have the next application that you need for installing WordPress: a basic text editor. On the Mac, it's called TextEdit; on PCs, it's Notepad. From here on, if you need to open a file to edit, you're going to use a text editor. All the files that WordPress uses are basic, plain text files. *Do not* open them in Word or another word processor or the text files will be changed so your web server cannot use or read them.

The files might end in extensions like .php or .css, but that's fine; trust me, they are just plain text files. If you really get into WordPress and start modifying your themes, you'll want to get text editors that are designed for programmers, but for now, TextEdit and Notepad will do just fine.

Manual WordPress Install

Installing WordPress by hand isn't hard, time consuming, or even fiddly. It takes only marginally longer to do than the one-click install, and it gives you some hands-on experience with the parts of WordPress that you'll be using throughout this book. Installing WordPress takes just a few steps:

1. Download WordPress from WordPress.org.

2. Extract and upload the files to your host.

3. Create a MySQL database for WordPress.

4. Edit and upload the configuration file.

5. Run the WordPress installer.

That's it. Nothing hard, nothing magic. Just five simple steps. Remember that WordPress is installed on a web server on the Internet, not your computer. This isn't like installing a new application on your computer. There is an exception to the "not on your own computer" statement, but that's a topic for Chapter 17, "Advanced WordPress Settings and Uses."

CAUTION If you have already installed WordPress using an easy install, or if you already have WordPress running in some way on your website, do not follow these directions. Just read along for your own edification and understanding. If you try to reinstall WordPress on top of itself, you could very easily wipe out your website without hope of recovery.

Downloading WordPress and Uploading It to Your Host

The first step is to go to WordPress.org and click the Download WordPress button (Figure 3.7). On the next page (Figure 3.8), you'll see the button to download the .zip file with all the files you need to upload to your host. Click that button and wait for the download to finish (probably just a couple minutes). Next, find the file (called wordpress-3.6.1.zip or something similar; the versions numbers are tacked on now) in your Downloads folder (or wherever you download files to on your computer). Unzip that file on your computer (double-clicking usually does the trick for most people).

FIGURE 3.7

WordPress.org home page. Note the Download WordPress button.

FIGURE 3.8

The download page for WordPress.

You should now have a folder in your downloads folder called "wordpress" (Figure 3.9). Here's where things might get a little out of your comfort zone; this is when we're going to fire up that FTP client and put it to use. When you were setting up your FTP client for your host, your host should have also indicated where your website files should go on the server. Each host is a little different in how it deals with directory structure. Sometimes when you connect to your account, you'll start off right where you need to be to start uploading files. Other hosts start you off where you can see all the websites you have, and then you open the folder for the website you'd like to work on. It's important that you know where your website files should go *before* you start uploading the files for WordPress. There's no point wasting time uploading files to the wrong folder!

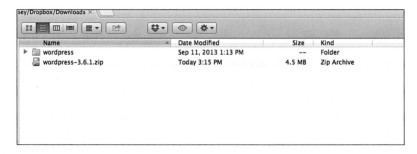

FIGURE 3.9

Downloaded .zip file and expanded folder containing the WordPress files.

FOR SAFARI USERS

One of the "handy" features of Safari is to open "safe" files automatically. This is convenient for many things, but not WordPress. The .zip files that we'll need to work with in Chapters 4 and 5 need to *stay zipped* to follow along. Safari automatically unzips zip files by default, so we need to change that behavior. Open your Safari preferences, and under the General settings is a check box at the bottom that reads Open "safe" Files After Downloading. Uncheck that box and close the preferences (Figure 3.10). The downside is that things like PDFs, movies, and other files won't magically open right after they download. The upside is that when you download themes and plugins for installing into your new site, you won't have to re-zip the files.

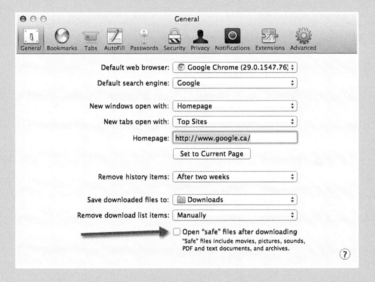

FIGURE 3.10

Unchecking the auto-open feature in Safari preferences.

After unzipping the file that was downloaded, open the folder called "wordpress" on your computer. You'll upload the *contents* of that folder to your host, not the folder itself. You'll upload the files to the *root* (that is the top level) of your website's directory. For this example, I'm going to be uploading to a new site I've created for this book with the URL abgwp.trishussey.com. I've gone ahead and created that subdomain within my DreamHost account, and Figure 3.11 is what I see when I connect to my account with my FTP program (for Mac users, the app is called Transmit, and although it's not free, it's worth every penny).

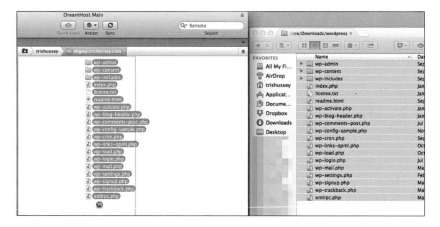

FIGURE 3.11

Uploading the WordPress files to my web host.

I navigated into the abgwp.trishussey.com directory. You notice it's empty, which is good, because I just made it. Now I'm dragging the files from the wordpress folder on my computer's hard drive to the root folder of this new site on my web host.

WHY NOT THE WORDPRESS FOLDER?

You might wonder why I didn't just drag the wordpress folder over. Seems a lot easier, yes? Not really. When you drag the *contents* of the wordpress folder over to the root of your server, the URL for the website (in this case) will be http://abgwp.trishussey.com/ if I copied the folder over, then the URL would be http://abgwp.trishussey.com/wordpress/. We used to see the structure a lot in the early days of blogging and WordPress because people wanted to keep their blog separate from the rest of their website (which was still written in plain old HTML). So people would upload the wordpress folder, change its name on the server to blog, and then install WordPress. Today, although some people do keep their blogs and websites separate, WordPress can be used to create your *entire* website—blog included—so we don't need to do the whole subdirectory (that's what a folder in a folder is called) routine any longer. If you *do* install WordPress into a subdirectory and then change your mind later, you can switch things around. We'll cover that case in Chapter 17, "Advanced WordPress Settings and Uses."

Depending on the speed of your Internet connection, uploading all the files will take between 5 and 10 minutes (there are *lots* of files to upload). This is a perfect time to move to the next step, which is creating your MySQL database.

Creating Your MySQL Database for WordPress

You'll create the database on your web host's control panel. On DreamHost, I find it under Goodies, MySQL Databases. Most hosts also give you a nice, convenient MySQL Database Wizard that walks you through the steps with a simple web form. You'll only have to provide the following:

- A name for the database.

- A name for the user who will access the database.

- A password for the user.

Remember all of these bits—we'll need them shortly for the configuration file part of the process. Yes, these are very similar steps to the easy install we just talked about, so all the same rules for database names, usernames, and passwords apply here as well. Remember, the manual install is just going through all the same steps as an easy install; you're just doing all the work to make it happen.

One key part of the MySQL database, as far as WordPress is concerned, is *where* the database is. Or rather, how will WordPress find the database and access it to make the WordPress magic happen? Many web hosts keep things simple and, as we'll get to when we get to the configuration file, the location of the database is just "localhost" (which means that the database software is on the same server as the web software). For some web hosts (like DreamHost), the server for your MySQL database isn't "localhost;" it's another name. On DreamHost, you give the host a name; on Rackspace, they give you a name that is related to your account; on GoDaddy, the name is assigned *after* you create the database and is *completely random* (which makes it less than fun to move to the install steps, because GoDaddy can take several minutes to set up a database and assign a name).

 TIP   I mention GoDaddy in this chapter not because I recommend it as a host—I don't, and neither does the WordPress community—but because lots of people use GoDaddy for domain names and hosting.

Figure 3.12 shows you what the creating a MySQL database portion looks like on DreamHost. Clicking Add a New Database Now gets the ball rolling and lets us move to the next step.

Create a new MySQL database:	
Database Name: Try putting your domain name in front of your database name if the name you want is already taken.	abgwp_db
Use Hostname:	mysql.trishussey.com ⟰
New Hostname: There is a delay while DNS updates for new hostnames (this can take up to a few hours). In the meantime, feel free to use any of your existing hostnames on the same service to connect to your database.	mysql . createyourownblogbook.com ⟰ *This domain must be registered and use our DNS (name servers)!*
First User:	Create a new user now... ⟰
New Username:	
New Password: Must be at least 6 characters	
New Password Again:	
Database Comment Optional - for your own organizational use!	
Your database will be created right away, however new hostnames will need time to propagate.	Add new database now!

FIGURE 3.12

Creating a MYSQL database on DreamHost. Notice the area to choose a hostname.

Editing the Configuration File

By now all the WordPress files should have finished uploading to your server, so we're ready to move on to the next step—editing the sample configuration file with your information. You can edit the configuration file if the upload is still going; you just have to wait until everything is done to move on from there.

 CAUTION   Watch out! At this point, we're going to start editing the files associated with WordPress. You'll notice that all the files end in .php. Remember, these aren't special files created by MS Word; they are just plain old text files. It's *essential* that when you open a PHP file, you use a text editor. Not Word, not ever. On Macs, the text editor is called TextEdit. On Windows, it's called Notepad.

On your computer, open either TextEdit (it's in the Applications folder) or Notepad (it's in the Utilities folder) depending on whether you use Mac or Windows. Go to the File menu and choose Open, find the unzipped wordpress directory (probably in your Downloads folder), and open wp-config-sample.php. Figure 3.13 shows you what this looks like within TextEdit on a Mac. We're going to be editing just a few things in this file: where the database is (if needed by your host), the name of the database, the username for the database, and the password for the database. The nice thing about the configuration file is that those spaces are noted for you to fill in.

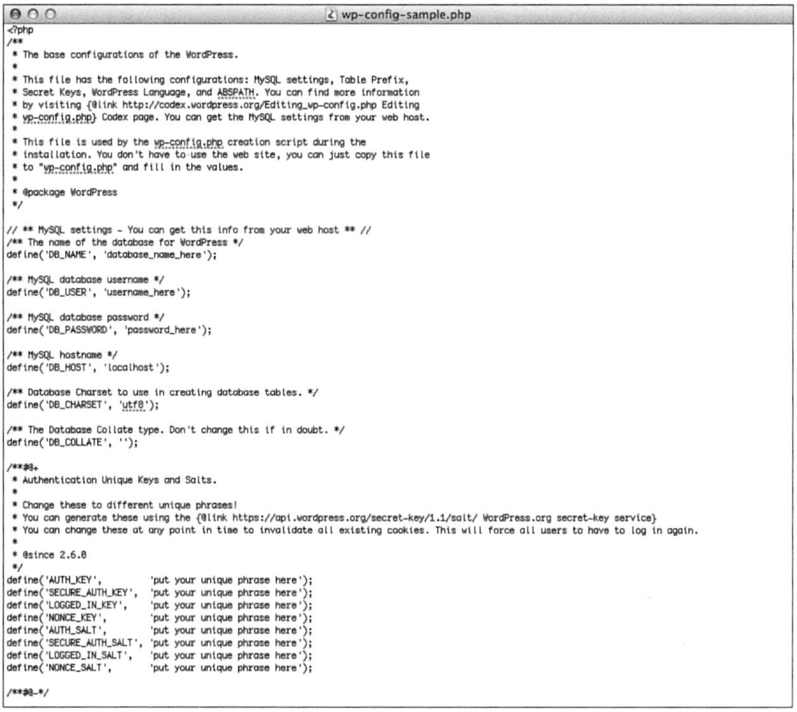


```
<?php
/**
 * The base configurations of the WordPress.
 *
 * This file has the following configurations: MySQL settings, Table Prefix,
 * Secret Keys, WordPress Language, and ABSPATH. You can find more information
 * by visiting {@link http://codex.wordpress.org/Editing_wp-config.php Editing
 * wp-config.php} Codex page. You can get the MySQL settings from your web host.
 *
 * This file is used by the wp-config.php creation script during the
 * installation. You don't have to use the web site, you can just copy this file
 * to "wp-config.php" and fill in the values.
 *
 * @package WordPress
 */

// ** MySQL settings - You can get this info from your web host ** //
/** The name of the database for WordPress */
define('DB_NAME', 'database_name_here');

/** MySQL database username */
define('DB_USER', 'username_here');

/** MySQL database password */
define('DB_PASSWORD', 'password_here');

/** MySQL hostname */
define('DB_HOST', 'localhost');

/** Database Charset to use in creating database tables. */
define('DB_CHARSET', 'utf8');

/** The Database Collate type. Don't change this if in doubt. */
define('DB_COLLATE', '');

/**#@+
 * Authentication Unique Keys and Salts.
 *
 * Change these to different unique phrases!
 * You can generate these using the {@link https://api.wordpress.org/secret-key/1.1/salt/ WordPress.org secret-key service}
 * You can change these at any point in time to invalidate all existing cookies. This will force all users to have to log in again.
 *
 * @since 2.6.0
 */
define('AUTH_KEY',         'put your unique phrase here');
define('SECURE_AUTH_KEY',  'put your unique phrase here');
define('LOGGED_IN_KEY',    'put your unique phrase here');
define('NONCE_KEY',        'put your unique phrase here');
define('AUTH_SALT',        'put your unique phrase here');
define('SECURE_AUTH_SALT', 'put your unique phrase here');
define('LOGGED_IN_SALT',   'put your unique phrase here');
define('NONCE_SALT',       'put your unique phrase here');

/**#@-*/
```

FIGURE 3.13

Sample WordPress configuration file ready to be edited!

Select the words like database_name_here and put in your information. Notice those single quotes around the words? Those still need to be there when you're done. Figure 3.15 shows what my wp-config-sample.php looks like just before I save it (yes, I blurred out the password). If the hostname for your database is different than localhost, put that in now. One more step and we're done. The last step is to visit https://api.wordpress.org/secret-key/1.1/salt/ in your web browser (Figure 3.14) and copy the randomly generated encryption keys (they are like passwords) and paste them into the file. Visit that link, copy the block of text (it's important to get all of it), and then scroll down until you find the section that looks like it. Select and delete that block of text and paste what you copied from your web browser. It should look the same as in Figure 3.15.

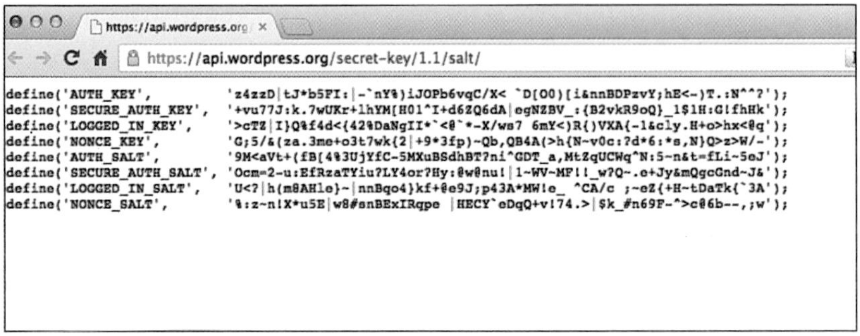

FIGURE 3.14

Encryption keys generated by Wordpress.org.

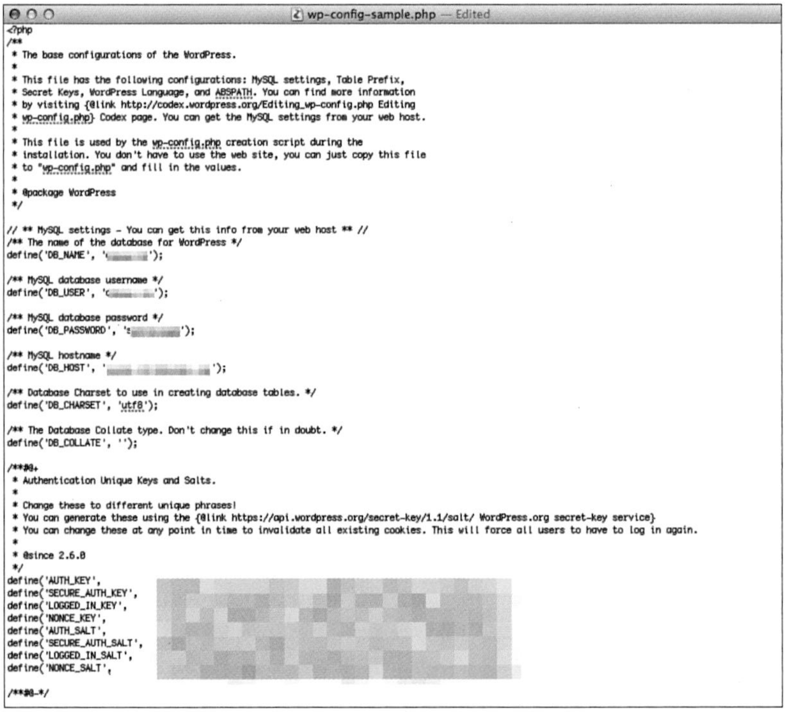

FIGURE 3.15

Edited configuration file.

The final step here in the editor is to choose Save As (Notepad) or Duplicate (TextEdit), and save the new file as wp-config.php (Figure 3.16). Your configuration file is now ready! Upload this new file to your host with all the other WordPress files in the root directory. If all your files have uploaded, you're ready for the next step: installing WordPress. (No, none of that uploading was actually installing anything.)

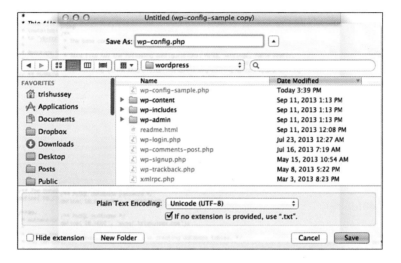

FIGURE 3.16

Choose Save As to create wp-config.php.

Installing WordPress

Assuming that your domain is all set on your web host and you can get to the site, we can install WordPress. If you get "host not found" or something like that when you try the next step, just wait a bit (especially if you *just* signed up for your web hosting account). If things aren't working by the following day, contact your web host for help.

To start the WordPress install process (and I promise that at this point, it's really painless), go to http://[yourdomain]/wp-admin/install.php in your web browser (for example, http://abgwp.trishussey.com/wp-admin/install.php). If everything has gone correctly, you should see something like Figure 3.17.

FIGURE 3.17

WordPress install screen.

TROUBLESHOOTING A MANUAL WORDPRESS INSTALL

If you get a funny-looking screen that has ads or links on it or get "not found," your domain updates might not have propagated yet. Wait 30 minutes and try again.

If you get an "Unable to connect to the database" error, double-check the information in your wp-config.php file and reupload if you need to.

If you get a "Cannot find wp-config.php" error, you didn't upload your wp-config.php file to the right place or didn't name it correctly.

If these don't cover your issue, check the WordPress help Codex: http://codex.wordpress.org/Installing_WordPress#Common_Installation_Problems

Fill out the form and click Install WordPress. You should see something like Figure 3.18. Click Login, and you should now see the WordPress Dashboard, as shown in Figure 3.19.

FIGURE 3.18

Success!

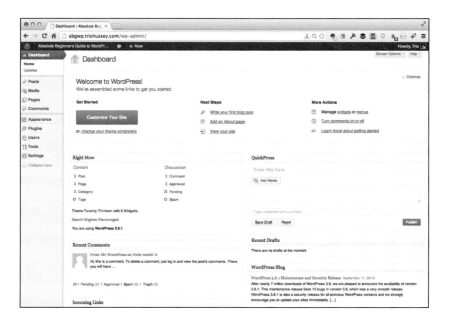

FIGURE 3.19

Welcome to the WordPress Dashboard!

That's it! You've installed WordPress manually, and we're ready to start rocking WordPress!

Quick Look at the WordPress Dashboard

I'm going to cover all the parts of the WordPress Dashboard over the course of this book, but for right now, I'm going to hit the major sections that will let you follow along with the next several chapters on plugins and themes (Chapters 4–7). By the time we hit Chapter 8, "All About Jetpack Settings," and start really digging into settings, you'll be an expert at navigating the WordPress dashboard. So, just what is the WordPress Dashboard anyway? It's what you first see when you log into your site, and it's the "backend" or administrative part of a WordPress website. From the Dashboard, you can navigate to the sections to create content, adjust settings, pick a theme (design) for your site, install plugins (how you add additional features to a WordPress website), manage users, and all the other parts of having a website that are "behind the curtain."

The first screen you see when you log into your website (which is, in case you ever forget, http://[yourdomain]/wp-admin/; for the example site, it's http://abgwp.trishussey.com/wp-admin/) is *technically* the Dashboard and the rest of the sections are just "areas" or "screens," but if you call the whole thing your Dashboard, that's fine. From the Dashboard proper, I like to break the sections into three basic groups that define what they do. The top part with the Dashboard link is where you click to get back to the main Dashboard and quickly access the Updates screen (we'll cover updates in Chapter 15, "Maintaining WordPress Sites"). Below that is what I like to call the "content section"; this is where you create and manage all the content for the site: Posts, Pages, Links, Media, and Comments. Chapters 11 and 12 will cover everything you have wanted to know about creating content within WordPress. The next group is a true administration area. This is where the sections for themes and templates (Appearance), Plugins, Users, and Settings are. We'll start getting into those in Chapter 4, "Installing WordPress Plugins," and continue on throughout the book.

From any point in your Dashboard, you can jump to another section by clicking the main heading or using the fly-out menus that pop out when you pass the mouse pointer over one of the headings. For example, to get to the Plugins install screen, you don't need to click Plugins and then Add New; you can just click Add New and be there in one click. An important part of using the Dashboard is to understand that as you install plugins and themes, the menu items on the side will change. If you compare the Dashboard from the brand-new WordPress install in Figure 3.19 and the Dashboard from my personal site (Figure 3.20), you'll see a pretty big difference. I have several plugins installed, themes, and even a special plugin to make my Dashboard easier to use on my tablet; however, the Dashboard still works the same way regardless. If I gave you access to my site to write a post, you'd still go and write a post in the same way as pretty much any other WordPress site. If you use WordPress.com, the Dashboard there and what you see when you install WordPress yourself look essentially the same. Learn one, and you know how to use the other.

FIGURE 3.20

The WordPress Dashboard for my personal website.

WordPress Directory Structure

WordPress has a pretty simple directory structure. As far as most users are concerned, you don't even *really* need to know about it, except that if you do know how things work, it's much easier to fix things when they are broken. Beyond the files that you saw being uploaded, there are three directories: wp-admin, wp-includes, and wp-content. Everything we're going to be working with will be in the wp-content directory (Figure 3.21). Within wp-content are directories for plugins, themes, uploads, caches, and database backups. The other directories, wp-admin and wp-includes, contain the nuts and bolts of WordPress. The only people who ever venture into those folders to work with *those* files are the people who develop plugins for WordPress and WordPress itself.

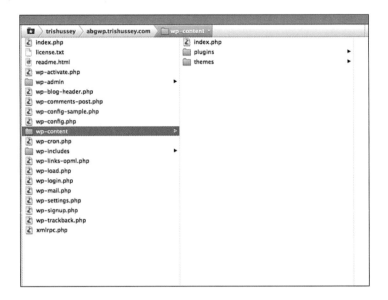

FIGURE 3.21

Basic WordPress directory structure showing the contents of wp-content as well.

One of the very handy things about WordPress is that if something goes horribly wrong with your WordPress installation, the *only* directory you need to worry about downloading and backing up is wp-content. All the other WordPress files are disposable. Sure, copying wp-config.php is *helpful*, but it isn't *essential* (you can always get the database name, username, and password in other ways). So remember when it comes to uploading things to your site and troubleshooting, we're going to be working in the wp-content directory, and that's pretty much it.

OTHER WAYS TO INSTALL WORDPRESS

Because geeks are geeks and we like to have several ways to do things, you can skip the whole uploading and downloading part of WordPress if you have shell access to your web host and are comfortable with the command line. All the information is here: http://wordpress.org/download/svn/. It simply involves using a tool called SVN to "check out" a copy of WordPress (it's like a library, but no one will "take it back," nor do you have to "return" it) and download it to your server. After that, you can usually edit your wp-config file remotely on the command line or through your FTP program.

If you're wondering, "huh?" at this point, don't worry—only developers use this tool because it allows them easier access to WordPress code that is in development. If you have the skills, however, this is (short of the one-click method) the fastest way to get WordPress onto a server.

USING FTP

One of the things about FTP (and FTP clients) that you need to know is that when you are connecting to the server and moving files around (you can move, delete, create, download, and copy files through FTP), *everything is live on the Internet*. If you delete a file that your website needs, your website will go down. If you are strolling through wp-content and delete the uploads directory, *all the images and files you've uploaded to your website will be gone*. FTP is a powerful, powerful tool, so you need to use it wisely.

FTP, in its most basic form, isn't the most *secure* way to move files around. Clever geeks (like yours truly) can intercept your FTP transfers and see what you're moving around (and get usernames and passwords in the process). To combat this, many hosts require you to connect through secure FTP (SFTP). This is no big deal, and both Cyberduck and FileZilla support SFTP. Your host will give you more instructions, but if given the option to connect via FTP or SFTP, choose the latter.

We'll be using FTP on and off throughout this book and especially in Chapters 4 and 5. You'll quickly get used to it. It's not hard; you just have to know what you're doing—and what not to do.

A Note About Users

I'll cover this in a lot more detail in Chapter 6, "Setting Up Your WordPress Site Right the First Time," but at this point you probably have just one user who has the role of "administrator." There can be more than one user with administrator privileges. Think of this role as the person who can do anything with the website. Change any settings, install themes or plugins, enable or disable themes or plugins, create, edit, or delete any content—the administrator role has the keys to the kingdom for the website. As you can imagine, with this great power comes great responsibility, because a user with admin privileges can make a website awesome—or wreck it completely. This is why if you need to create more user accounts for your website—for example, if other people are blogging for you or helping you manage the website—you need to match that person's role to the correct level of user permissions. WordPress has five user levels that have fewer and fewer privileges to do things on the website. The roles are (in order of decreasing power):

- **Administrator**—You know about this one.

- **Editor**—No access (generally) to settings, changing themes, and so on, but can create content and edit anyone's content on the site. Editor is a great role for many users to log in to day to day, as long as they don't need to use the settings at all.

- **Author**—Can create and post content of their own without the approval of an Administrator or Editor. That's it—just writing.

- **Contributor**—Can create content, but it won't be live on the website until approved by an Editor or Administrator.

- **Subscriber**—Just receives posts and comments by email. Can't see or do anything else.

For right now, you're logged in to the site with an administrator-level account. We're going to keep it that way for a while—remember, only admins can work with settings, themes, plugins, and other sitewide tasks—so we can continue on with working with your new website. In Chapter 6, I'll go into more depth about user roles, creating users, and how to manage permissions to different aspects of WordPress.

Conclusion

In this chapter, we've learned about how to get WordPress running on your website. If you've been following the chapters in order, you have a basic, functioning website. It might be simple and generic, but it's functional and ready for content. It works, and if you skipped down to Chapter 11 and started creating all the content (words and stuff), you'd be fine. Stopping by at Chapters 6 and 7 might be good to first get a few settings out of the way, but it's not *required* for your website to function.

This is one of the best things about WordPress: After it's installed, it's pretty much ready to go. The install process is simple, and because nearly every web host you come across will support it, it's an easy choice to make to start building a blog, website, or anything else you dream of to put yourself online.

INSTALLING WORDPRESS PLUGINS

Now that we have WordPress installed, it's time to start adding the features you want (and sometimes need) for your website that don't come with WordPress out of the box—it's time to install some plugins.

NOTE Remember, if you've decided to go with a WordPress.com blog, installing plugins isn't in the cards for you. Don't worry—the folks at Automattic are adding new features all the time.

One of the reasons I chose WordPress over other blog engines—and why I keep using it—is how flexible WordPress is because of the massive ecosystem of plugins and themes. Instead of trying to develop everything that users might need, WordPress is designed to be *extensible* so other developers can build the additional parts that people need, which can be added only *when they need them*. Those additional parts are plugins. Some early plugins have become a core part of WordPress itself, and now that WordPress has become more mature, there are less-commonly used functions that are being spun off into separate plugins you can choose to install if you need them (such as import-export functions and posting by email).

Before we get into finding and installing WordPress plugins, let's talk about what plugins actually are and what they do within WordPress. WordPress plugins are like tiny programs that add features, functions, or capabilities to WordPress that it can't do otherwise. For example, there are plugins to automatically tweet your posts on Twitter. There are plugins that make your website *instantly* mobile-friendly. There are plugins to create a forum right within your website. Some plugins are simple and others are very complex. Many of my favorite plugins I just turn on and don't ever have to worry about ever again; other plugins are designed to become a part of your daily routine. Here's how I explain plugins to students in my classes.

Imagine that you bought the most basic model of a car available. The car goes, but there isn't an extra bell or whistle at all. So you go to a tire store and get some better tires. Next, you get a new stereo that also wirelessly connects to your iPhone so you can listen to music and make calls. While you're at it, you upgrade the speakers in the car, too. Finally, you really, really wanted a sunroof, so you have one put in. Now imagine how complicated it was to upgrade each of those features. Tires are pretty easy. New stereo and speakers, harder and more complicated. Sunroof? Well, you had to have a hole cut into the roof of your car that wasn't there before. All of these are like WordPress plugins. Some are simple and easy (pretty much all WordPress plugins are very easy to install) and don't need a lot of attention; others are more complex. Some plugins make only minor changes to your website, but can have a big positive effect (like tires on a car). Others really get into the core of WordPress and intertwine with it (like a sunroof). Like car stereos, tires, and sunroofs, there are good, bad, and mediocre plugins, so caution is warranted when downloading and installing plugins. However, there are some amazing and fantastic plugins available, for free, through WordPress.org. Essentially, when people ask if they can do x, y, or z with WordPress, my answer is usually "I bet there is a plugin for that!"

In this chapter, we'll be going through finding and installing plugins, some tips on working with plugins, and I'll share a few of my favorites. We'll talk about configuring various plugins throughout the rest of the book, but mostly in Chapters 7, 8, 11, 12, and 13. Let's start with the first part of using plugins—finding them.

Choosing WordPress Plugins

Finding Plugins

Before we start off looking for plugins, let's talk about where you get them. A dedicated group of volunteers from the WordPress community maintain the plugin repository found at WordPress.org (from the Plugins menu). Although computers do most of the work listing the plugins for you, real people vet the plugins at a very basic level. Before a plugin can be included in the repository, the code is checked to be sure that it meets general guidelines for coding and quality and that it passes a basic security check that the plugin doesn't do anything intentionally bad to your site. This means that you can consider free plugins you find, download, and install from WordPress.org to be safe. Free WordPress plugins you find elsewhere should be, as a general rule, considered unsafe. We'll talk about plugins you pay for later in this chapter—that's a little more complicated. For this chapter (and the following one on themes), we'll be searching through the repository on WordPress.org for plugins. The Easy Install system for plugins and themes within WordPress relies on this repository, as well. For the two-step and fully manual installs, we'll use plugins that we find and download from WordPress.org.

When you're looking for a new WordPress plugin, you don't have to venture any further than your own Dashboard. Just pass your mouse pointer over the Plugins section and click Add New. At this point, you can search for a plugin based on a keyword (such as "slideshow") or click the links at the top of the page for Popular, Featured, or Newest. The Popular and Featured sections are great ways to find plugins that are almost always a safe bet and that thousands of people find helpful. You won't need all these plugins by any stretch of the imagination, but it's a safe bet that'll you'll wind up installing a bunch of them. The Newest plugins are the ones that have either just been updated (so an existing plugin with a update) or are brand new.

Let's start with the Search option and search for "slideshow" (Figure 4.1). For this example, we're looking for a plugin that will let us embed a slideshow into our site. Looking at the results, you see that each plugin has Details and Install links below the name, version, a star rating, and a description. The plugin author submits the description, so some are better than others. Let's look at the Details for the first plugin named Slideshow (Figure 4.2).

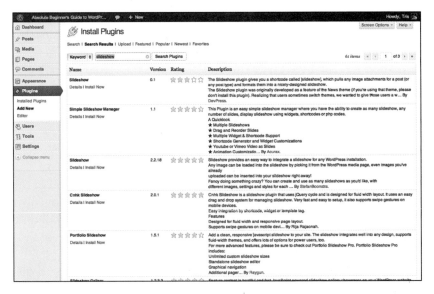

FIGURE 4.1

Search for "slideshow" plugins through the Dashboard.

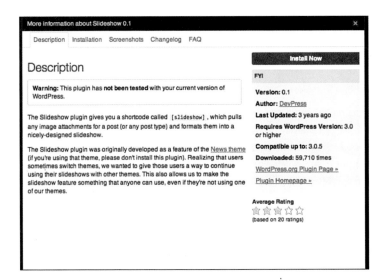

FIGURE 4.2

Details for a slideshow plugin.

Huh. That doesn't look so great. Regardless of the description, it hasn't been updated for three years. A lot has happened within WordPress in *three years*, so there is no guarantee that the plugin will even work! Looking more closely, you'll see that it was downloaded a lot when it was current, but didn't get many (or very good) star ratings. Now let's compare this with the plugin below that one, also called "Slideshow" (Figure 4.3).

FIGURE 4.3

Results for a different slideshow plugin.

This is a horse of a different color! It was updated two weeks ago from when I took the screenshot (September 2013). It has been downloaded an order of magnitude more than the other one and has solid five-star ratings. Chances are this plugin will be a better bet for us if we want to install it. When you're looking for plugins through a regular search, look at when it was updated, how many times it has been downloaded, its compatibility with the current version of WordPress, the star ratings, and how many other plugins the author has in the repository. This last point is important when you are looking at brand-new plugins, but one that is from a person who has released many other popular and successful plugins. Those are often safe to try out. When Apple comes out with a new iPhone, even though it's "new," you know what to expect from Apple and the things it makes. Using the Featured (Figure 4.4) or Popular (Figure 4.5) links gives you information similar to Search (name, version, description), but has more focus than regular search. Featured plugins have been handpicked by the curators of the WordPress plugin repository as great ones to download and use (if you need that feature or function). The Popular list changes all the time but is generally the plugins people download and install the most.

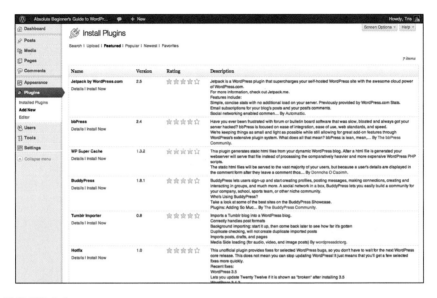

FIGURE 4.4

Featured plugins.

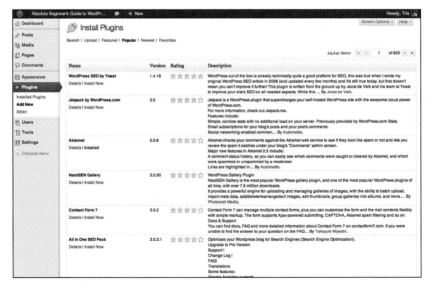

FIGURE 4.5

Popular plugins.

You should notice that a lot of great plugins, including ones that I'm going to recommend to you in this chapter, don't have 5 out of 5 stars. What these plugins do have instead are thousands of downloads. People don't download a plugin that doesn't work, nor do they recommend it to anyone else. Over time, and as you start to tune into the WordPress community, you'll quickly see which plugins are recommended and which are not. Some great plugins are great for everyone, and others only for experienced users tackling very specific challenges. So if you look at a plugin overall, the star ratings might mean less in general if the plugin is downloaded and installed by thousands of users. Okay, you've found a plugin that sounds like it will do the job, and it has been downloaded a lot and is compatible with your version of WordPress. What's the next step in choosing? Installation and configuration options. When I'm looking for a new plugin after those first "sniff tests," I look at the documentation provided. I want to know if there are any special things I need to do to get the plugin to work. Does either the installation or configuration seem complicated and laborious? I also like to see some effort with screenshots and a website for extra help (if it's a somewhat complicated plugin).

Although searching for plugins through the Dashboard area is easy and convenient, I often go to http://WordPress.org/plugins/ and search from there (Figure 4.6). You get all the same information, but I find it easier to parse through lots of plugins that way. In the end, it really doesn't matter too much; it's almost as easy to do the "easy install" as the two-step install (if you download the plugin from Wordpress.org), as you'll see in a minute.

FIGURE 4.6

WordPress.org plugins page.

Installing WordPress Plugins

There are three ways to install a new plugin for your site. First is the "Easy Install"; just a couple clicks and you're done. Everything is done through the screens you just saw. The two-step method involves downloading the plugin from the WordPress repository (or one that might have been included with a theme), and uploading the .zip file. The final way is the original manual way using FTP with downloading, unzipping, and uploading. In case you're wondering, none of the three methods are intrinsically better than the others. All will get you to the same end result: a plugin ready to be activated and configured. I tend to do the easy or two-step method most of the time. I don't have to open another app (my FTP client), and I just need my web browser to make it all happen.

Easy Install

The Easy Install is as simple as clicking the Install Now link either right below the plugin's name or in the popup Details window. It's that easy. The plugin files will be downloaded directly from the WordPress servers to your web host (nothing touches your computer), unzipped, and placed in the right spot within wp-content (wp-content/plugins as you might expect). You'll get a nice little set of messages as it happens, and when the process is complete, you can activate (turn on) the plugin right then or go back to finding and installing more plugins. Choosing to activate right away or not is up to you. It just depends on how many more plugins you want to install. If I have at least another couple plugins to install, I'll usually wait until they are all installed and then activate them (one by one—I'll get to that shortly). Let's pick Jetpack from the Popular list (Figure 4.6) as an example. Clicking the Install Now link gives you a little warning (Figure 4.7).

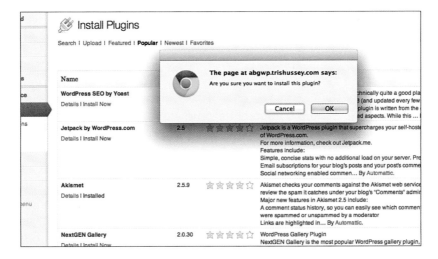

FIGURE 4.7

Installing Jetpack.

Then you see Figure 4.8 when it's all done. Elapsed time? About 5 seconds.

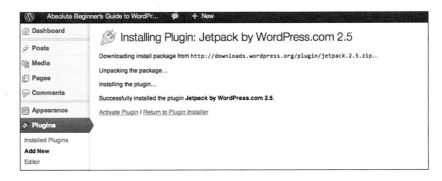

FIGURE 4.8

Jetpack installed!

Two-Step Install

The two-step install is only marginally harder than the easy install. This is when you've downloaded a plugin from WordPress.org and then you upload the .zip file containing the plugin yourself to your site. It works like this. You go to wordpress.org/plugins/ and search for the plugin(s) you want. You'll notice that the search results, Popular, Featured (Figure 4.6), and Newest sections have the same results as you see from your Dashboard. They draw from the same data set, so don't worry that you're missing out by using one or the other. When you find a plugin you are interested in, you click its name from the list and come to a page like this one for bbPress, the WordPress forum software (Figure 4.9). You'll see all the same information you would see from the Details window from within your Dashboard, but instead of Install Now, you see Download Version. When you click that button, a .zip file containing the plugin and all its files are downloaded to your computer (Figure 4.10). Don't double-click to open (expand) the .zip file. It needs to stay as a compressed file for the installing step.

FIGURE 4.9

The bbPress plugin details page. Notice the Download button.

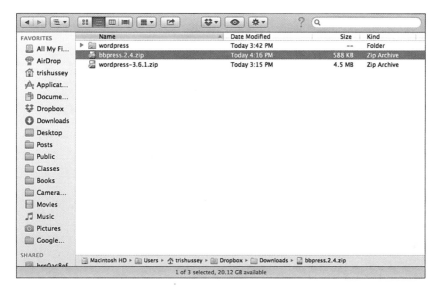

FIGURE 4.10

Downloaded .zip file for bbPress.

Now return to your Dashboard and the Add New Plugins screen. At the top, you'll see a link, Upload. Click that link and you'll see the standard upload button (Figure 4.11). Click Choose File, browse to where you downloaded the .zip file a moment ago (probably in your Downloads folder), select it, and click Open (Figure 4.12); then back at the Upload screen, click Install now. You'll see the same series of steps you saw through the Easy Install (Figure 4.13). Again, activate or return, whichever you choose at this moment.

FIGURE 4.11

Upload screen for plugins.

FIGURE 4.12

Locating and uploading the plugin.

FIGURE 4.13

Done!

Why use the two-step install when the Easy Install is so easy? If I find myself downloading several plugins at once and installing them, the two-step way can be marginally faster if you know where to go to get the plugin on WordPress. org. The other main reason is when I'm researching a new plugin and I'm reading about how it works (and doesn't) and how to configure it. Generally I've started that process from WordPress.org and might have gotten to the website for the developer or plugin. By that time, it's often easier to download the plugin from WordPress.org because the tab is probably already open. Again, does it matter in the end? Nope, not at all.

Manual Install

The manual install is the absolute, will-always-work way to install a plugin. Sometimes, much more rarely now, the easy and two-step procedures don't work. Or the upgrading procedure doesn't work (we'll talk about updating plugins in Chapter 15, "Maintaining WordPress Sites," but the update/upgrade system works like the install system) and you have to kick it old school and use FTP to upload the plugin files yourself.

Like knowing how to manually install WordPress, knowing how to manually install plugins (and themes) gives you an edge on fixing problems when they come up. You know where the files are, what they are called, and how to delete them. Here's how to manually install a plugin.

First, follow the steps for the two-step method so you have a .zip file for the plugin on your computer. We're going to download WP Super Cache for this example (Figure 4.14). Next you need to double-click the .zip file to uncompress it (Figure 4.15). Now launch your FTP client and connect to your site. From the root of your WordPress site, double-click wp-content to open the directory, and then double-click plugins to open that directory. You'll see a few folders already in there—that's good. Next, drag the plugin folder from your computer (as a folder, not as a group of files like we did when installing WordPress) into the plugins directory on your server (see Figure 4.16).

FIGURE 4.14

Download page for WP Super Cache.

FIGURE 4.15

WP Super Cache downloaded and expanded.

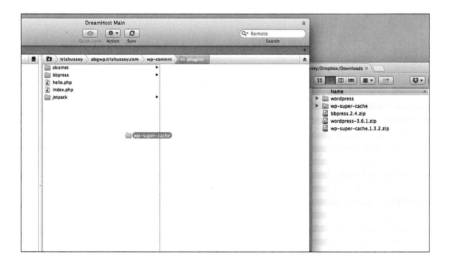

FIGURE 4.16

Uploading WP Super Cache to wp-content/plugins/.

After the upload is complete, the plugin is installed! No, you won't see a little Activate Now link, but it's all ready. To activate the plugin, go to your Dashboard and click the Plugins button (Figure 4.17). You'll see a list of all the plugins you've installed. Click the link that says Activate to turn on the plugin.

FIGURE 4.17

Installed and ready to be activated on the main Plugins screen.

It's that easy. You can see, however, why the easy or two-step method is better. Less fuss, less time, fewer steps. In the end, it's still done, and if that's the only way to install plugins on your host…then that's how you have to do it.

Plugin Tips

I'm not going to get into configuring plugins here (those tips come in Chapters 6–8), but I'll discuss some general tips when installing plugins into your site. First is that when you're just learning how to do things and setting up your site, turn on one plugin at a time, configure it, and then activate the next one. Plugins are intended to run together, and most WordPress users have about a half-dozen different plugins running all the time, but turning them on one by one lets you see what's working and what isn't. You also get a chance to configure the new plugin and see if you're going to like it before moving on.

Next, there are a lot of plugins that do similar or the same things. For example, Jetpack by Automattic can replace an easy half-dozen different plugins in one fell swoop. This means that you should turn off plugins that have duplicate functions to avoid conflicts. For plugins that handle caching (for making your site load faster) or Search Engine Optimization (SEO), you need to pick one plugin to try (one caching or one SEO) at a time. Running two caching programs or two SEO plugins can cause your site to crash, stop loading, or just generally look strange. It's also especially important that if you are testing different caching or SEO plugins, when you deactivate them, you follow the directions. Caching plugins especially have special instructions to ensure that they are completely uninstalled. If you don't uninstall a caching plugin correctly, and then you install another caching plugin to test (this, by the way, is normal; I often test different caching plugins on different web hosts to see which ones work the best), you could wind up with a broken site to fix.

Finally, don't go crazy with installing plugins. Each plugin you install taxes the server just a little more. Most plugins aren't a big drain on a server, but like loading up a car, one child won't do much, but a kindergarten classfull will be too much to handle! Pick the fewest number of plugins to do the job you need done. Watch out for plugins that have overlapping functions and manage that (usually through the plugins' settings). Also, don't fall victim to all the latest fads in site design and layout. At the time of this book's writing, a lot of websites are using "Featured image/post sliders" on the home page and coupling those with really long home pages that try to contain as much information as possible on one page. At some point, featured image sliders will fall out of fashion, and so will extra-long pages. Not to mention, sometimes plugins used to create these styles can drag a website's performance down into the basement. I'm not saying don't use them— I'm just saying be careful.

Recommended Starter Plugins

Get any group of WordPress folks together and it won't take long before someone asks about a plugin, talks about a new plugin, or both. WordPress and plugins go hand in hand. There are thousands of plugins in the WordPress.org plugin repository, and everyone has favorites. Although I could dedicate an entire chapter just on the subject of plugins and how to configure them, that's a little excessive. What I will do, however, is mention here my favorite "starter" plugins that I think everyone should install. Over the course of the rest of the book, I'll talk about setting up these plugins; I might mention a few extras here and there (for specific things like slideshows or e-commerce or social media), but to start with, here is my list of must-have plugins:

- Akismet (for comment spam, a free account is required for activation, already installed by default)

- WP Super Cache or W3 Total Cache (one or the other, not both)

- WP DB manager

- WordTwit

- WPTouch

- All in One SEO Pack or WordPress SEO (one not both)

- Google XML Sitemaps (not needed if you use WordPress SEO)

- Jetpack (which can take the place of both WordTwit and WPTouch, requires a WordPress.com account)

This isn't an exhaustive list by any stretch of the imagination, and I'm sure someone will say, "Hey, what about…" after the book comes out, but to start with, this is a solid list. Like I said, we'll add to this list as we work through the book, but for now picking up all of these is a good idea.

Commercial Plugins

What about plugins that *aren't* free and *aren't* in the WordPress.org repository? Are there "commercial" or "for pay" plugins that are safe and worth buying? My friends at BraveNewCode (http://www.bravenewcode.com/) make a Pro version of their popular (and recommended) WPTouch plugin. There are also plugins for running membership sites, e-commerce, and many other "niche" needs. So are they worth it? Yes, in many cases they are. Here are some tips about commercial plugins that will help you vet them and make sure you get what you pay for:

- Check for a free version and try it first. The free versions will give you an idea of how well the plugin was made, how easy it is to use, and how helpful the help files are.

- Check the refund policy. Try before you buy can be hard in the commercial plugin (and themes) world, but make sure that you're not paying $100 for a plugin that, if it doesn't work, you can't get your money back for.

- Ask (Google) around. Do a little research. Search the WordPress.org forums about the plugin and see what people say. You might even find a free option that you might have missed.

The majority of WordPress sites run entirely on free (or more common now—donationware plugins, where something in the tip jar is appreciated) plugins. However, there are good reasons for developers to offer their plugins for sale. If you find you need the extra features or support a commercial plugin brings, then the price is probably worth it.

Conclusion

Plugins are one of the things that makes a WordPress site move from good to great. WordPress plugins help WordPress do lots of things it can't do out of the box, and the fact that there are thousands of free plugins makes it even more awesome for WordPress users. As you've learned in this chapter, finding and installing WordPress plugins is fast and simple. In just a few short minutes, you can turn your basic, bland WordPress website into a powerhouse that can handle thousands of views, be SEO friendly, keep the huns at bay, and look cool to boot. This, and we haven't even changed the default theme yet!

Just remember that WordPress.org should be the only place you download free plugins from, you can have too many plugins running (active, not installed), and if you need to pay a little coin for something better, that option is available to you, too.

5

INSTALLING WORDPRESS THEMES

Depending on your perspective, either WordPress themes are second only to plugins as the most awesome feature of WordPress, or vice versa. Regardless of whether themes rank number one or two in your mind, WordPress themes are *awesome*. Why? Frankly because of the near limitless design options that are available to you—including thousands of amazing themes available for free through WordPress.org. In just a few minutes, you can install a new theme, check it out, see how it looks on your site, activate it, and your website can have a completely new look in seconds. Don't like the theme? Find another, activate the new one, and, ta-da!, another new look! I've worked with a lot of different blog engines and CMS systems over the years, and I think WordPress has absolutely the easiest theme and template system going.

Like plugins, the best (free) themes are found on WordPress.org (wordpress.org/ themes/), and this is also the *only* place you should download *free* themes from. There are commercial/paid themes—I use them all the time—and there are many great theme foundries out there that I can recommend—and WordPress.org has even more. We'll cover paid themes at the end of the chapter. This chapter is structured very much like Chapter 4, "Installing WordPress Plugins." In fact, I could almost give you just a few basic tips and send you on your way because the general process for finding and installing themes in WordPress is the same as for installing plugins. In this chapter on themes, we'll cover finding and choosing the right themes to try out for your blog and how to install them. In Chapter 6, "Setting Up Your WordPress Site Right the First Time," I'll cover how themes work, and in Chapter 7, "Setting Up Your WordPress Site the Right Way: SEO, Social Media, and More," you learn how to set up a theme. We'll also talk about themes in Chapter 10, "Tweaking, Tuning, and Customizing Your WordPress Site," Chapter 11, "Using WordPress: Content," and Chapter 14, "All About WordPress.com." Let's start things off with how to find themes.

Choosing the Right WordPress Theme for Your Website

It's fair to say with more than 2,000 themes in the WordPress.org theme repository as of the writing of this book, there is probably a theme in there that will suit any WordPress user to start with. This doesn't even get into the hundreds of themes you can *buy* from reputable theme foundries. That's a lot of choice. How do you start? What's the right way to vet themes? The answer is pretty simple—just start looking.

 NOTE As with plugins, there are paid and volunteer staff who thoroughly *check every single theme* that is submitted to the WordPress theme repository. These dedicated people make sure that the themes aren't just coded to rigorous standards, but they are also safe. So, like plugins, don't download free themes anywhere else than from WordPress.org.

When I'm working on a new site, the first thing I do is think about what kind of style I'd like site to have *and* what features I might need. Do I want minimalist or offbeat or colorful? Do I need a portfolio feature? Do I need a customizable home page? Starting off with an idea of both form and function helps me pick and choose what themes will make the first cut and which ones aren't even in contention. Usually I have other sites in mind when I'm starting a new site (or a site redesign), sites I'd like to emulate stylewise; in fact, I'll share a trick for figuring out not only which of your favorite websites are running WordPress but also what theme they are using. It might seem strange that after talking about style and features, the first thing I narrow down in my field of choice is color. However, I find that starting with color is a good start because finding the perfect theme with all the right features and a killer style isn't helpful when it uses all the wrong colors. Yes, in the end, you should decide on things like number of columns, SEO features, and design, but I've found that people gravitate to color first. If you really don't like the color green, then no theme, no matter how awesomely built it might be, will never be the right one for you if it has a green color scheme.

DOESN'T WORDPRESS COME WITH THEMES ALREADY?

Hold the phone—am I saying that before you can even start using this WordPress thing that you have to spend time looking for and picking a theme? Absolutely not. WordPress comes with two themes preinstalled for you (Twenty Thirteen and Twenty Twelve), and one will be activated for you when WordPress is installed. Truth be told, lots of people use one of the default themes (even the older ones Twenty Ten, Twenty Eleven, and Twenty Twelve) quite happily and don't do anything more than customize the theme to their liking (see Chapter 10, "Tweaking, Tuning, and Customizing Your WordPress Site").

So you don't have to look for a new theme right now at all. If you want to jump to Chapter 9, "How WordPress Themes Work," to learn how themes work and proceed from there—that's great. You can come back to this chapter when you need to start working with new and different themes.

You can start looking for themes right from your WordPress dashboard. Just click on Appearance from the sidebar, then click Add New at the top. What you see first is the theme feature filter/search (Figure 5.1), but you can jump right into the thick of things by clicking the Featured link, which will show you some themes that the folks at WordPress.org think are pretty cool (Figure 5.2). If you want to get back to the Feature Filter/Search screen, just click Search at the top of the screen.

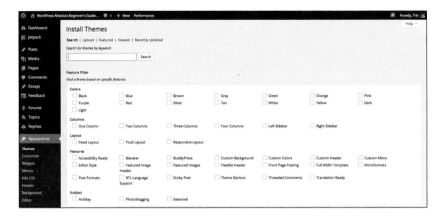

FIGURE 5.1

Feature Filter and Search page for themes.

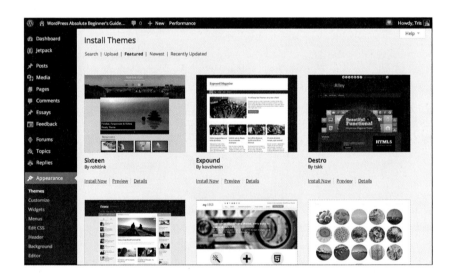

FIGURE 5.2

Featured themes.

Although some of the featured themes are awesome—and we'll hit a few of those later as install examples—let's come back to the feature filter and start looking for our theme. First, let's start with a color. I'm going to check off Light (I know Light isn't a color, but it's a great option for finding themes in a range of colors) and click Find Themes. Figure 5.3 shows what I got for results.

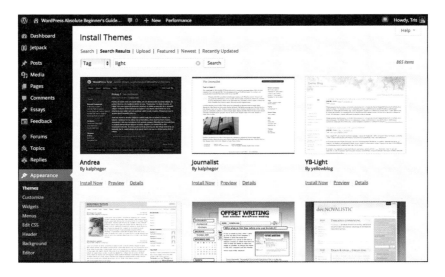

FIGURE 5.3

Light themes.

This is great, but I'd like to narrow things down a bit. So clicking Search again, I return to the feature filter and check off Light for color and then check off Full-Width-Template and Theme-Options under features. This is what I get (Figure 5.4).

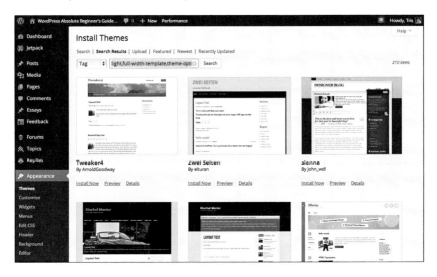

FIGURE 5.4

A more refined list of themes.

If you're looking for something very specific, you can use the search box and enter some keywords (Figure 5.5), such as "magazine."

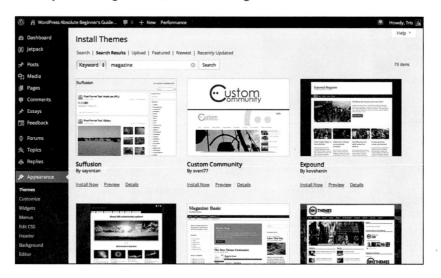

FIGURE 5.5

Searching for "magazine" as a keyword.

At this point, I'd pick about five themes that I think look good and have the features I need. I also make sure that all of the themes in contention have been updated in the past year or so—each new WordPress version includes more features and enhancements just for theme developers and designers, and you need to be sure that your theme is up to snuff. Like plugins, you are probably wondering if the ratings or downloads matter when picking a theme. The answer is the same for themes as it was for plugins. Look at the information and judge if this five-star theme with a few hundred downloads is a brand-new theme from a respected theme designer or some one-off project from a kid in design school (not that those aren't good). I go for downloads almost every time. Ratings are a good indicator, but having 10 ratings and the average 4.5 stars suggests to me that the designer's friends did most of the rating. Downloads show how often people have picked a theme given all the other options. A metric that would be great, but very hard to actually pull off, would be how many blogs have the theme active (not installed, *active*. I have lots of themes installed at any given time that aren't active). That would get a little dicey to gather and figure out, but suffice it to say if there are tens of thousands (or more) downloads, that's a good indicator that the theme has some legs.

Themes are one of those things, like plugins, that you don't really know how good it is until you install it and use it. Yes, you can click the Preview button on the theme's information page, but that view gives you only a partial look into how the theme works. I've lost count of the number of times I've downloaded a theme with high hopes only to find that the content column is narrower than I like (I like 500 pixels wide or wider) or that some of my plugins or widgets look strange on it. This is why I pick several themes that I think I like and try them. That said, after years and years of using WordPress, I have a few "go-to" themes and theme designers I often start out with. Sure, I'm always on the lookout for new, cool themes, but I tend to stick from theme designers I already know and trust.

One of the challenges you're going to face is that if this is a new blog, you don't have a lot of content to test the theme against. There is an easy solution for this—demo content. Many of the commercial themes I buy include demo content you can import, but if the theme you have doesn't come with demo content to import, what do you do? Easy—just download some! The official WordPress theme testing demo content is here, http://codex.wordpress.org/Theme_Unit_Test, but I'll warn you now—there is a lot of content there. Far, far more than you might need to just get a sense of a theme. Other free WordPress content sites have come and gone, so in the end you might just have to do what a lot of people do—create a lot of placeholder content in the interim.

I'll cover how to import content in Chapter 10; go there now and come back if you like. It's important that while testing themes, you have some content to work with to help you see how all the different types of content look and work in the theme (even the default ones). You should also plan on spending a little time working with each theme, configuring it, testing the features that you need before you decide on the theme you're going to go with. There are no shortcuts for this. You just have to tweak and fiddle with it until you're satisfied that the theme will probably work. I'll be covering all the basics of using themes in Chapters 9 to 11, so after you have picked a few themes (and installed them), those three chapters will help you learn how to quickly configure and test your themes.

Installing Themes on Your Blog

By now you've installed a few plugins, so you have everything you need to know about installing themes. Not only can you install them manually the same way (except themes go into the themes folder, not plugins), but you can install them through the Dashboard the same way. There is a theme browser that connects to the WordPress.org repository to install directly as well as being able to upload a ZIP archive to install if you downloaded a theme already.

Just like with plugins, after you have the theme uploaded and installed, you need to activate it. Clicking the Appearance button will give you a list of the themes you have installed. Now, you can activate the theme with one click, but if you're trying out a theme for the first time, click Preview first. Sometimes all I need to see is the Preview (which shows you what your blog will look like with the theme, using all your content and widgets) to decide that the theme won't be a keeper. If, on the other hand, you're happy with what you see, click Activate Theme and check out your new look!

Unlike plugins, you can have only one theme active at a time (not including mobile themes, which I'll talk about in Chapter 14), and although turning themes on and off is easy, you'll often need to do a little reconfiguration each time you switch. I'll talk more about how this works in Chapters 9 and 10. Let's get right into installing themes with the Easy Install.

Easy Install

I think using easy install for themes is much more fun and satisfying than installing plugins. There is something about clicking a few times and giving your website a brand-new look that is just amazing to me. So, what makes this install so easy? Let me show you.

First, it starts with picking the themes you're interested in. In truth, you're probably going to go from picking to installing in one fell swoop. Figure 5.5 showed the search results for "magazine" themes, so let's start there. The actual results you see when you do this now is almost surely going to be different from what I'm seeing now, but that's okay—the names might be different, but the steps are the same.

First (if you're not already in the Appearance section), click Appearance from the Dashboard menu. At the top you'll see the Install tab; click it. Again, we're going to enter "magazine" into the search box. If you want to use the feature filter or browse through the featured or newest themes, that is fine. When I did my search for "magazine," a theme called Fresh Ink Magazine caught my eye, so I clicked Details below it (Figure 5.6).

FIGURE 5.6

Details for Fresh Ink Magazine.

When I click the Preview link, what you see in Figure 5.7 comes up. You'll notice that in both Figures 5.6 and 5.7, there is a link or button called Install. Clicking that at any point in the process will do the same thing—install the theme on your website. Let's do that now from the Preview window. The result, just like when we did the easy install for plugins, is in Figure 5.8.

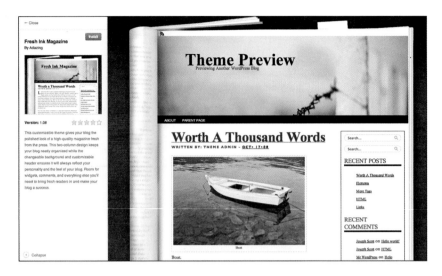

FIGURE 5.7

Previewing the theme.

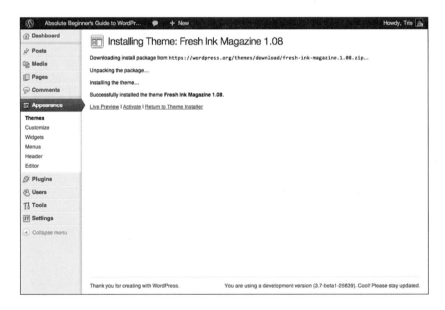

FIGURE 5.8

Fresh Ink Magazine installed!

At this point, you can click Live Theme Preview to see what the theme will look like on your site before activating it. You can activate the theme right away, or you can return to the theme installer. Because we have the two-step install to do next, we're going to click Return to Theme Installer. As you have figured out by now, that was easy. Let's move onto the two-step install now.

Two-Step Install

Just like the two-step install for plugins, the two-step install involves downloading the .zip file for a theme and uploading it to your website. Let's head over to word-press.org/themes/ and find something to download. The Theme Directory lists the featured themes first; scrolling down, I found one called Customizr that I thought looked interesting (Figure 5.9). You'll notice that if you're immediately enamored by the theme, you can download it right from this page, but we're going to check out the theme first.

FIGURE 5.9

Customizr, one of the featured themes.

On the page for Customizr (Figure 5.10) (http://wordpress.org/themes/customizr if you're interested), you can read more about the theme, and if you click the Preview button, you can see what the theme looks like with the standard WordPress demo content (Figure 5.11).

FIGURE 5.10

Detail page for Customizr.

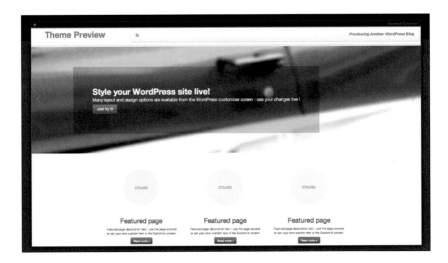

FIGURE 5.11

Preview page for Customizr.

Again, you see the download link in the upper-right corner. If the theme looks perfect, you can click that and the download the .zip file. I closed the Preview window by clicking the little x in the upper-left corner, and then I downloaded the .zip file from the link you saw in Figure 5.10. Now we're ready to install it.

Go back to your site's Dashboard and go to Appearance and click "Add New" again. Just like installing plugins, click the Upload link. You should see something like Figure 5.12.

FIGURE 5.12

Theme Upload screen.

Clicking the Choose File button gives you the same file browser as you saw with plugins (Figure 5.13).

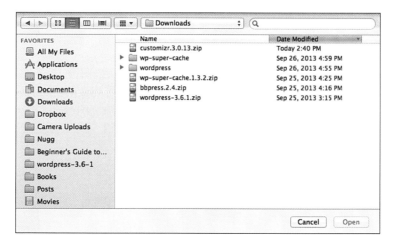

FIGURE 5.13

Uploading the new theme.

After you click OK and then upload, again just like with plugins, you'll see that the theme has been uploaded, installed, and is ready to be previewed or activated (Figure 5.14).

FIGURE 5.14

Customizr successfully uploaded.

That's all there is to it! By this time, I'm sure you've figured out how the manual install is going to go, but I'll walk you through it regardless.

Manual Install

I've gone back to WordPress.org/themes and picked another of the featured themes to use as the example for the manual install. I've picked one of my favorite themes I use in demos and classes—Responsive (http://wordpress.org/themes/responsive), shown in Figure 5.15—and downloaded it to my drive and unzipped it (Figure 5.16).

FIGURE 5.15

Responsive theme page.

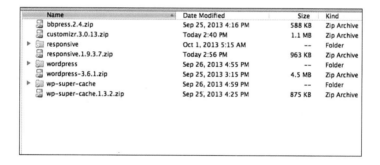

FIGURE 5.16

Downloaded and unzipped theme.

Now I just launch Transmit (my FTP application); this time I browsed for the file in the left pane to find where the file is on my computer and then dragged it over to wp-content/themes/ (Figure 5.17).

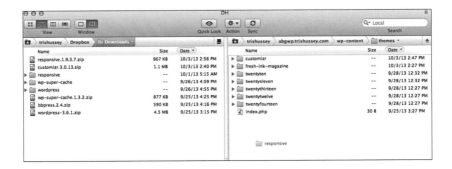

FIGURE 5.17

Uploading the theme.

In a couple minutes, the theme was uploaded, and in Figure 5.18, you can see all the themes that I've installed this chapter (as well as the ones that came preinstalled with WordPress).

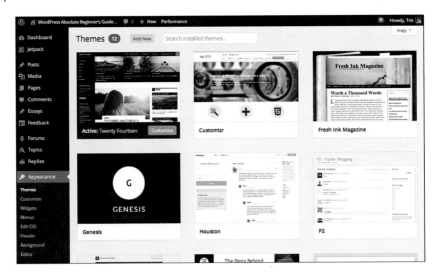

FIGURE 5.18

All my themes ready to test, configure, customize, and try out.

That's it for installing themes. Like plugins, if for some reason installing themes the easy or two-step method doesn't work, the manual method will *always* work. If you ever get started with developing and customizing themes (more than what I'll be covering in this book), you'll get used to using FTP to upload new themes, parts of themes, and generally moving files around. For now, however, that's it. We're done installing themes.

Recommended Starter Themes

Although we've spent this entire chapter talking about looking for and installing themes, in truth we didn't need them for you to get a lot out of WordPress or create a really great site. The default themes installed with WordPress are great (Twenty Eleven is my personal favorite). For the next several chapters, we're going to be using Twenty Thirteen as the test bed for customizations, tweaks, and tuning. Twenty Thirteen is a great responsive theme (we'll talk about what responsive themes are in Chapter 9, "How WordPress Themes Work"), and if you're going to focus on blogging, Twenty Thirteen and its successor Twenty Fourteen are great choices. Both of those themes were designed with a focus on being "blog style" themes. If you plan on using WordPress to create a "website" (in the traditional sense), all the default themes work, but other themes are better suited to that purpose. Twenty Twelve, in fact, was designed to be used to build a "regular" website around. By regular website, I mean one that doesn't have a blog front and center as the content of the homepage. We'll dig into this in Chapter 17, "Advanced WordPress Settings and Uses."

Commercial/Premium Themes

Just like plugins, maybe even more so, people always want to know if commercial or premium themes are worth it. I have one simple answer for you: on the whole, yes. WordPress.org has a list of recommended, commercial theme foundries—http://wordpress.org/themes/commercial/ (Figure 5.19)—that you can check out for yourself. I've used themes from StudioPress, Woo Themes, Graph Paper Press, and Press75 and have been very happy with the themes I've built using those themes.

FIGURE 5.19

List of the recommended theme foundries.

Those are just four of many, many foundries, so how do you choose? Here are my tips:

- Look at the various foundries and see what you like. No sense in using a foundry that I'm recommending if you don't like any of the themes there.

- What do you get for your money? Premium themes cost money, so see what you're getting for your dollars. Lifetime upgrades? Free support? Access to other resources?

- How many sites can you use the theme on? This is more for people who are developing lots of sites on WordPress, but it's a good idea to check to see if you can use the same theme on more than one website.

- Can you return it? This is the big one for me; if I don't like a theme (or plugin), I want to be able to get my money back. Because there is no way to "try out" a premium theme, you have to gauge if the theme will work from the descriptions, previews, and other information on the website. Being able to get your money back is important—actually essential—for me to use a theme foundry.

There are great commercial foundries and bad ones, which is why I have to hedge and say that on the whole, yes, commercial themes are worth it. I have, unfortunately, had to help clients who bought pretty bad themes that were really difficult to work with and customize. However, the majority of my experiences have been excellent. The quality of the premium themes (and some of the extra features they are coded with) have made my life a lot easier and my websites cooler.

Advanced Tip: How Do I Find What Theme a Website Is Using?

What if you find a site that looks awesome and you'd like to know what theme it uses so that maybe you can use it, too? Can you do that? You certainly can! This *isn't* downloading a copy of their theme for you to use. That is actually very hard to do without the site owner's permission. You probably wouldn't want to do that anyway. The theme could have been modified a lot from the original to tailor it to the owner's needs or the owner could have spent good money developing or buying the theme (so your taking it would be like stealing). What I'm talking about here is looking at the source code of the website to peek behind the curtain.

We'll use my website as the example. I'm using Google Chrome for Mac as my browser, but all browsers on Mac and Windows can do this trick (it's nearly as old as the web itself and it's actually how most of us learned how to make websites ourselves). First, here is my website (Figure 5.20).

FIGURE 5.20

My personal website.

In Chrome, what I'm looking for is under the View menu. Click Developer, View Source (Figure 5.21).

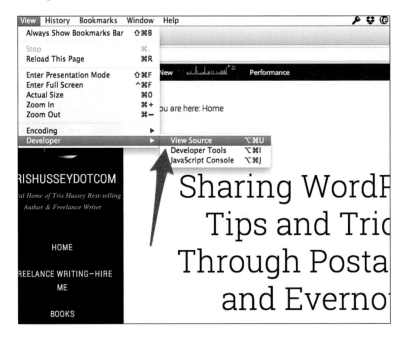

FIGURE 5.21

View Source command in Google Chrome for Mac.

Check the Help menu in your browser for information on finding the View Source command. When you view the source of my site, you'll see something like Figure 5.22.

FIGURE 5.22

The source for my website.

The trick is to look for the subtle indicators that a website is using WordPress and then where you might be able to discern what the theme is. The easy one for my site is that if you look closely, you'll find this line:

```
<meta name="generator" content="WordPress 3.6.1" />
```

That's a dead giveaway for WordPress. A lot of websites pull this out because it can tip your hand to hackers if your version of WordPress is out of date. Regardless, you can also look for things like /wp-content/plugins (or wp-content anything) to see if the website is running WordPress. For the theme, you'll need to look for something like this:

```
href="http://www.trishussey.com/wp-content/themes/sixteen-nine-pro/
```

This line tells you that my theme is called Sixteen Nine Pro. You can speed this up (and not strain your eyes) by using the find command (usually command or control-F) to look for /wp-content/themes/ on the page. Now that you know the theme, what's next? A quick search for that name in Google gives you the information (Figure 5.23).

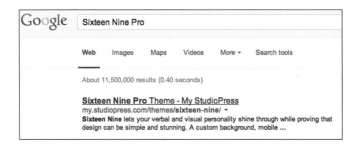

FIGURE 5.23

Google search for Sixteen Nine Pro.

If the search turns up more than just WordPress themes, add "WordPress theme" to the search. There you go—now you know that I'm running the StudioPress theme Sixteen Nine Pro (which is here, by the way: http://my.studiopress. com/themes/sixteen-nine/). Now you know how to see if a website is running WordPress and how to figure out what theme the site is using.

Conclusion

As you learned in the preceding chapter on installing plugins, most of the work, time, and energy you spend on themes is going to be looking for them and configuring them. Installing themes is easy and fast. Just remember: Download free themes only from WordPress.org, and buy themes from reputable and recommended foundries, and you'll be in good shape.

In Chapters 9 and 10, we'll be covering how themes work and how to use the various theme options to make even the default WordPress themes more of your own. Before we get there, though, let's get your website set up right—the first time.

IN THIS CHAPTER

- Basic WordPress settings to start with
- Setting up Akismet
- Setting up and managing users

6

SETTING UP YOUR WORDPRESS SITE RIGHT THE FIRST TIME

Part I of this book was all about getting WordPress running: installing things, getting themes in hand and ready to test, picking plugins to add extra features to your site. Now in Part II, the rubber hits the road and it's time to get your WordPress site really working for you. The first step is all about settings. The good thing is, there aren't many settings you need to worry about. In fact, many of the steps and tasks here are: download this plugin, activate it, configure it, and then forget about it (just keep it updated). Although I'll describe and show you all the main (default) settings screens, we're going to change settings on only two of them, and even those aren't going to be much of a change.

Basic WordPress Settings

From your Dashboard, the Settings button is where all the action for the basic WordPress settings happens. As we add and activate more plugins, some of those settings will appear under there as well. Some plugins and themes create their own buttons on the sidebar. It's nice in some ways, but annoying in others. When you turn on a plugin, sometimes it feels like a game of hide and seek to know where the settings are going to appear (if there are any to begin with). Figure 6.1 shows the Settings button with the fly-out menu. We're going to start with General settings, which you can pick from the fly-out menu, or just click the Settings button.

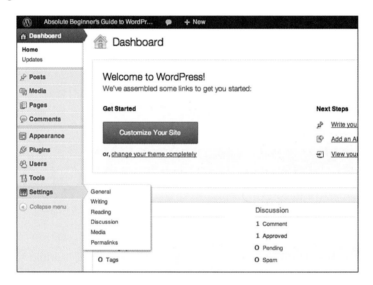

FIGURE 6.1

The Settings menu.

General Settings

Our first stop is General Settings. You need to look at only a couple things on this screen. First is the tagline. The Site Title you've already set, but if you'd like to take another stab at the title now, be my guest. The tagline helps describe the site a bit more for readers *and* search engines. Keep it to a short sentence at most. For the most part, you won't ever need to worry about the Site URL or WordPress Address—unless you move the website or something like that. I'll cover those instances in Chapter 17, "Advanced WordPress Settings and Uses," but for the time being, those are settings best left alone. Really—*alone*. Messing with those settings might not only take down your website, it could make it *really* hard for someone to help you fix it. If you need to update or change the email address for the site, here's where to do it. This is where things like new comments, notifications when users sign up, and password reset instructions are sent. This address gets all those emails.

Unless you're running a restricted members-only site or forum, you don't need to worry about the Anyone Can Register box or the default member role. These come in handy when you want people to register to get access to certain parts of your website, but that's about it. Visitors can still leave comments and read the public content of your site without being "a member" of the site.

The next section focuses on Time and Date. Of all the settings (how you format the date and time are self-explanatory), it's the time zone that's most important. Make sure you pick the time zone based on your city. Why? Because this makes sure that when you schedule posts or just plain old post, the timestamp of the post matches what you expect. It's really odd to see the post you just wrote show up at 5 a.m. the following day when it's really evening where you are. It's all about the time zone. WordPress doesn't really care what time it is, but you do! Figure 6.2 shows you all the settings and changes I made.

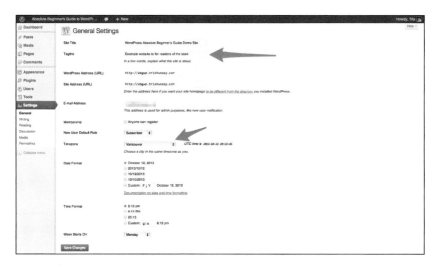

FIGURE 6.2

General Settings.

When you're done, don't forget to click Save Settings, or they won't be saved! That goes for all these settings screens, by the way.

Writing Settings

On this screen, you might, at some point, want to change the default category all posts will be assigned to if you don't assign a Category when you create the post. This will make a lot more sense in Chapter 11, "Using WordPress: Content," but for the moment, we can leave this setting alone. The Default Post Format (Standard/Normal, Aside, Quote, and so on) is going to be *theme dependent*. A theme will or won't support Post Formats (again, more in Chapter 11) and if your theme *does* support them, here is how to choose which Post Format will be selected when you start a new Post in the Editor. The Press This bookmarklet is very handy if you like to start a Post based on something you see online. After you drag the bookmarklet to your browser's menu bar, the next time you're on a site or post you'd like to include in new post, just click the bookmarklet and a little new post window pops up. Figure 6.3 shows you what this looks like.

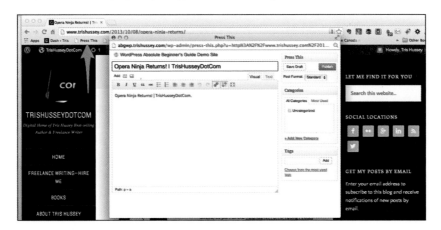

FIGURE 6.3

Using Press This to start a new post.

The section on Post by Email is an interesting one. Very few people take advantage of this feature. You can, believe it or not, send an email to a specific email address and it will appear as a post on your site. Yes, there could be issues with this (if someone got a hold of that address or spam was sent to it), but it *was* handy for a time. Starting in WordPress 3.9, this is one of the core WordPress features (like the Import-Export function several versions ago) that will be pulled out of the WordPress core, and if someone needs the functionality, it can be installed as a plugin. To you, this means that chances are that you won't even see this feature and probably didn't need it anyway.

The final section, Update Services, is one that, again, most users don't even know is there or what it's for. Way back in the early days of blogging, it was essential to use a service like Ping-o-matic to help get the word out. Today, it's helpful, but not required. Why is it still there? Because there is some benefit to using it to help search engines and other services know you have new content. Autoposting to Facebook and Twitter (which we'll cover later in this chapter) has almost entirely replaced Ping-o-matic and RSS for finding content online, but the majority of Internet users start a new search for something on Google or another search engine. Ping-o-matic: gone but not forgotten. You can see all the settings in Figure 6.4.

FIGURE 6.4

The Writing Settings screen.

Reading Settings

Although you might not go into the Reading Settings very often—or at all—this settings screen manages one of the most important parts of your website: what the home page will look like. Right at the top (Figure 6.5), you can see Front Page Displays and the choices Your Latest Posts or A Static Page. Here's what's going on there. Your latest post means your last 10 (that's the default number, and you can change it below) posts will make up the home page. However, this doesn't mean that your home page is limited only to posts. All this means is that a specific part of your WordPress template is set as the home page. That template part can do a lot of amazing things, more than just showing posts. A lot of "magazine style" themes need you to set Your Latest Posts as the setting so it can pull in all sorts of other dynamic content.

On the other hand, a static page means one page (we'll get to posts versus pages in Chapter 11) will be the home page. Whatever that page's content is will be there. It's great for creating a "traditional" website where you want the same sort of landing page content for all your visitors. Below that option button, you see the menus to choose which page will be the Front Page and which will be the Posts Page. I'll show you how all this works in Chapter 17, "Advanced WordPress Settings and Uses," but for the time being, if you pick the static page option, you need to set only the Front Page menu. We'll talk about what the Posts Page does later.

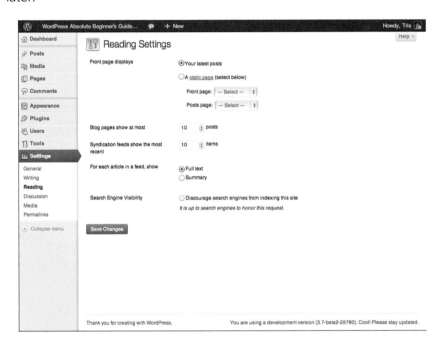

FIGURE 6.5

The Reading Settings screen.

Below those settings are the choices for how many posts are on the home page (assuming that's the option you chose) and how many posts are included in your RSS feed. You might have noticed if you've visited my personal site, http://trishussey.com, that I have only five posts on the home page. Why? I used to have 10, but lately I've been writing closer to two to three times a week instead of two to three times a *day*. I felt that showing the latest five posts gave readers a more current post list than doubling that number. Another bonus is that with half as many posts on the home page, my site loads marginally faster than it did with 10 posts. How many posts to show on your home page is up to you; pick the number that seems to match the frequency of your updates. I've seen more and more blogs with only the single newest post on the home page, but that selection also covers the subsequent pages, so I think paging through a blog a single post at a time is tedious.

As for the RSS feed choice, I'd leave it at 10 regardless of how many posts are on your home page. I've put a discussion about RSS on the sidebar, but essentially RSS is a computer-readable version of your posts (not pages). The number of posts you set determines how many of your posts people who use RSS to find and read blogs will see at a given time. RSS and RSS Readers never hit the mainstream, but they are still used and loved by the tech set to find, share, and read new content from websites. As for the choice of full text or summary in your feed, that is more complicated—and beyond the scope of this book—what it comes down to is whether the people reading your posts through an RSS reader will be able to read the entire post in their reader or have to click through to your site after the first few sentences. I pick full-text myself because I prefer to have people read my entire post in their RSS reader. However, I do experiment with switching to summaries to see if that changes my website traffic. I also publish the last 15 posts in my feed instead of the usual 10.

WHAT IS RSS?

RSS stands for Really Simple Syndication or Rich Site Summary or RDF Site Summary (depending on whom you ask) (http://en.wikipedia.org/wiki/RSS), but what the letters stand for doesn't matter as much as what it *does*. RSS was developed to allow people to publish a computer-readable list or feed of the recent content from their blog so people (and other websites) could subscribe to the feed and read the articles without having to visit the website. To use RSS, you need an RSS Reader, a piece of software that allows you to subscribe to feeds, have them checked periodically, and convert something computer-readable to something more human readable.

Figure 6.6 shows what my RSS feed looks like in its native format.

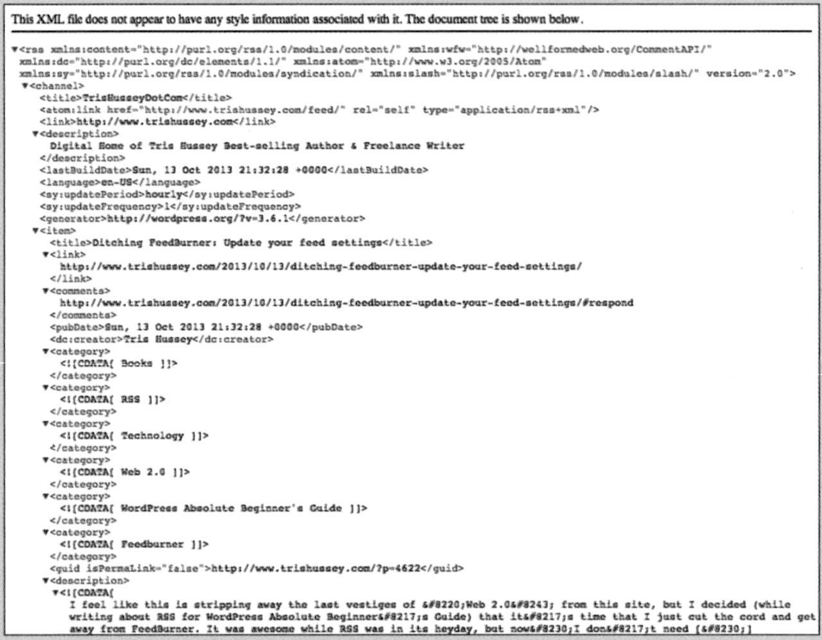
This XML file does not appear to have any style information associated with it. The document tree is shown below.


```
▼<rss xmlns:content="http://purl.org/rss/1.0/modules/content/" xmlns:wfw="http://wellformedweb.org/CommentAPI/"
 xmlns:dc="http://purl.org/dc/elements/1.1/" xmlns:atom="http://www.w3.org/2005/Atom"
 xmlns:sy="http://purl.org/rss/1.0/modules/syndication/" xmlns:slash="http://purl.org/rss/1.0/modules/slash/" version="2.0">
 ▼<channel>
    <title>TrisHusseyDotCom</title>
    <atom:link href="http://www.trishussey.com/feed/" rel="self" type="application/rss+xml"/>
    <link>http://www.trishussey.com</link>
   ▼<description>
     Digital Home of Tris Hussey Best-selling Author & Freelance Writer
    </description>
    <lastBuildDate>Sun, 13 Oct 2013 21:32:28 +0000</lastBuildDate>
    <language>en-US</language>
    <sy:updatePeriod>hourly</sy:updatePeriod>
    <sy:updateFrequency>1</sy:updateFrequency>
    <generator>http://wordpress.org/?v=3.6.1</generator>
   ▼<item>
     <title>Ditching FeedBurner: Update your feed settings</title>
    ▼<link>
       http://www.trishussey.com/2013/10/13/ditching-feedburner-update-your-feed-settings/
     </link>
    ▼<comments>
       http://www.trishussey.com/2013/10/13/ditching-feedburner-update-your-feed-settings/#respond
     </comments>
     <pubDate>Sun, 13 Oct 2013 21:32:28 +0000</pubDate>
     <dc:creator>Tris Hussey</dc:creator>
    ▼<category>
       <![CDATA[ Books ]]>
     </category>
    ▼<category>
       <![CDATA[ RSS ]]>
     </category>
    ▼<category>
       <![CDATA[ Technology ]]>
     </category>
    ▼<category>
       <![CDATA[ Web 2.0 ]]>
     </category>
    ▼<category>
       <![CDATA[ WordPress Absolute Beginner's Guide ]]>
     </category>
    ▼<category>
       <![CDATA[ Feedburner ]]>
     </category>
     <guid isPermaLink="false">http://www.trishussey.com/?p=4622</guid>
    ▼<description>
     ▼<![CDATA[
       I feel like this is stripping away the last vestiges of &#8220;Web 2.0&#8243; from this site, but I decided (while
       writing about RSS for WordPress Absolute Beginner&#8217;s Guide) that it&#8217;s time that I just cut the cord and get
       away from FeedBurner. It was awesome while RSS was in its heyday, but now&#8230;I don&#8217;t need [&#8230;]
```


FIGURE 6.6

An RSS feed in all of its XML glory.

But when I read it in my RSS reader, it looks like Figure 6.7.

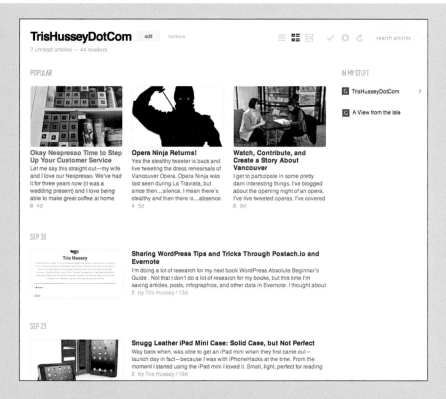

FIGURE 6.7

My feed items in a RSS reader.

That's a pretty big difference, I'd say. RSS never broke into the mainstream for *most people* to use, but RSS is still essential for tech journalists, sites that index and analyze content, and other tech-focused users. Those of us who make our livings by getting the most information we can put our hands on at any given moment *need* RSS to avoid having to jump and visit every site we're interested in to see if there is anything new to read.

The last part of the screen is whether you tell search engines to index your website. The box is unchecked by default because most people want search engines like Google to index their site. If you check the box, you're telling search engines not to index the site or visit again. When you uncheck the box, and save the settings, search engines *will* index the site again after you remind them you're around. We'll cover search engines and search engine optimization (SEO) later in this chapter. For the moment, just remember this is where the setting is if you need it.

Discussion Settings

The Discussion Settings page is jam-packed with check boxes and decisions, but in reality you probably won't ever need to visit it—the default settings are fine. I'm going to suggest a change or two, but even if you don't take my advice, things will be just fine. Really. Based on user feedback, the default Discussion Settings have been tweaked and tuned over the years, so they really have the best settings for 95% of bloggers and site owners. Let's start at the top with the Default Article Settings (Figure 6.8).

FIGURE 6.8

Discussion Settings (top half of the page).

The first two settings—Attempt to Notify Any Blogs Linked To from the Article and Allow Link Notifications from Other Blogs (Pingbacks and Trackbacks)—have to do with how your site interacts with other sites. If the first check box is checked, then whenever you post something, WordPress (at the server level) will attempt to let that other site know you've linked to it so that article can be included in the comments section of *its* site. The second box refers to how *your* site handles those same requests. Should you check them? (By default, the first one is not and the second one is.) If the first box is checked, you are helping to let other sites (and the people that run them) know you've linked to them, but the downside is that it can slow down how quickly your post is posted (by a second or two) if you link to a lot of different sites. The second box is more interesting. It is checked by default, and when someone links to your site, that link is listed as a "comment." That can look strange when there aren't any "comments" (real people leaving words about the post), but a number of comments is shown. It used to be that it was considered good blog citizenship to make sure both of these options were active, but today I don't believe it's as important. I've unchecked both of the boxes on my own blog. This doesn't mean that people can't link to my site—you can't stop that by the way—it just means that their links don't show up as comments (nor to mine on their sites). I'm willing to accept that for a little less clutter on my posts.

The last check box in this section, Allow People to Post Comments on New Articles, has to do with whether people can leave comments on posts. This is on by default, so your Posts and Pages will accept comments. As you see below the section, you can change any of these settings on a per article basis (either before or after you publish it). If you decide to leave this option checked and allow comments, and then change your mind later, there will be no comments allowed on future Posts and Pages. This isn't a retroactive change, so you will need to go back and turn off comments on your Posts and Pages manually. There are quick ways to do this, and I'll cover those in Chapter 11.

The Other Comment Settings section is pretty self-explanatory, but I'd like to mention one of the settings: Users Must Be Registered and Logged In to Comment. You might be tempted to require people to register an account on your site before they can leave a comment—resist this temptation. If you want people to leave comments, you need to make this as easy as possible. I think requiring a name and email is the right balance. By requiring someone to create an account, you *will* reduce the number of comments you will receive on your site. I know this from personal experience. Before I switched over to WordPress in 2005–2006, I used a great (and ahead of its time) engine called Blogware run and owned by Tucows. Blogware required—and there was no way around it—people to create a Blogware account to leave a comment. It was a royal pain for everyone. I probably would have received an order of magnitude more comments on my posts back then (and this is when I was blogging a *lot*) if there hadn't been an artificial barrier to commenting. Take my advice—leave this unchecked *unless* you need to require more information from people (for instance, if it's a restricted members-only site).

The email settings, by default, make sense. It lets you know when someone leaves a comment or there's a comment in moderation. Speaking of comment moderation, that's what the next several sections focus on.

Comment moderation means that before a comment will appear on your site, it has to pass through some steps. By default, the first time a "person" leaves a comment, it is held for you to review before it goes live. After that first approved comment, whenever that "person" leaves a comment, it will be posted immediately. I put "person" in quotes because, like email, blogs and websites receive comment spam. Special programs (called bots) comb through the Internet looking for blogs and sites they can leave comments on. The comments might *seem* real, but they contain links for illegal download sites, online pharmacies, and pretty much anything you get in your email spam. This could make approving comments a little tricky. What if you read a comment that *sounds* real (and the comment spam comments are getting better and better) and you approve it? Then that bot will know it can post spam comments willy-nilly on your site. Ouch. You might then be tempted to check to manually approve *all* comments *all* the time. Resist this temptation. We use plugins like Akismet to help protect our sites from spam. I'll talk more about Akismet later in this chapter, but for now, taking the step to require that you read and moderate *everything* is extreme. I can foresee cases where this would be a good idea, but in general, it's an extra burden on you that you don't need.

The boxes for Comment Moderation and Comment Blacklist (Figure 6.9) allow you to automatically flag (or block) comments that are submitted to your site. The number of links triggering moderation is a safety net in case you accidentally approve a spammer. Spam comments often contain lots of links (generally two or more) to the sites they'd like your visitors to fall victim to (and Google to index), so even if you've approved a comment from someone, if future comments contain two or more links, the comment will be thrown back into moderation. The box below that section allows you to enter words or phrases that automatically trigger moderation. You can put in any words you like, or leave it blank and allow Akismet to do the work for you. The Comment Blacklist section allows you to automatically dump comments with particular words, email addresses, and so on into spam. This is a blunt (like sledgehammer blunt) instrument, so use it with caution. I don't have anything in my comment blacklist—I haven't needed to—and if someone is going to inundate my site with spam, either Akismet will take care of it or they will be smart enough that trying to block their email or IP address (the computer where the comment was sent) will be fruitless.

FIGURE 6.9

Second half of the Discussion Settings screen.

The final section covers whether you will allow little pictures next to the comments people leave. The pictures are called avatars; you have choices on how tame or racy people's avatars can be (I leave my settings at "G") and if someone doesn't have an avatar, what to assign them. How do you get an avatar to show up with your comments? You just use Automattic-owned Gravatar (Figure 6.10) and register your name and email address. WordPress (and WordPress.com) will automatically pick up and pull in the picture you set. If you have lots of email addresses, you can include those in your profile and assign different pictures to different addresses. Figure 6.11 shows you all my avatars (or Gravatars) for my email addresses. Yes, it's the same picture; I like to be consistent with my photo around the Internet. Setting up Gravatar (it's free, by the way) is a great way to personalize your site for visitors. It gives a face to the words.

That does it for discussion settings. Remember, the default settings are fine, so if you never visit this settings page again, you'll be fine.

FIGURE 6.10

Gravatar homepage.

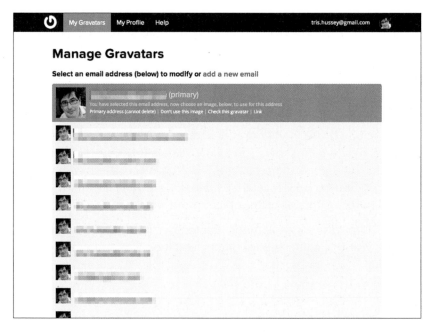

FIGURE 6.11

All my Gravatars...yes, all the same picture, but it doesn't have to be that way.

Media Settings

Media settings *don't* manage or control what you can or can't upload, but rather how images are handled when you upload them (as well as other media types). Figure 6.12 shows the settings for this page. Let's jump to the bottom of the settings and the check box Organize My Uploads into Month- and Year-Based Folders. I suggest you keep this checked. Figure 6.13 shows you what this looks like when you use FTP to connect to your site and look at the uploads directory. All the images are nicely organized. Figure 6.14 shows you what it looks like when you *don't* check the box. Day to day, will this make a difference to most users? No. Most WordPress users don't FTP into their sites to look for images very often; however, if you do need to look for an image, this is a much easier way to do things.

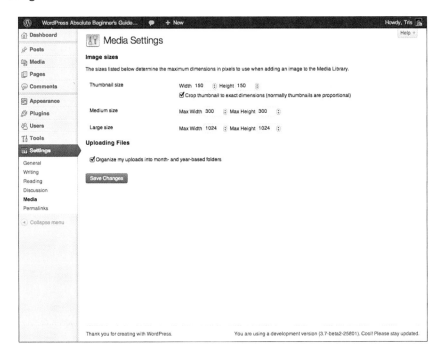

FIGURE 6.12

Media settings.

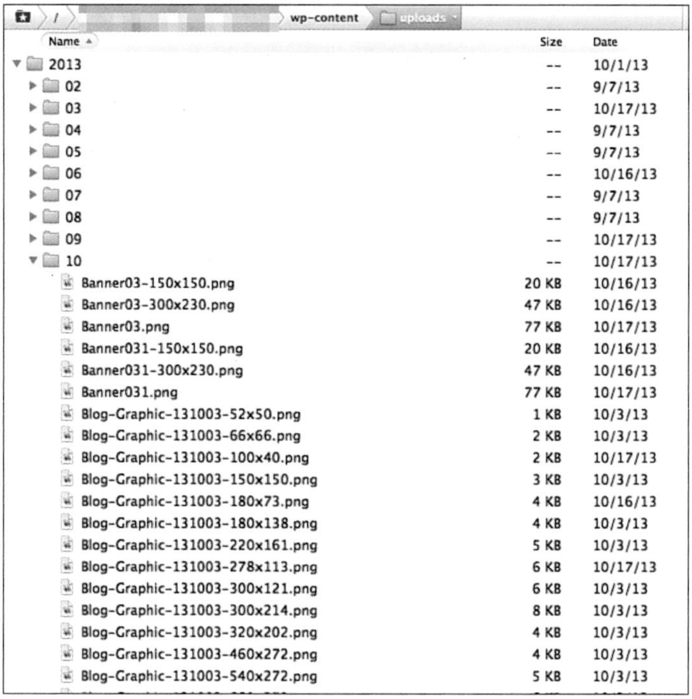

FIGURE 6.13

Organized uploads.

Name ▲	Size	Date
2010-02-01_21-thumb.38.091-150x150.png	12 KB	2/1/10 10:28 PM
2010-02-01_21-thumb.38.091-300x174.png	26 KB	2/1/10 10:28 PM
2010-02-01_21-thumb.38.091.png	32 KB	2/1/10 10:28 PM
2010-02-01_21-thumb.49.22-150x150.png	12 KB	2/1/10 10:28 PM
2010-02-01_21-thumb.49.22-300x135.png	18 KB	2/1/10 10:28 PM
2010-02-01_21-thumb.49.22.png	22 KB	2/1/10 10:28 PM
2010-12-17_11-31-40-150x150.png	7 KB	12/17/10 12:17 PM
2010-12-17_11-31-40-300x188.png	22 KB	12/17/10 12:17 PM
2010-12-17_11-31-40-940x198.png	71 KB	12/17/10 12:17 PM
2010-12-17_11-31-40-1024x644.png	229 KB	12/17/10 12:17 PM
2010-12-17_11-31-40.png	84 KB	12/17/10 12:17 PM
2010-12-17_11-32-47_2-150x150.png	21 KB	12/17/10 12:17 PM
2010-12-17_11-32-47_2-300x182.png	48 KB	12/17/10 12:17 PM
2010-12-17_11-32-47_2-940x198.png	134 KB	12/17/10 12:17 PM
2010-12-17_11-32-47_2-1024x624.png	421 KB	12/17/10 12:17 PM
2010-12-17_11-32-47_2.png	421 KB	12/17/10 12:17 PM
2010-12-17_11-32-47-150x150.png	27 KB	12/17/10 12:17 PM
2010-12-17_11-32-47-300x270.png	86 KB	12/17/10 12:17 PM
2010-12-17_11-32-47-682x198.png	90 KB	12/17/10 12:17 PM
2010-12-17_11-32-47.png	208 KB	12/17/10 12:17 PM
2011-01-06_11-12-32-150x150.png	30 KB	Jan 6, 2011 4:55 PM
2011-01-06_11-12-32-300x248.png	78 KB	Jan 6, 2011 4:55 PM
2011-01-06_11-12-32-940x198.png	113 KB	Jan 6, 2011 4:55 PM
2011-01-06_11-12-32.png	619 KB	Jan 6, 2011 4:55 PM
2011-01-06_11-13-50-141x300.png	54 KB	Jan 6, 2011 4:55 PM
2011-01-06_11-13-50-150x150.png	29 KB	Jan 6, 2011 4:55 PM
2011-01-06_11-13-50-483x1024.png	488 KB	Jan 6, 2011 4:55 PM
2011-01-06_11-13-50-940x198.png	150 KB	Jan 6, 2011 4:55 PM
2011-01-06_11-13-50.png	1.3 MB	Jan 6, 2011 4:55 PM

FIGURE 6.14

Disorganized uploads.

Now back to the top of Media Settings.

When you upload an image to WordPress, WordPress *automatically* tries to make three copies of your image: thumbnail, medium size, and large size (WordPress won't make copies that are larger than the original image). This means if you upload an image that is 600×700 pixels, WordPress won't create the Large size image, only the Medium and Thumbnail sizes. Why does WordPress do this at all? Flexibility and speed. In Chapters 11 and 12, we'll talk more about media and how to use it, but here's the gist of it.

When you want to insert an image into a page, WordPress gives you the option of choosing from these predefined sizes. This helps you match the size of the image to what you what to show (flexibility), but instead of inserting the full-size image scaled down for the screen, WordPress uses an image that is actually *smaller* (dimensions *and* file size). For example, a picture from an 8-megapixel camera produces images that are about 2448×3264 pixels and 4.7 megabytes. When you upload that image to WordPress, copies of that image are created with those new dimensions—the same as if you opened the image in an image editor, scaled the image down, and saved the smaller image. Figure 6.15 shows you what happens when I uploaded my 4.7 (rounded to 5) megabyte picture to WordPress. I have the Original, Large, Medium, Thumbnail, plus an extra size for Featured images. Note that it isn't just the *dimensions* that are smaller, but the *file sizes* are smaller as well. Smaller files download faster and load faster onscreen. One of the old ways of making an image *look* smaller was to load the original image but scale it onscreen to the size you need. This would mean that the same 5-megabyte image would need to download regardless of how small or large the image appeared onscreen. Nice trick, but it made for slow-loading websites.

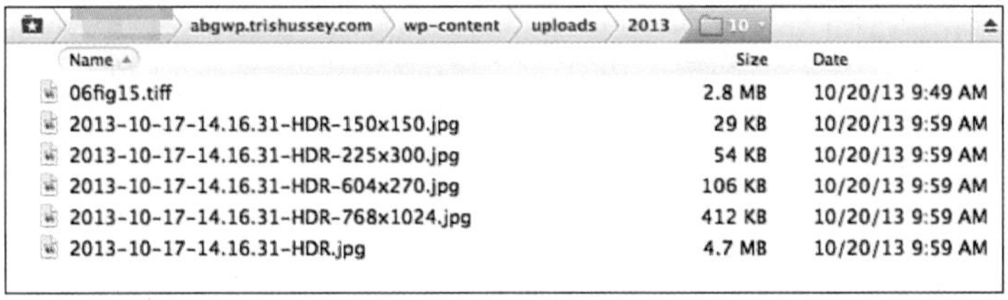

Name ▲	Size	Date
06fig15.tiff	2.8 MB	10/20/13 9:49 AM
2013-10-17-14.16.31-HDR-150x150.jpg	29 KB	10/20/13 9:59 AM
2013-10-17-14.16.31-HDR-225x300.jpg	54 KB	10/20/13 9:59 AM
2013-10-17-14.16.31-HDR-604x270.jpg	106 KB	10/20/13 9:59 AM
2013-10-17-14.16.31-HDR-768x1024.jpg	412 KB	10/20/13 9:59 AM
2013-10-17-14.16.31-HDR.jpg	4.7 MB	10/20/13 9:59 AM

FIGURE 6.15

See how the file sizes are different?

Often, people change these size settings based on their theme or preference. The check box below the Thumbnail size means that the image will be cropped to those (square) dimensions. If you uncheck the box, the thumbnail will be cropped based on the longest side and the other dimension in proportion with the original image. So a rectangular image will have a rectangular thumbnail with the longest side at 150 pixels.

Permalinks

The final default setting (before activating any plugins) is permalinks. Your first question is probably, "What the heck is a permalink?," which is a good question because it gets to the heart of why WordPress and other modern Content Management Systems (CMS) are much, much better than ones that came before (including the commercial ones that cost tens of thousands of dollars).

Back when people first realized that it was much more efficient to manage a web-site when the content was stored in a database and the theme kept separate, it was an amazing innovation. It made managing large websites much easier for Webmasters and administrators. People could update content, and there was little risk of something going wrong that could take down the site. The problem was that the URLs (the addresses you see in your browser's address bar) were created only when a user—an individual human user—clicked a link to visit that page. If you tried to bookmark that page, it wouldn't work; often you'd wind up back at the home page (if done well) or with a page not found error (if handled poorly). Why? Because that original URL *didn't exist any longer*. This gave rise to two problems: One, people couldn't bookmark websites. Annoying, but not a killer. Two, Google couldn't index the website beyond the home page. Google's index-ing robots often couldn't find or follow the links from one page to another. And if it did follow them, subsequent visits would return different URLs for the same pages. This was a search engine disaster for site owners. Then came the idea of "permalinks," or *permanent links*. Instead of the posts you write and publish hav-ing a different URL whenever someone visits the post, it will always have the same URL. Also, when any page is rendered for visitors or Google's indexing bots, the code uses regular HTML links that can be followed, indexed, and bookmarked. The permalink meant that CMSs that use them would be treated by visitors and Google as "regular" websites, while still reaping the benefits of keeping content in a database and themes safety out of reach.

The Permalink Settings screen (Figure 6.16) allows you to set how the permalinks are set and created for your site. The default is pretty ugly and looks like this: http://abgwp.trishussey.com/?p=123. This is a problem because the URL doesn't give any indication of what the post or page's title is. Maybe that's not a big deal to people, but the URL name *does* matter to Google. The examples on the set-tings screen—at least the ones I recommend—all include the post name as part of the link. There is a trend—and recommendations from many SEO experts—that the setting Post Name is the best choice for most people. Although this is true, just having the post name doesn't give your visitors a clear sense of when that post was written. Including a combination of year, month, and day fixes that. Is it better? That is an answer best left up to you. I had the Day and Name setting (including year, month, day, and post name) for a long time, but recently changed to Post Name. I think Post Name looks cleaner and pleasing to visitors (as well as better for search engines). Don't worry, WordPress won't allow for duplicates in the Post Name field—that's an automatic thing handled when you create a post or page.

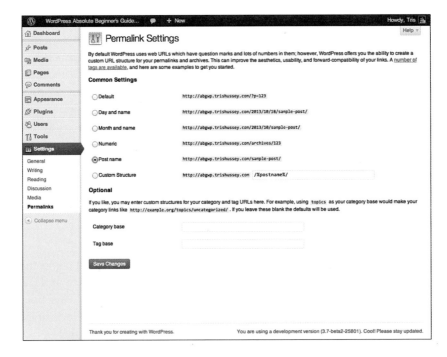

FIGURE 6.16

Permalink Settings screen.

NOTE What if I change my mind? I mentioned that I had one Permalink setting and then changed it. So, is that a problem? Not if you handle it correctly. What you have to do is make sure that search engines that have recorded the URLs of all your posts *and* people who have bookmarked a particular post will get to the right post. This is handled with a *redirect*. There are plugins to help you with permalink redirects, but the most efficient way to manage them is to edit your .htaccess file yourself with the right code. Which brings up the next question: What is the right code? That's a little more complicated because it depends on what you had and what you are changing to. I used a handy tool from SEO expert Joost de Valk (http://yoast.com/change-wordpress-per-malink-structure/) that let me enter what the previous permalink structure was before switching to Post Name; it then generates the code so no visitors (human or computer) would lose their way. Other tools will let you change from any permalink structure to another, but because the trend (and my preference) is now Post Name, this is what I'd suggest you try. Or just start with Post Name to begin with.

The last section of the setting screen is an optional one and allows you to change what visitors see when they are reading a category or tag archive. The default would be like this: http://abgwp.trishussey.com/category/about-wordpress/. You could change it to read http://abgwp.trishussey.com/topic/about-wordpress/. A subtle difference, but it matters in some cases. We'll talk more about Category and Tag archives in Chapter 10, but remember where this setting is if you decide to change it later.

Like all settings, before you leave the page, you need to click Save Changes. Unlike other settings, your Permalink Settings edit a file on the server—the .htaccess file—which tells the web server how to create the URLs for posts, pages, visitors, and search bots. Generally, when you click Save Changes, you will see a yellow bar at the top of the screen that says Permalink Structure Updated, but if WordPress can't modify the file on the server, you will be told you have to do it manually. Don't worry—you're given the code to do it, but this means you will have to use FTP connect to your site, open the .htaccess file in a text editor (you will probably need to tell your FTP client to show invisible files; .htaccess is a file the servers like to keep hidden), copy the code from the Permalink Settings page, paste it into .htaccess, and save it back to your server. The good thing is that this error happens much more rarely now that it did in the past. If you get stuck on this part, don't worry—it will be easy to find someone close by to help you.

Akismet

This is the only plugin-specific setting and section that we're going to tackle in this chapter. Akismet is a free plugin from Automattic that is preinstalled (not activated) with WordPress. Akismet's entire purpose is to keep your blog free of comment and trackback spam. Believe me, you want to have Akismet activated and configured on your blog. Without it, you risk spammers leaving comments and trackbacks on your posts and pages that you do not want there; also, links to bad sites lower your search engine ranking on Google. Turning on Akismet is easy. Just go to the Plugins screen and click Activate. The next step is to request an Akismet key from Akismet.com (Figure 6.17).

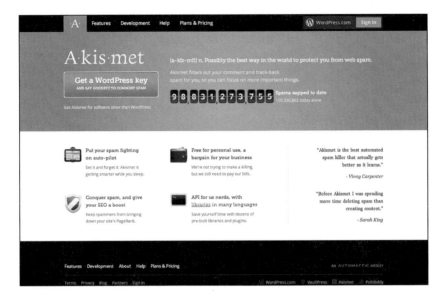

FIGURE 6.17

Akismet.com.

Akismet works through a network of servers that *constantly* monitor sites for spam comments. As users mark comments spam (or not spam), Akismet learns so it can improve. As you can imagine, this kind of processing horsepower doesn't come cheap, which is why Akismet has pricing plans for users. There are plans ranging from free to enterprise level (Figure 6.18).

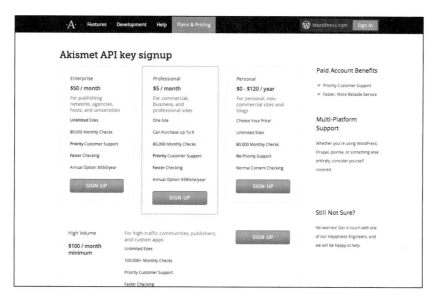

FIGURE 6.18

Akismet pricing plans.

For personal users, picking the free level is fine, but if you'd like to chip in a little to help, that is better. Companies and people using Akismet for business should purchase a plan so they get better support, faster spam checking, and other benefits. The Akismet settings screen (Figure 6.19) is pretty straightforward. Except for putting the number of comments approved by each commenter's name (I'd leave that one off), there isn't anything to do. The default is to automatically delete spam comments on posts more than a month old (which helps keep clutter down). Before you can get to this point, however, you need to get your Akismet key.

FIGURE 6.19

Akismet settings screen.

When you first turn on the plugin, you'll see something like Figure 6.20.

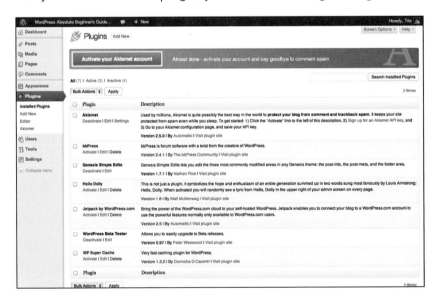

FIGURE 6.20

Akismet on the plugins screen.

When you click the button, you get to Figure 6.21.

FIGURE 6.21

Next step, requesting a key!

If have your Akismet key already (when you request or buy your key, you receive it in email as well as onscreen), click the link below (Figure 6.22).

FIGURE 6.22

Entering your Akismet key.

If the key is valid, you should see a page similar to Figure 6.19. That's it! Akismet should be ready and running, and you won't have to think about it again.

Setting the Right User Roles

In Chapter 3, "Installing WordPress," I talked briefly about users and user roles. Now I'm going to delve a little deeper into the topic and give you the full story on how to create and manage users. First, here are the five main WordPress user roles/types:

- **Administrator**—Somebody who has access to all the administration features within a site.

- **Editor**—Somebody who can publish and manage posts, including the posts of other users.

- **Author**—Somebody who can publish and manage his or her own posts.

- **Contributor**—Somebody who can write and manage his or her own posts but cannot publish them.

- **Subscriber**—Somebody who can only manage his or her profile.

When you installed WordPress, the Administrator role was created for you. User number one is always an Administrator—at first. You can have more than one user given Administrator privileges on the site, but make sure the people who have these privileges *need* them and *you can trust them not to break things*. The Administrator role has enough privileges to do your site serious harm if used carelessly (or maliciously). Administrators can change all the settings, add and remove plugins, add and remove themes, and create and delete content. Administrators can do everything on the website. I've worked with a lot of people who've set all the people who need to post or contribute to a site with Administrator (or Admin, for short) privileges. One of the first things I suggested was to audit who needs to do what and adjust their roles as needed. Because Admins can do *everything* on a site, and that's not always a good idea, who should have the previously described roles? First let's look at the user-creation process; then we'll talk about the promoting and demoting aspect of this.

From the Dashboard, pass your mouse pointer over the Users button, and from the fly-out menu, choose New User (Figure 6.23).

FIGURE 6.23

Add New (User) from menu.

The Add New User screen (Figure 6.24) is straightforward, and the only things you need to set right now are the user's email address, username (you can use capitals and spaces, so "Tris Hussey" is an acceptable username), the password, and role. Although WordPress 3.7 brought in a better password strength meter, there isn't an option for a random password to be assigned for the user. If you're the sort who'd like your site to be secure, using good, strong passwords is a must. I use a random password generator through my password manager program, but if you don't have access to one of those, here are three places you can generate random passwords for users:

- RANDOM.ORG—Password Generator (random.org)

- Norton Identity Safe Password Generator (https://identitysafe.norton.com/password-generator)

- Symantec/PCTools Password Generator (http://www.pctools.com/guides/password/)

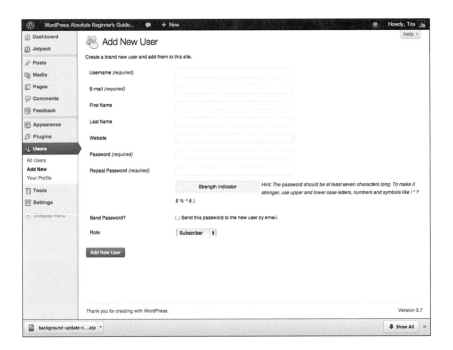

FIGURE 6.24

Add New User screen.

I also check the box to have the password emailed to the user. The only downside to that approach is that the email doesn't include the URL to log in to the site (which is http://[siteurl]/wp-login.php—that is, http://abgwp.trishussey.com/wp-login.php). Which means you either send two emails to each user or one email, but you send it manually. I'd go for the latter option in many cases, unless you're dealing with people who are old hands at WordPress and will be able to figure out where to go.

Now let's talk about who should have which roles on your site. Admins should only be the people who need to change settings, manage updates, install plugins, install themes, manage users, and have the final say over content. On most sites, this should be one or two people (maybe three). Just having one admin (and if the rest of the team doesn't know the login) is too risky for me. I like to plan for the "hit by a bus" scenario; there needs to be a backup to the admin in case something goes wrong and the primary admin isn't available. Yes, for your own personal site, this is overkill, but for a company or group, it's absolutely critical to have a backup admin, even if that backup admin is there only for emergencies.

The Editor role is what even admins only need to use day-to-day. Editors have complete control over all the content on the site. They can publish (or unpublish) content from any user on the site. The person in this role can be trusted that when content is published live, it is good, has been proofread, and is acceptable. You can have multiple editors, of course. For a lot of sites, this is probably a handful of people you trust with content decisions, but not with administering the website. I tend to set the boss as Editor so she feels in control of all the content, but can't accidentally do something to completely break the site.

There is a good case to be made—and a common security recommendation—that even for a personal site, you should log in to an admin account only when you need to administer things (updates, settings, and so on) and use an editor account the rest of the time. I've tried this myself and find the switching back and forth to be too much of a hassle. Usually when I'm running a site, I'm doing admin things pretty often (especially plugin updates), so the back and forth thing doesn't work for me—which means that I have to be extra careful with my passwords and how (and where) I log in to my site.

The Author role is for people you trust to be able to write and post content on their own, without an Editor needing to give it a once over first. This is a standard, general role for most site users. If you work in a team where *everyone* needs to be able to work on *all* the content, you'll have fewer Authors than Editors, but if you have just a core of writers, the Author role is perfect. Authors can manage only their own content, not other Authors or Contributors.

Contributors can write whatever they please, but the content can't be published until an Editor or Admin does it. This is the kind of role you use for writers who need to have a quick read of their posts before they go live.

Subscribers are "members" of the site, but can't create content at all. They are just readers/viewers of the site. If you're creating a private site, which I'll talk about in Chapter 17, "Advanced WordPress Settings and Uses," this role will let people in to read the content of the site.

If you need to change someone's role, first click All Users under Users (or just click the Users button itself). Then click the Edit Link that appears when you pass your mouse pointer under the user's name. Figure 6.25 shows the top of the Edit User screen.

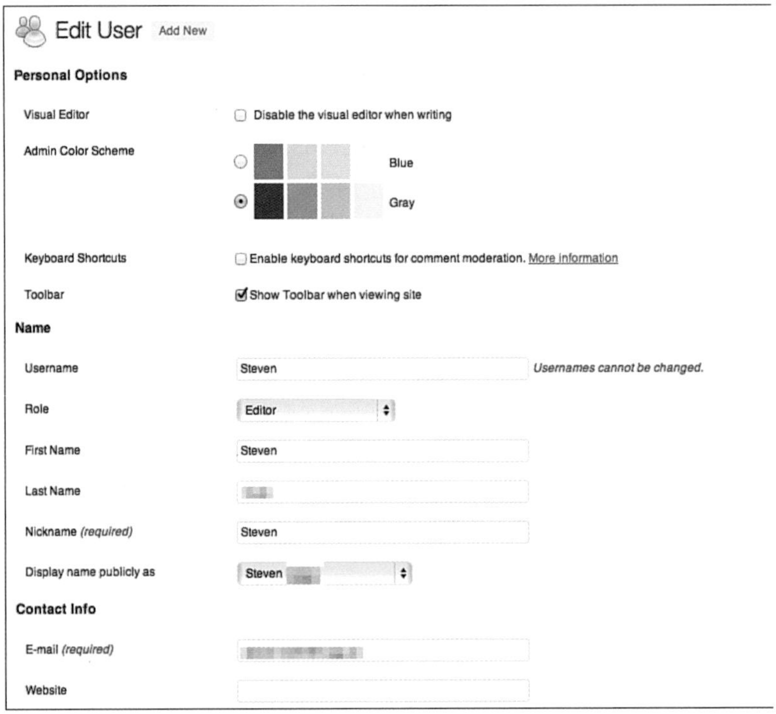

FIGURE 6.25

Edit user screen.

From this screen, you can edit everything about the user that you need to—as long as you're an admin. As an admin, if you need to demote another admin, you can do that as well, but you can't demote *yourself* from being an admin. You can change anything else about your user profile, except your own role.

The rest of the Edit User screen (or Edit Profile, if you're editing your own account) covers things like what color scheme you'd like to use for the Dashboard, your nickname, how to show your name publicly, website, and bio. Other plugins add fields like Twitter ID, Google+ profile, and other social media links. At the bare minimum, I'd have people make sure their first name, last name, nickname, and how to display their name on the site are all set.

That's all about users in a nutshell. As the admin, you can reset people's passwords, delete them, and do all sorts of things. Use that power wisely or you might wind up with your site in a world of hurt.

Conclusion

This chapter is just the first part in a settings chapter trilogy that sets the stage for you to have a really great site. In this chapter, I've covered the basic settings you need to get going. If you were to stop here and jump ahead, you'd be okay for a while—we have the important, basic things all covered. The next two chapters start to dig into the nitty gritty of setting your site up the right way—the first time. In Chapter 7, "Setting Up Your WordPress Site the Right Way: SEO, Social Media, and More," I'll cover making sure your site is found and indexed by search engines, how to connect your site to social media, how to make your site load as fast as possible, and finally, include a little discussion about backup and security. Chapter 8, "All About Jetpack Settings," is all about the very powerful—and a little contro-versial—plugin Jetpack by WordPress.com. Yes, a whole chapter on a single plugin. The funny thing is, I cover only the *best parts* of the plugin in the chapter. There is so much more to the plugin that it could have a book all its own.

So we've got the basic settings done, and I'm sure you're ready for more tweak-ing and tuning. So—on with the next chapter in the settings trilogy: SEO, social media, and more.

IN THIS CHAPTER

- WordPress SEO tips and settings
- Connecting WordPress to social media
- Helping WordPress load your website faster
- WordPress security tips

7

SETTING UP YOUR WORDPRESS SITE THE RIGHT WAY: SEO, SOCIAL MEDIA, AND MORE

Chapter 6, "Setting Up Your WordPress Site Right the First Time," did the ground work for this chapter. Our site has all the basic—and essential—stuff done, so we can move on to more detailed topics. This chapter covers the things that separate good sites from great ones: managing search engines, making sure your site loads quickly, using social media, and security. All these tasks are essentially optional, but I believe you'll come to realize that this chapter might be the most important chapter in the whole book. This is the chapter that will help you make sure your site can stand above the rest and be a rock solid platform for your words, your business, or your hobbies.

Doing WordPress SEO the Right Way

Right off the top, I'm going to give you some good news about WordPress and search engine optimization (SEO)—from the start, WordPress is about 90% optimized for search engines. Right, before you do *anything*, WordPress has things well in hand. In fact, even if you do just a few simple things in your writing and the General settings, you're 95% there. In this section, I'm going to get you to 100% and you'll be happy to know that even that last 5% is pretty easy. Let's start with the first 5% to bring you closer to 100%—settings and writing.

Settings

Earlier in this chapter, I talked about General settings, and if you flip back to Chapter 6 and look at Figure 6.2, you see the first settings you need to think about: Site Title and Tagline. If your site name is "My site" and your tagline is something like "Just another site built on WordPress," you're missing out on a great SEO opportunity. First, make the site title something short, but descriptive. For the demo site, you've been seeing my screenshots: "WordPress Absolute Beginner's Guide Demo Site." It's pretty descriptive and sums up what I want casual visitors to know about this site (essentially that it's not a "real" site that will have any content). The site tagline in Figure 6.2 says: "Example website for readers of the book," which begs the question: Which book? That's in the title, but I'd like Google to associate this site with the book (or at least I would if I planned on this site having a long life). So while writing this chapter, I took the opportunity to change the tagline to: "Example website for readers of the book WordPress Absolute Beginner's Guide" (trust me, I changed it; you can look at the demo site and see). Much better! Now search engines and visitors will connect "book" with "WordPress Absolute Beginner's Guide." Applying this to your own site, make sure the tagline is a short sentence or phrase that describes *exactly* what the site is about and what you'd like people (and search engines) to expect.

The next setting, which you should have already taken care of, is make sure you're using "pretty permalinks." Like in Figure 6.16, I have this site (and all the sites I manage) set to Post Name under Permalinks Settings. This setting makes sure that when visitors look at the URL in your address bar, there is a bit of a cue about what the post is about *and* search engines have some starter keywords to begin indexing and categorizing your post or page (for the record, Pages always use the Post Name setting regardless of your Permalinks setting). That's it for settings and SEO—for now. When we install some SEO-related plugins, they will have their own settings to manage, but if you don't install them, use the preceding settings and the writing tips I'm going to talk about in a moment. You're going to do pretty well in the search engine front.

Writing

Writing for SEO is *not* about *keyword stuffing* (artificially adding into the post a lot of keywords, sometimes unrelated to the topic); it's about adopting a mindset to write your posts and craft titles while considering both what search engines and people are looking for. None of the suggestions I'm going to give you will get you in trouble with Google. In fact, these suggestions are based on Google's own Matt Cutts' suggestions. Matt is responsible for keeping spam results out of Google search results—so if this is what he recommends, it's going to be okay.

Descriptive Titles

Let's start at the top: Post and Page titles. I'll get to the mechanics of writing and posting in Chapter 11, "Using WordPress: Content," but for now accept that Posts and Pages need titles, people read them, and search engines index them. They matter. A lot. Here are some titles for posts that I wrote about the same time I've been working on this chapter. See if you can tell what the post is about:

- 5 Real Tips to Get More Done at Work

- Encouraging Attention to Detail Starts at the Top

- Why Email Is Terrible for Updates

- Proud to Be a Gleek

- iWork for Free Might Mean the End of MS Office Tyranny

- I'm a Mercenary Writer and Here's How I Can Help You

- 10 Tips to Break Through Writer's Block

I'm confident that if you just read the title of the post, you'll have a good idea of what the post was going to be about—and so would Google. All these titles are *descriptive*; the words I chose describe what the post is about. Tips for getting more done at work, tips for breaking through writer's block (near and dear to my heart), iWork, MS Office, all these have *meaning* to you. Now here is another set of post titles:

- Do People Want to Work for You?

- Failure Is the Only Goal and Option

- Transparency: I Can See Right Through You

- Go Exploring, Get Inspired

I wrote these titles to be *less* about description and *more* about catching attention. This isn't bad, but you don't want to indulge your inner punster or "too clever by half" sense of humor too often. These titles were written to get *clicks* more than to be descriptive. You'll notice, though, that there are still keywords in the titles—keywords that I'd like people to find my posts based on. The key is to make titles that describe what the post is about, while being interesting for people to click on if they see the title on Facebook or Twitter. This isn't always easy. It's never easy to write good titles, but with practice you'll get it.

Write Normally

Moving down from the title to the body of the post, let's talk about *how* you write your posts. It comes down to this: be normal. Write descriptively (make sure people know what your post is about as they are reading it), write using synonyms for ideas and phrases (this lets Google associate your post with the rich breadth of language that exists), don't try to include all the keywords for a topic in your post. If the words naturally flow into your writing, fine. If you're forcing extra words in, that's bad. Google might not penalize you right away, but your writing will sound robotic, stilted, and just…off.

Normal writing is rich in keywords and ideas. Consider this section. How many different ways have I said pretty much the same ideas? Is it boring? Does it flow and sound normal? No and yes (at least I hope so). That's what you're going for in your own writing.

Use Headings

One of the new realities of our online world is how we're reading things. Reading online is much different from reading on a physical piece of paper. You probably already know this in your gut if you hadn't noticed it. Online, people skim pages more, and their eyes jump around the page. Large blocks of text seem like daunting masses that you need to mentally gear down in order to read. So here's a trick for both SEO *and* to help people get more out of your writing: use headings.

Already built in to the WordPress Editor is the capability to set heading levels from 1 (usually the title) to 6. When you change in topic—sometimes even a minor one—throw in a heading. Personally, I don't usually do more than heading levels 2 or 3, but a big document might need more. Look at this book. There are headings, subheadings, and even sub-subheadings to help you find your place in the flow of the section and chapter. When you do this within your post, both your readers and Google pull the context out of that heading (because labeling something Heading 2 means that text is important) and ensure it is part of the metadata (the data that Google interprets about a piece of content) for the post. So while readers just acknowledge "oh, this is what this section is about," Google records that information as part of the index of the post—and in relation to all other posts.

Like Post or Page titles, use descriptive headings and subheadings as well.

Descriptive Links

If you do a search on Google (or any search engine) for "click here," you will get a lot of different results. In fact, few of them are even related to each other. When I did a search (just for kicks), the results were so awesome that I had to make it into a figure (Figure 7.1).

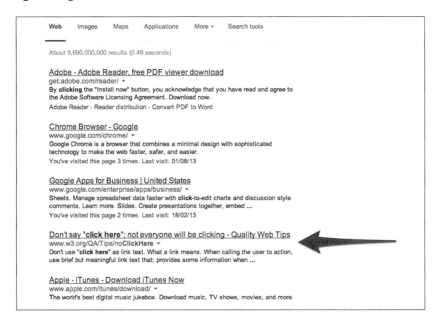

FIGURE 7.1

Search on Google for "click here"; note the result with the arrow.

The W3C is the group that sets the standards for HTML and how web pages work online. The highlighted page from the results (http://www.w3.org/QA/Tips/noClickHere) talks about how and why to use descriptive links so well that you need to memorize it. It boils down to this: Click here doesn't really *mean* anything. You don't know what you're getting or going or why. It's the difference between "To learn more about me click here" and "Learn more about my background, skills, and publications." Which makes more sense? Which gives you context? If the link text gives you context and makes sense to you, it's also good SEO. Simple as that. Don't use "click here" unless there is no other way around it. Make the text of your links something that gives an indication of the destination after clicking.

ALT Text for Images

I'll show you *how* to do this in Chapter 12, "Using WordPress: Images, Videos, and Other Media," but for now we're going to talk about the *why*. When you insert an image into a post or page, there is a little part of the code called the *ALT tag*. ALT stands for alternative and is supposed to be text that the visitor can read if the image isn't loaded. Something like "header graphic," "[company] logo," "screenshot of General settings." This text can serve several purposes. For the visually impaired, the software that reads their web pages aloud will read the image ALT text to give the listener something more than "image" to go on. For Google, ALT tags add more context and data to the post or page so it can put that piece of content into context with all the other pieces of content on the Internet.

Everything about this writing section is about *context for your readers and Google*. There are billions of pieces of content spread across hundreds of millions of websites. For people to find your particular piece of content, you need to make sure Google knows as much about it as possible. The better your titles, the better you write, the more descriptive your links—all these combine to give Google the context it needs so that when someone searches for tips to break writer's block, for example, there is a good chance readers will find my post.

Categories and Tags

We'll talk more about categories and tags in Chapter 11, "Using WordPress: Content," but as far as SEO goes, they are an essential part of Google understanding the context of your content. I'll show you all about creating and managing them later; just file away "Tris said to use categories and tags" and think of them as keywords for your posts. In addition to helping you organize your content for your readers and visitors, categories and tags help Google and other search engines put all the content of your site into context with itself *and* all the other content out there.

Plugins

In order to bring your SEO efforts to 100%, the last bit is handled by one or more plugins. From Chapter 4, "Installing WordPress Plugins," you can probably guess that I'm going to recommend using either All In One SEO Pack *or* WordPress SEO by Yoast. It's *essential* that you do *not* run both of these plugins at the same time. They will conflict with each other and generally mess things up. One of the things I like most about both plugins now is that neither of them needs much in the way of configuration to work. In fact, for both of them, I suggest looking at the home page title and description settings. All In One SEO Pack works off a (mostly) single page configuration screen, and the home page section is close to the top (Figure 7.2).

FIGURE 7.2

The settings home page for All In One SEO Pack.

For WordPress SEO, the similar setting can be found under the Titles & Meta section under the Home tab (Figure 7.3).

FIGURE 7.3

WordPress SEO settings home page.

Under both plugins, you can set a different, maybe more descriptive, title and description (the meta information search engines index) for just the home page of your site while keeping the "regular" site name and tagline the same for all other parts of your site. Why bother with this? It gives you a chance to optimize your home page for people searching for particular keywords and ideas without cluttering up the titles of the other pages.

Both of these plugins do an array of amazing SEO things for you in the background—I highly recommend you take advantage of these:

- Rewrite Post and Page titles on the site so the title of the content comes before the site name. This is an essential SEO step; search engines only record the first so many characters of a title, so you don't want them indexing your site name and only *part* of the title over and over. This forces the title to come first and be indexed; the site name stays the same, so that's not as important.

- Create XML site maps for your site. WordPress SEO does this automatically for you. All In One SEO Pack has a separate option to turn it on (under Feature Manager, Figure 7.4).

- And a lot more under the hood changes to ensure your site is tuned for Google and all other search engines.

FIGURE 7.4

XML sitemaps in All In One SEO Pack.

 NOTE If you turn on the XML site maps feature, you don't need Google XML site maps or a similar plugin. One plugin per job!

SEO is one of those crucial parts of running a website, so there tends to be *a lot* of plugins, tricks, and tools out there to "help" you. I've tried a lot of the tools and talked with a lot of colleagues about SEO: I believe if you go with either of these two plugins (and make sure you enable the XML site map feature in All In One SEO Pack), you are in good hands. These plugins work—they don't do anything devious to your website, they follow Google's rules/recommendations, and they are in active development (which means they are updated frequently). My advice is to try both of these plugins for a while (one at a time, remember!) and see which you like more and which you think gives you the best results—increased search traffic to your site.

The suggestions and settings in this section aren't SEO voodoo. These aren't things that you're doing to try to game Google. Trying to game Google will only get you penalized by Google. What I recommend are solid, proven SEO techniques that are easy to follow and, in fact, add a lot of value to your content (descriptiveness, context, categorization). Yes, there are a lot of other things you can do to help your SEO, but that's beyond this chapter. It's time to move on to the next set of settings: social media sharing.

Using Social Media Sharing Tools

There are two kinds of social media sharing tools that you need to look for. One is letting people share your content to their social network, and the other is automatically sharing your content to *your* social network. If you use Jetpack for WordPress (Chapter 8, "All About Jetpack Settings"), both of these aspects are covered for you. Love it or hate it, Jetpack makes social sharing pretty darn painless (more in Chapter 8 on all that). If you don't want to use Jetpack for your social sharing, there aren't as many options as there used to be. Twitter changed a lot of its rules on posting, and Facebook is always Facebook (changing the rules as often as they change underwear), so the options for the best plugin(s) to use change all the time. So I'm going to shock you and tell you this: Unless you're using Jetpack, don't bother with them and use HootSuite instead. For sharing to other networks, the options are quite varied, but I'll hit a few of my favorites here.

Posting to Your Social Network

HootSuite is a tool for posting and managing your social media profiles and networks. It supports Twitter, Facebook, LinkedIn, Foursquare, Google+, WordPress.com, and mixi (a Japanese social network), and you can add up to five of these networks to your HootSuite account for free. Included for free is being able to use your site's RSS feed post to up to two social networks. I have HootSuite post to Twitter and LinkedIn, and then I have Twitter post directly to Facebook. Three networks, all automatic, done like dinner. Here's an overview of how you do it:

- Sign up for HootSuite at HootSuite.com.

- Connect your social networks to your account (I suggest setting up Twitter, Facebook, and LinkedIn to start with).

- Use the HootSuite publisher tool to read your site's RSS feed on a periodic basis and then post to your desired accounts.

- Enjoy.

A couple of notes about this: Because HootSuite is reading your RSS feed to find what's new to post, there is a time delay. The shortest amount of time you can set HootSuite to check your feed is hourly (probably more than enough for most people), but this means that it could be up to 59 minutes before your post appears on your social networks. If it's something urgent, you might consider posting manually. For more information on HootSuite (and the details on how all this works), visit HootSuite.com. You don't have to tell them Tris sent you, but you can if you like. If you use Jetpack, there is no delay between when you publish and that post appearing on your social networks. If instant distribution to your social networks is important to you, Jetpack might be a good choice.

Now let's talk about helping your readers/visitors share your content to *their* social networks.

Helping Visitors Post to Their Networks

Again, Jetpack does a great job at this function. It's simple, clean, has an elegant use of space, and includes all the major social networks. However, if you're not using Jetpack, a myriad of other options are available to help site visitors share *your* content to their social networks. From Share This… to Digg Digg, there are plenty of options to choose from (see Chapter 4, "Installing WordPress Plugins," for my recommended choices), so the better question here is, how do you choose the right plugin for your site? I've found the right social sharing plugin for your site comes down to two factors: how it looks and how it works.

For looks, it's important that sharing options are visible to people but don't distract from your content *or* clash with your site design. A lot of sites use (and I often appreciate) the floating vertical bar that Digg Digg (http://bufferapp.com/digg-digg) offers. I used to use Digg Digg myself, until I found that it didn't work with a new theme I started to use (by the time you read this, I might be using it again, so who knows). Nothing against Digg Digg; it just didn't work for my site (for the time being). Simple Share Buttons Adder (http://www.simplesharebuttons.com/) offers several different (and stylish) options for how your buttons can look. These styles are different from the official styles offered by Twitter, Facebook, LinkedIn, and others. I happen to like the choices, so that's my plugin choice for the time being. Beyond the initial style and how well the plugin looks within your site, you need to be able to tweak and tune it so it *really* fits into your site. The first site I used, Simple Share Buttons Adder, needed a little more space between the button bar and the content above and below. Handy for me, the author had simple settings for adding padding around the bar. Some plugins allow you to *really* tune the sharing buttons to match your site, if that's what you need—awesome. Myself, I just go with general fit and the capability to fine-tune as needed. After I have the bar looking the way I'd like, I tune it for how it will work on my site.

Now by "work," I don't mean what happens when someone clicks one of the buttons. I mean can I arrange the buttons in the order I want? Can I turn some services on and off? Can I put in frequently used—for my site—services under an "other" menu? For my site, I make sure email, Facebook, Twitter, LinkedIn, and

Google+ are the main options visible. Why those? Because those are the services that I've found most of my shared traffic comes from—even when I have lots of other share options available. Although Pinterest is great for sites with fashion, crafts, recipes, and images, my site isn't like that. It doesn't make sense to take up space with a Pinterest button. For your site, it may be different. The "how you know this" comes up in the next section on finding out how many visitors come to your site. Regardless, it isn't the choice of plugin or how you configure it that matters; it's how the plugin works, looks, and if it has the sharing options you need. Whether you choose to have the button above your text, below your text, or both, also doesn't matter—except to you. The most important part of the sharing buttons and sharing your posts to your social network is that they are there and they *work*. Simple as that. Jetpack has a great (and easy) set of options, but so do a lot of other plugins. Try a few out, see which one you like the best, and run with it.

Finding Out How Many People Visit Your Site

Knowing how many people come to your site, what they read, and how they got there in the first place is an essential part of managing a successful website.

This is another area where Jetpack really shines. The WordPress.com-powered stats through Jetpack are really good. The Dashboard view gives you several weeks of traffic data at a glance, the top pages from the current and previous day, and where people came from (current and previous day as well). You can drill down into the stats a bit more if you need or want to, and for many site owners, that's enough. Although, WordPress.com stats aren't power user stats by any reckoning, they are functional, informative, and *live*. Yes, live. You can see from moment to moment how many people have been to your site that day (though not how many people are there right at that moment). The benefit of WP.com stats is that after you activate Jetpack, the data starts being gathered. You'll have solid results the next day. They work, it's simple, and you don't have to fuss around with anything else. The stats are pretty basic, which presents a problem for people who have bigger questions that need answering: what did they see/read, where did they go, did they do a particular action that I'd like them to do (fill in a form, download a PDF, request a quote)? For that kind of detail, you need Google Analytics.

Like WordPress.com Stats through Jetpack, Google Analytics (GA) is free. Go to http://www.google.com/analytics/ to get started. This section isn't a tutorial on how to set up Google Analytics or how to use all the insanely powerful tools there. This part of the chapter discusses how you hook GA into your WordPress website. It's pretty simple, but there are some common pitfalls that I want to make sure you avoid. Like WordPress.com stats, GA works by putting a tracking code into every page on your website. Usually it's in the header of the page (so it's loaded right away) and is a little JavaScript with a unique identifier in it that tells Google that the page belongs to you and your Google Analytics account. Now comes the interesting part: How does one get this magical code into one's pages?

At first, we used to all put the GA code into the header file of our theme. We'd copy, paste, save, and upload the code. That was dandy—until you wanted to change themes or the theme was updated. Either of those two things could cause the code to no longer be loaded or connected to your site. Not good. I've done it myself when I've updated or switched themes. If you don't notice right away, then you could lose days, weeks, *months* of site traffic data (this also why sometimes I run both WP.com stats and GA—to have the assurance that I'll always have some data). So, hard coding the GA code into your theme files is a bad idea. Got it. But what if your theme offers you a space to put the code in through settings? Also not good. What if you decide to switch themes? Your GA code is still tied to the specific theme you're using for your site. Switch themes, still gone. The only sure way to make sure you have uninterrupted GA data is to use a plugin that is independent of your theme to insert the code into the header of your site.

Many SEO plugins (All In One SEO Pack and WordPress SEO included) either allow you to enter just your site's unique ID number, and the plugin will write the correct JavaScript around it, or let you paste in code that will be loaded into the header (in which case, you'd paste the entire JavaScript you get from Google Analytics when you set up your site). My preference, though, is to use a plugin like Google Analyticator (http://www.videousermanuals.com/google-analyticator/) or Google Analytics by Yoast (http://yoast.com/wordpress/google-analytics/), which allows you to connect to Google Analytics, pick your site from the list, and then do its magic. I find plugins that let you connect directly to Google to be more reliable than trying to make sure you copy and paste the right code into the right place, the right way. I'm all about easy and automatic.

Whether you choose WordPress.com Stats through Jetpack (simple, easy, fast, and basic) or Google Analytics (powerful, rich, needs your help to hook up to your site), it doesn't really matter. For a while, I ran both systems on my site, just to see how the data compared, and I liked the up-to-the-minute data that WP.com stats gave me. When I wanted to understand more about my site and its traffic, I'd turn to Google Analytics. Later I turned off Google Analytics to see if WP.com Stats alone was enough—it wasn't. I turned GA back on, but I have a pretty large gap in my traffic data. That's the price you pay for being your own guinea pig. Experiment with each, see which fits the bill, and go with it. If you change your mind, then switch. It's as simple as that. Very little of what you're doing in WordPress is set in stone. WordPress is a pretty flexible and adaptable tool—it will grow with you as long as you know where to look and how to do it.

Helping WordPress and Your Site Run Faster

Out of the box, WordPress runs efficiently and can handle a pretty heavy traffic load (exactly how many visitors per minute depends on too many factors to detail here, but let's leave it at "a lot"). However, you can do some simple things to not only help your site handle an unexpected spike in traffic but also help your site load faster. The best part is that all the work to make this magic happen is managed by plugins and requires you to do very little work after the initial set up. To make your site load quickly and be able to handle a sudden influx in traffic, such as if a celebrity tweets out a link to your website, we focus on two things: caching pages so the server needs to do less work and optimizing your theme and code so all the pages download faster.

HOW DO I KNOW IF MY SITE IS FAST ENOUGH?

When I need to know if my site is loading quickly, I use the Full Page Test from Pingdom (http://tools.pingdom.com/fpt). Just put in the URL of a website, click Test Now, and watch the results. Figure 7.5 shows you what the results for my personal site are.

FIGURE 7.5

Whoa, that's fast!

Sometimes when I run the test, it is a lot slower, and yours will be, too. That is normal and happens if there is a lot of traffic on the Internet between your server and the

Pingdom server, if you just emptied your site cache, or if the web server is having issues. When I get a really high test, I wait a few seconds and try again. Usually the numbers drop down to normal. If they don't, and testing a few minutes later gives you the same slow loading issues, it's time to look into things to see if something else is going on. This might be a good time to contact your web host's support line.

Caching

Caching your site means creating static copies of your most recent and most popular pages so that when visitors view that page, the web server, database, and WordPress don't have to work as hard to display the pages. When websites were first invented, all the content was static, and the load on a web server was pretty minimal, but as we discussed, WordPress (and other modern websites today) relies on databases and a series of scripts to "appear" for viewers. To load and run the scripts, load your theme, load the images, and do whatever your plugins do takes memory and processor time, just like launching and using a program on your computer does. You can run only so many programs and do only so many things on your computer at once before *everything* starts running *very slowly*. Caching tools and plugins were created so that semi-static copies of key parts of your site are saved and load quickly. I say *semi-static* because if you update the page in some way, or if there are comments on a post you need readers to see, caching plugins discard the cached versions of the pages after a certain period of time *or* when there is an update to the page.

It sounds pretty complicated to pull off and, yes, it is, which is why caching is pretty hard to do well and probably has something to do with the fact that there are only two real WordPress caching plugins that people use. From Chapter 4, you already know my two recommendations: WP Super Cache or W3 Total Cache (W3TC), and you also know that you pick *one* of these plugins to use at a time. If you want to test one and then the other, you need to follow the directions for how to uninstall the plugin properly so your site will still function. This is essential. Running both of these plugins at the same time or not completely uninstalling one before trying the other *will very likely cause your site to crash*. No kidding.

 CAUTION I'm not joking around here. I've had to clean up the mess left behind when people run both of the plugins at the same time or don't switch between them cleanly, and it's not pretty. Read the instructions for how to disable the plugins and double-check that you've done it right.

For both of these plugins, after you activate them, there is a short walkthrough to turn on caching, and the plugin takes care of the rest. The out-of-the-box settings for both plugins are pretty good, so starting there is fine. That's not to say there aren't a few tips I can pass on for each plugin.

The General settings for W3TC have a tempting-looking check box at the top that says: Toggle All Caching Types On or Off (at Once). Don't do it. Many of the settings that you'll turn on require accounts and settings for other services—services you might not need, want, or be ready for. What you need right now is to enable the following:

- Page cache with the cache method set to Disk: Enhanced

- Minify with auto mode, disk caching, and the other default options

- Database cache with disk as the cache method

- Object cache (disk method)

- Browser cache

Turning these on with the default settings will give you a huge boost in how quickly your pages load and how much traffic your site can handle before your web host starts calling you in a panic.

When you activate WP Super Cache, there is a message to go to the settings page for the plugin and turn on caching. The recommended settings under the Easy tab are fine, but switching to the Advanced tab gives you more options. Generally, it's safe to choose all the recommended options for the web hosts that WordPress recommends. If you are unsure, don't sweat it. If you do turn on Use mod_rewrite to Serve Cache Files, after you update the settings, you'll see a dire message that you need to modify your rewrite rules in your .htaccess file. Don't worry; for most hosts now, all you'll need to do is scroll down the page to click the button Update mod_rewrite Rules and you'll be done.

You might have noticed that I didn't mention anything about minify with WP Super Cache; that's because WP Super Cache doesn't include that function. Let's cover what that means for your site now.

Optimizing Your Theme

When developers and programmers write code, we need to be able to go back and reread and recheck and fix our code. To do this, we insert blank lines, tabs, and other things that make the code readable to people, but the computers running the code couldn't care less. Sort of. The extra blank lines, tabs, and other human-readable things still have to be "seen" and ignored by the computer. Something like "code, code, code, blank line (skip), code, code, code" that pause to deal with the blank line (or extra spaces or tabs) takes a moment to handle. Also, believe it or not, other extra returns, spaces, and tabs start to add up in a file. To make things run faster (and download faster), programmers use tools to "minify" their code to remove all the extras that make it easy to read, but the computer will ignore. The code runs better, the files are smaller (spaces add up folks!) and no one notices—except that the site is faster.

W3TC comes with built-in minifying tools; you just have to turn them on. Figure 7.6 shows you what the code for the home page for the demo site looks like without minifying the code.

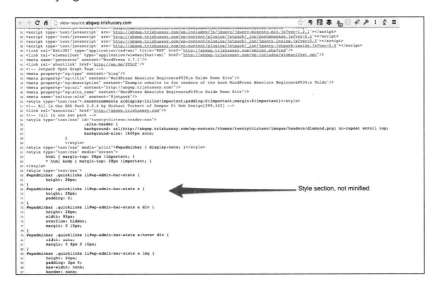

FIGURE 7.6

Home page code not minified.

Now this is the same page with minified code (Figure 7.7).

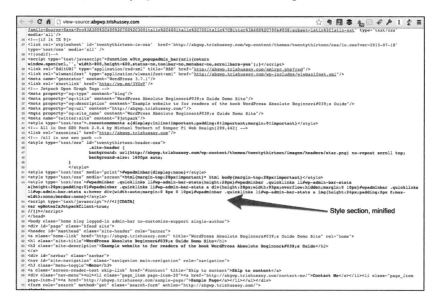

Style section, minified

FIGURE 7.7

Minified code.

In Figure 7.6, you can't even see all the style code that the arrow is pointing to. In Figure 7.7, you can see all of it. That's just a small portion of the code that makes up the home page. Now, as you add more plugins, more content, and just plain *more*, the minified code will download and run faster for visitors (especially style code, which is run by your web browser on your computer, not the web server). Because W3TC includes minifying, it is an easy choice if you want to run fewer plugins. The gotcha is that the plugins that you could use in concert with WP Super Cache to minify your code aren't being updated in active development. It makes for a tough choice. If WP Super Cache works better for your site, you'll just have to do without minifying your code.

There's one last thing to help improve your website's loading time—optimizing your graphics.

Optimizing Your Graphics

Sometimes it's hard to wrap your head around how fast our Internet speeds are compared to a few years ago. Not long ago, the thought of uploading or downloading a 2 megabyte photo you just took of your kids would be insane. Today we take pictures like that and upload them from our *phones* to Facebook, and think nothing of it. But just because things are faster now, it doesn't mean that we shouldn't at least try to make the images we upload to our sites as small as possible. One of the first and easiest things to do *before* you upload your images to your site is to reduce the size of the image to only what is really necessary. An 8-megapixel image is roughly 2400×3200 pixels. Chances are you're only going to want to use an image half that size on your site. Although WordPress can help you with this, using Preview on the Mac or Paint.Net on the PC can quickly make an image smaller in dimensions and a smaller file to upload (and download). To take things to the next level of cool, and automatic, you can employ the plugin WP-Smush.it (http://wordpress.org/plugins/wp-smushit/), which uses a Yahoo! service to compress JPEGs, PNGs, and GIFs so they load faster. When you upload an image, WP-Smush.it automatically tries to make the image smaller *before* WordPress makes the scaled versions of the image. Nice, handy, and always good—automatic! The only downside is that the image you *upload* has to be 1MB or less for the plugin to work (it's a limit on the Yahoo! Service, not the plugin). For many small images, that 1MB limit isn't a problem. Digital photos? Getting those down to 1MB can be tough. It can be worth it, though, if you can speed up the load time on your site by a few seconds.

For starters, reduce the size of the images you're uploading, then give WP-Smush.it a try to see if that speeds things up.

Backups and Security

Throughout these discussions of settings (Chapter 6, "Setting Up Your WordPress Site Right the First Time," and this chapter), I've talked a lot about changing this, changing that, and occasionally warned you about breaking something. Although I cover troubleshooting problems with WordPress, themes, plugins, and your database in Chapter 18, "Troubleshooting Common WordPress Problems," it's always good to make sure that if there *is* a problem, you have a safety net—a backup of your site. It's an interesting thing to back up a WordPress site. You don't have to back up WordPress itself—that's easy enough to redownload. You don't even really have to back up plugins; those are easy to download and reinstall. Even if you bought a premium theme, you can download that again, too. So what *do* you need to back up? Very simple:

- Your database

- Your uploads

- Your theme if you modified it

- wp-config.php if you really want the extra protection

But why would you need this? Well, for lots of reasons. If you install a plugin that really goes sideways, sometimes you need to clear out your database and start over. If you get hacked, you will almost certainly need to roll back the clock on your site to *before* the hack to fix the damage done. Finally, you'll have peace of mind that if your web host has a major hardware failure and it loses everything, you can get back up and running. For all the disaster scenarios you can possibly think of, having a backup of your site is a good idea.

The first step—and if nothing else, do this—is to back up your database. I use the plugin WP-DBManager (http://wordpress.org/plugins/wp-dbmanager/) for this task. It isn't updated often (it doesn't really need to be) and offers a lot more than backing up your database (it can periodically repair and optimize your database as well), but for backing up my database, this is the tool I make sure I have installed and configured right away. After you install and activate the plugin, you see a dire-sounding warning message at the top of the screen (Figure 7.8).

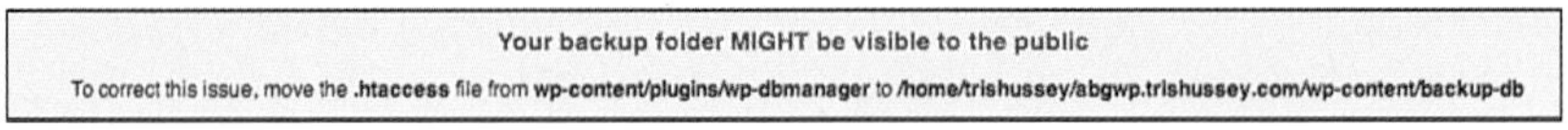

Your backup folder MIGHT be visible to the public
To correct this issue, move the .htaccess file from wp-content/plugins/wp-dbmanager to /home/trishussey/abgwp.trishussey.com/wp-content/backup-db

FIGURE 7.8

Yikes—a big warning in red!

Fixing this is very easy. All you need to do is launch your FTP program, navigate to wp-content/plugins/wp-dbmanager, and look for the file htaccess.txt. Then you're going to copy the file into wp-content/db-backup/ and rename it to .htaccess. Simple. If your FTP program doesn't allow you to use a copy-and-paste command or drag and drop to move the file, download htaccess.txt onto your computer and then upload it to the right place. The file is teeny tiny, so it will take less than a second to download. Figure 7.9 shows you what it looks like when it's done and the first database backup for the demo site.

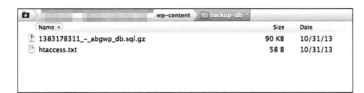

FIGURE 7.9

The .htaccess file in place and first database backup.

That's step one. The next step is even easier and just as fast—simple configuration of when to back up your database. Figure 7.10 shows you what the bottom half of the DB Options screen looks like with the options you need to see (you can't see the Save Changes button, but that's there, too). I like to back up my database once a day, compress it (GZIP set to Yes), but not have it email the file to me. I don't need to clutter my email with copy after copy of my database; that's just too much.

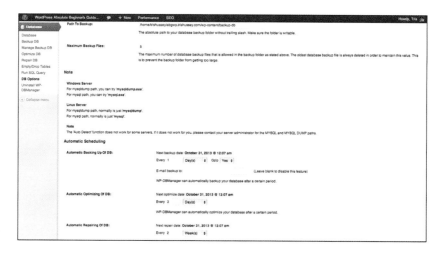

FIGURE 7.10

DB Options screen.

Generally, I keep only five to seven database backups at a time. That's about a week's worth of content and settings that I can roll back to if I need to. I also leave the automatic repair and optimization set to 3 days to optimize and 2 days to repair. This keeps my site running in peak form and condition. This covers my database, but what about the other critical files? For that, I use a handy plugin called WordPress Backup to Dropbox (wpb2d—http://wpb2d.com/) to automatically download a copy of my critical files to my Dropbox account. Dropbox is a cloud-based storage service that gives you several gigabytes of space to store whatever you like for free, and then you can earn more free space by referring friends to the service (if you'd like to sign up, you can use this link https://db.tt/vG7Jlzi and you'll get an extra 500 megabytes of storage on me!). I have my backups there set to back up the core files (the ones I listed previously) once a day in the middle of the night. The files are compressed and sent over to Dropbox for me, and I get an email when it's all done or if there is a problem. (Note: I paid extra for those two services from the creator of the plugin.) I keep about a week's worth of backups on Dropbox, because although I have plenty of space on Dropbox to have more, a week is plenty for my sense of security.

You can always use your handy FTP program to download your uploads directory and database backups manually, but who really wants to have to *remember* to back up their website? Exactly. Let the computers do that kind of work for us. Before wrapping up this section, I want to touch on the last aspect of keeping your website running: security.

Keeping WordPress secure isn't very hard. A lot of the burden is going to fall on your web host to make sure that their servers are secure and don't allow malicious people into them. Then there are simple things you can do, too. First—passwords. Don't give out your web host account password, FTP password, or WordPress admin account passwords to just anyone who asks for them. Plugins and themes don't (and shouldn't) need to ask for them. If you're asked for any of those passwords while setting up a plugin or theme, stop and don't continue. Period. Still on the password front, use good, strong passwords. Don't use simple passwords; use longer phrases with numbers, uppercase letters, and lowercase letters mixed in. These passwords are harder for hackers to guess through their automatic password guessing programs. Also, don't give hackers half of your username and password combination by using "admin" as a username within WordPress. Use pretty much anything other than that and you've made a hacker's job harder.

The last thing to do is keep WordPress updated. Thankfully, starting with WordPress 3.7, the smaller point updates (like 3.7.1, which came out a couple days after 3.7) will be automatically installed for most WordPress users. Often each WordPress update includes security fixes as well as bug fixes. The security fixes are crucial because after the fix is available, clever hackers can find ways to exploit the security flaw in sites that *haven't* updated yet. Even if your site or host doesn't support automatic updates, you can still update WordPress with just a click.

Keeping WordPress updated, using good passwords, and being cautious about who you give access to your site will go a long way to keeping your site secure. Yes, there are certainly a lot more security measures you can take; however, for most sites and most people, these will do just fine.

Conclusion

This second of three settings chapters has been focused on some pretty heavy, but crucial, topics. Making sure your site ranks well in search engines, connects to social media, loads quickly, and is backed up, secure, and tracking visitors might not be required for your site to *function*, but they are required for your site to be successful. Don't feel too daunted by all the things in this chapter, either. Remember things like caching, social media connections, and a lot of SEO are tasks you set up and then don't need to worry about. For backups, make sure that they are set up, and you can forget about those, too. It's as simple as that. If you don't want to worry about dealing with caches or even social media or SEO right away, don't worry. You can start working these into your plans over time.

In the next chapter, we spend time talking about a single, powerful plugin: Jetpack. It's a plugin that can do a lot of things for you and your site. Because it's so powerful and multifaceted, it needs a chapter of its own.

8

ALL ABOUT JETPACK SETTINGS

Jetpack from Automattic is a plugin designed to allow DIY WordPress users to have many of the same features found on WordPress.com—all built in to one plugin. This makes Jetpack very powerful, very complex, and, potentially, something that could *slow* down your site. Remember, all plugins come with a cost. Every plugin you install requires server resources to run. Using a lot of plugins might not only use more resources than your web host allocated to you (and believe me, your host will let you know when that happens), but your website might load a lot slower than you'd like. This is what makes Jetpack a very interesting plugin to discuss. On one hand, it can replace an easy half-dozen other plugins (mark in the plus column). On the other hand, because it is so large and complex, it can put a drain on your site—if you try to turn on *all* of its features. Figure 8.1 shows just the top third of the Jetpack options screen. There are two more screens full of options below that one.

FIGURE 8.1

The first third of Jetpack options.

Let's back up for a moment and talk about what happens when you first activate Jetpack on your site. Figure 8.2 shows the handy message that you see at the top of the Plugins page (and throughout the rest of your site until you complete the next steps).

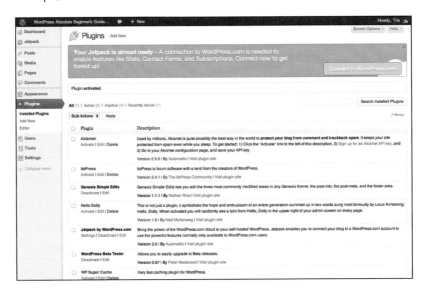

FIGURE 8.2

A message letting you know that you need to connect Jetpack to WordPress.com.

When you click the button, you'll be asked to log in to your WordPress.com account. Don't have one? Well, you should. It's very handy for this kind of thing, and for being able to experiment with WordPress.com if you feel like it. After you're logged in to WordPress.com, you'll be asked to authorize Jetpack (Figure 8.2) (on that site—you can use Jetpack on as many sites as you'd like) to connect to your account. After you're connected, come back to your site and you'll see Figure 8.3.

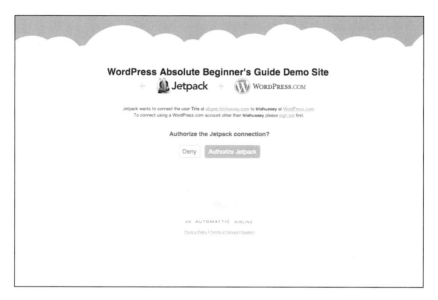

FIGURE 8.3

Connecting Jetpack to WordPress.com.

Now comes the hard part: settings. It's not that any of the settings are terribly hard to use or even configure—it's that there are so many that discussing them all could be a book all to itself! Rather than discuss all the features of Jetpack, I'm going to cover in detail only a few of the most common (and handy) features. For more details, I encourage you to visit www.Jetpack.me. Even giving you a simple list of all the features isn't easy—new features are constantly being added to Jetpack to make it more powerful and useful.

Here are the features that Jetpack includes as of this writing (from the Jetpack.me FAQ):

- **Beautiful Math**—Mark up your posts with the LaTeX markup language, perfect for complex mathematical equations and other über-geekery.

- **Carousel**—Transform your standard image galleries into an immersive full-screen experience.

- **Comments**—Give your readers the capability to comment using their WordPress.com, Twitter, or Facebook accounts.

- **Contact Form**—Insert a contact form anywhere on your site.

- **Custom CSS**—Customize your site's look without modifying your theme.

- **Enhanced Distribution**—Share your public posts and comments to search engines and other services in real-time.

- **Extra Sidebar Widgets**—Add images, Twitter streams, and your site's RSS links to your sidebar.

- **Featured Content**—The Featured Content module allows you to display specific posts in a highlighted area on your site's home page, letting you draw attention to your most important content.

- **Google+ Profile**—Show a link to your Google+ in the sharing area of your posts and add your blog URL to your Google+ profile.

- **Gravatar Hovercards**—Show a pop-up business card of your users' Gravatar profiles in comments.

- **Infinite Scroll**—Learn how to add infinite scroll support to your theme.

- **JSON API**—Allow applications to securely access your content through the cloud.

- **Likes**—Likes are a way for people to show their appreciation for content you have written. It's also a way for you to show the world how popular your content has become.

- **Mobile Push Notifications**—Get notified of new comments on your Apple device.

- **Mobile Theme**—Optimize your site for mobile devices.

- **Omnisearch**—Search once, get results from everything! Omnisearch is a single search box that lets you search many things.

- **Photon**—Accelerate your site by loading images from the WordPress.com CDN.

- **Post by Email**—Post by Email is a way of publishing posts on your blog by email. Any email client can be used to send the email, allowing you to publish quickly and easily from devices such as cell phones.

- **Publicize**—Publicize makes it easy to share your site's posts on several social media networks automatically when you publish a new post.

- **Social Links**—This module is a canonical source, based on Publicize, that themes can use to let users specify where social icons should link to.

- **Sharing**—Share your content on Facebook, Twitter, and more with a few simple clicks.

- **Shortcode Embeds**—Embed content from YouTube, Vimeo, SlideShare, and more into your site, no coding necessary.

- **Spelling and Grammar**—Improve your spelling, style, and grammar with the After the Deadline proofreading service.

- **Subscriptions**—Allow users to subscribe to your posts and comments to receive notifications via email.

- **Tiled Galleries**—Display your image galleries in three new styles: a rectangular mosaic, a square mosaic, and a circular grid.

- **Toolbar Notifications**—Get notified of activity on your site, right from the toolbar.

- **Widget Visibility**—Control what pages your widgets appear on.

- **WordPress.com Connect**—Let users log in with their WordPress.com credentials, through WordPress.com Connect.

- **WordPress.com Stats**—Monitor your stats with clear, concise reports and no additional load on your server.

- **WP.me Shortlinks**—Enable WP.me-powered shortlinks for all your posts and pages for easier sharing.

Yeah, wow. I'm going to talk about the features that I think you will get the most out of *and* you might have questions about. Many of the settings for these options are merged with other settings (for example, Gravatar Hovercards is found under Discussion), so when I cover the settings for these, if you think you're seeing some familiar screens—you are. I've also grouped some of these options together that have separate tiles on the Jetpack screen (Publicize, Sharing, and Google+ specifically) but all go to the same settings screen for configuration. One final note, although it says on the Jetpack.me FAQ:

> I don't want to use all the features. Can I turn some of them off?

> Sure! You can deactivate any feature you don't feel like using, and reactivate it at any time.

> To turn specific features off, first head to the main Jetpack page in your dashboard. In the box explaining the feature you'd like to turn off, click the 'Learn More' button. A 'Deactivate' button will appear. Click that button and that feature will be completely deactivated.

This isn't entirely true. You can't, for example, disable WordPress.com Stats without turning off Jetpack entirely. Which means that if you have Jetpack enabled, you will have some features loading on your site whether you want (or need) them or not. This "feature" has caused a bit of controversy within the WordPress community because sometimes new features (that you can't disable) conflict with a critical plugin or your theme. Mark Jaquith wrote a plugin to help prevent new Jetpack features from automatically turning on when they are introduced (http://wordpress.org/plugins/manual-control/). It doesn't, however, give you the capability to manually turn features off that don't appear to have an off switch.

WordPress.com Stats

A few features of Jetpack are well worth the price of admission, and WordPress.com Stats is one of them. WP.com stats are simple, elegant, and *live* so you can see moment to moment what the traffic is like on your site without having to leave the Dashboard. I'll talk in more detail about stats and tracking later in this chapter, but as far as WP.com stats goes, there isn't much to configure. The only thing you might need to adjust is which logged-in users to count and who can see the stats (Figure 8.4). Why might you want to count logged-in users? Because if you're running a membership website or a WordPress site using bbPress (the forum plugin), those users are logged in, but you'd still like to know what they do and see on the site. WP.com Stats is an elegant stats package that works nicely on its own, but is also a nice complement to the tremendous amount of detail that you get from products like Google Analytics.

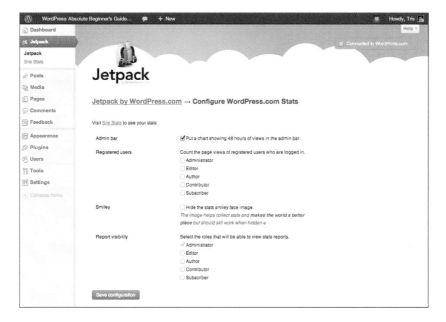

FIGURE 8.4

WordPress.com stats through the Jetpack settings.

Publicize and Sharing

Another of the awesome features of Jetpack is how smoothly and easily it allows you to connect your site to your various social media profiles and let your visitors share your posts on social media sites. Figure 8.5 shows the top half of the Sharing settings screen where you click the button next to the service you want to add, go through the steps required (for most sites, this just means logging into the site and clicking an Authorize button), and you're done! Connecting Google+ is a little different and means something different than the other connections. For Twitter, Facebook, and LinkedIn, the connection is used to allow you to automatically post new Posts to your profile on those social networks. For Google+ (or G+) it's to claim *authorship on Google* for the posts you write on the site. Don't worry, if you have more than one author on your site, each person can claim authorship of his or her posts as well. Why would you bother to do this? For better Google search results on the posts you've written. Figure 8.6 shows what a Google search result that found one of my posts looks like.

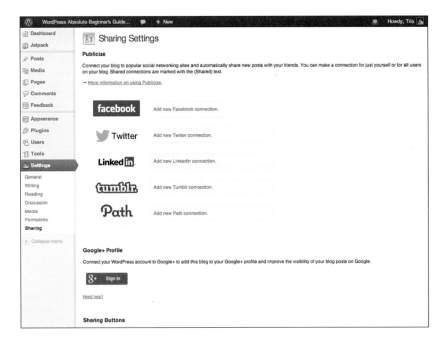

FIGURE 8.5

Sharing Settings.

FIGURE 8.6

Google search result with Google authorship claimed.

Not too shabby. My name, picture, and other profile information are all right there for searchers to see and use.

The bottom half of the Sharing screen powered by Jetpack is all about helping people share *your posts and pages* on social networks (Figure 8.7). Just drag the service icons you want to the area below (noted with Drag and Drop Available Services Here) in the order you want them; then save them, and you're done. I like to keep the number of visible searches pretty tight (for my site, I focus on Twitter, Facebook, LinkedIn, and email) and place the extras in the other box to appear as a Share menu. You can experiment for yourself which services are used the most by your visitors and adjust accordingly. WP.com stats can help you determine which services are working best for you.

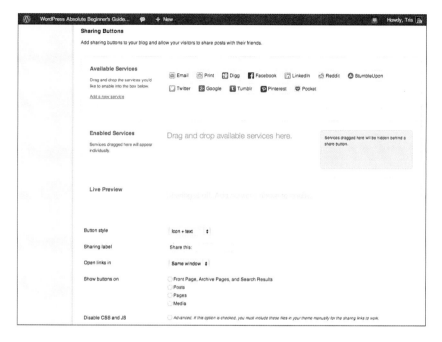

FIGURE 8.7

Sharing settings, part 2.

Below the button layout area are the settings for where the sharing buttons should appear on your Posts and Pages and what they should look like. As you change the settings, you can see a preview of the layout before you click Save Changes and seal the deal. Personally I have sharing buttons only on Posts, not on the Front Page, Pages, or Archives. Why? Because I only want people to *share* posts, and because my home page shows only an excerpt of the post, it doesn't make sense for sharing to happen *before* someone reads the entire post. But that's just me. The beauty of these kinds of settings is that you can try different ones and measure the results for yourself. My suggestion is to start off with the settings that you think *look* and *feel* right to you. Then keep track of the results through WordPress.com Stats or Google Analytics and adjust if you need to. The most important thing is just having social media sharing options available. Sharing content through social media is essential to the success of any website.

Subscriptions

Although we geeks might think everyone should use RSS to receive updates from our favorite sites and blogs, the majority of people either visit the site manually, see it on Facebook, see it on Twitter, or receive an email when there is new content. This is why Subscriptions is a popular Jetpack feature that many blogs can't live without. Subscriptions makes it easy—just fill in your email address and click—for site visitors to receive an email whenever you publish a new post (remember we still have to talk about Posts versus Pages, but this is one of the key differences; new Posts are included in RSS and Subscriptions, but Pages aren't). The settings (there are only a couple) for Subscriptions are under Discussion settings right at the bottom below Avatars (Figure 8.8).

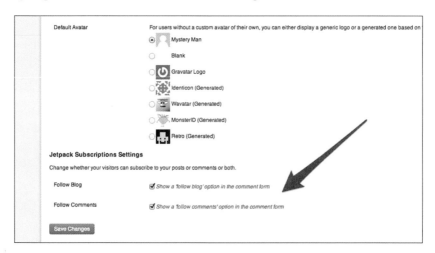

FIGURE 8.8

Subscription settings.

These check boxes allow for readers to sign up for updates when they are leaving a comment on one of your Posts (or Pages). To allow visitors who aren't leaving a comment to subscribe, you need to use the Blog Subscriptions widget. We'll talk about using widgets in Chapter 10, "Tweaking, Tuning, and Customizing Your WordPress Site," but Figure 8.9 shows you the options available in the widget. Essentially the settings are the title, what message you'd like to entice potential readers with, the text for the button, and if you'd like to show the number of people who subscribe to the site (I'd opt for no on that, unless you have thousands of subscribers).

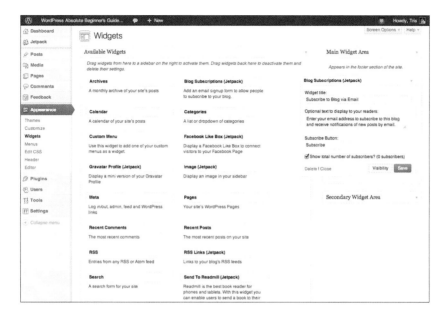

FIGURE 8.9

Blog subscriptions widget and settings.

Subscriptions are an easy way to encourage more people to receive updates from your site. Again, one of the modules that is worth the price of admission to Jetpack.

Likes

If you'd like to have star ratings below your posts, activating Likes is the way to do it. Likes is one of the Jetpack modules that you have to activate before you can use them (unlike Stats, Subscriptions, and others), and after you do, the settings appear under the Sharing settings screen (Figure 8.10).

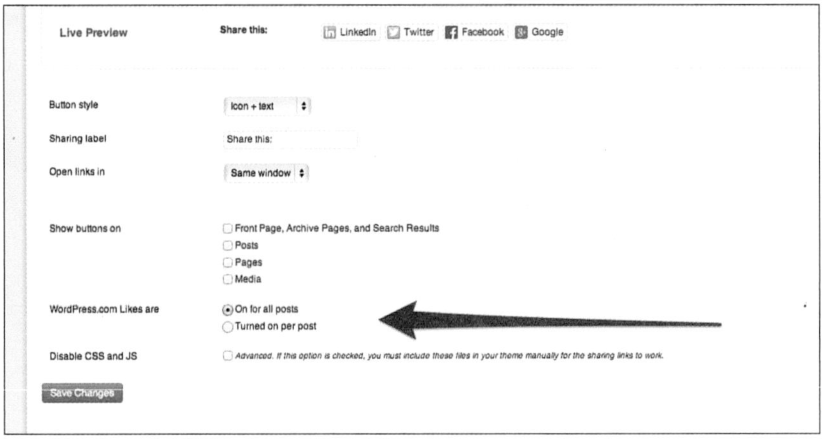

FIGURE 8.10

Likes now added to the Sharing settings.

Again, these are very simple settings, either on for all posts or on a post-by-post basis. My take on Likes is that if you have an audience who will Like your posts on a regular basis, great. If not, it's another thing cluttering up your posts that might draw people's attention away from the content. (Read: Gee, no one has Liked this post—maybe it isn't very good.)

Spelling and Grammar

Some people don't need spell check. Some people don't need to be reminded of grammar rules. Then there's the remaining 99% of writers. The spelling and grammar tool takes the built-in spell check and includes grammar and proofreading options powered by After The Deadline (http://www.afterthedeadline.com/). What is checked (beyond spelling) is enabled on a user-by-user basis on the user's profile page (Figure 8.11). I'm not saying that I'm great at proofreading, grammar, or editing (the editors of this book can attest to that!), but I didn't find the suggestions helpful. Probably because I'm a writer and I think my way is right. I have my own style, quirks, and "Tris-isms" that I like to spice my writing with. Other writers—especially beginning writers—might appreciate the safety net of some proofreading help. There is no harm in trying a few of the settings to see whether they are a help or a hindrance.

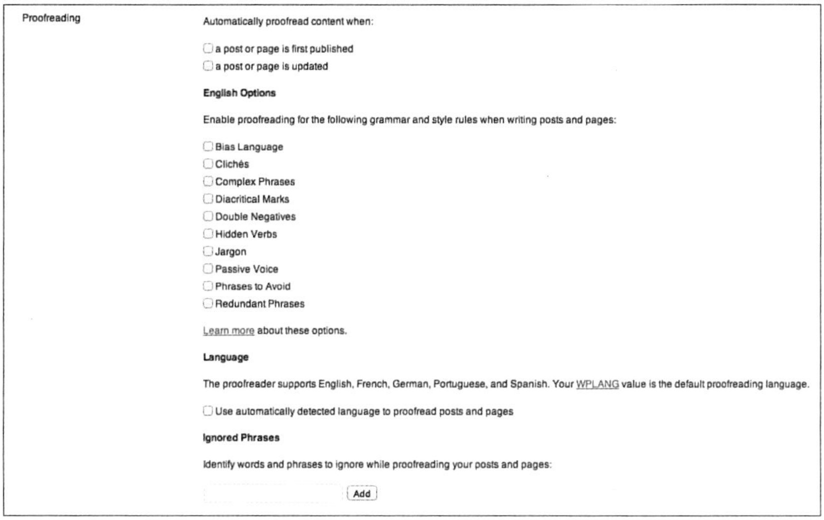

FIGURE 8.11

Spelling and grammar settings on a profile page.

Contact Form

Having a contact form on your website is critical to people running websites for a business. If you don't need to hear from your readers, you might not need this. However, because more and more people are using WordPress to power their business sites, the contact form tool is essential. Creating contact forms (or any form) can be maddening. Getting the right short codes, creating the page, embedding the form—although there are plugins that make it *pretty* simple, there's nothing like Jetpack Contact form for making it just *plain* simple (Figure 8.12). Contact form is one of the Jetpack features that is automatically on when you activate Jetpack—which also means you can't disable it, either. The feature is made up of two parts. One is the button in the Editor to allow you to create and insert a contact form into a post or page (my preference is page, but it doesn't matter which you choose); the other is the Feedbacks section of the Dashboard, which will gather all the contact form submissions in one place (in addition to them being emailed to you).

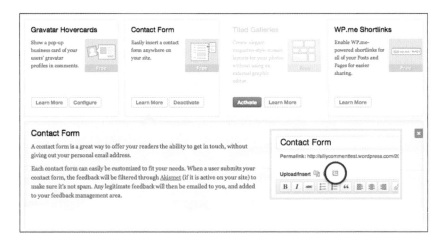

FIGURE 8.12

Contact Form info on the Jetpack screen.

As I said, inserting a form is about as drop-dead easy as it can get. In the Editor window—don't worry, we'll get further into this in Chapter 11, "Using WordPress: Content"—click the Add Contact Form button; then, if the default fields are okay with you, click Add This Form to My Post. If you need to add, remove, or reorder the fields, you can do that before you insert the form (Figure 8.13). The code for the form looks pretty intense at first, but on closer inspection, it does make sense. Don't worry about that, though; if you're done, click Publish and the result should look something like Figure 8.14.

FIGURE 8.13

Adding a form to a post or page.

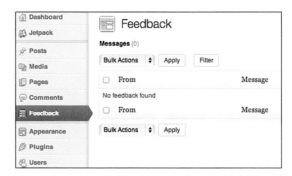

FIGURE 8.14

Completed form on a page.

As I mentioned previously, when the contact form is submitted (and after it passes through Akismet to make sure the submission isn't spam), you'll be emailed the submission, and all of the submissions will be gathered together in the Feedback section of the Dashboard (Figure 8.15).

FIGURE 8.15

Feedback from within the Dashboard.

I don't think there is a simpler way to collect and gather feedback on your site. Jetpack Contact forms might not be the most full-featured of contact tools out there, but it is certainly the simplest one I've ever used.

WP.me Shortlinks

Since Twitter emerged on the scene in 2006, people suddenly became aware of how long their links were. When you only have 140 characters to say your piece, having a URL like http://www.trishussey.com/watch-contribute-and-create-a-story-about-vancouver/ is really long, which is why link shorteners were invented. All link shorteners do is create a shorter form of that link (usually with a really short domain like wp.me) that still points to the original post so you can post to Twitter or other social networks (short links also tend to look tidier, as well). For example, the shortlink for the contact form page in Figure 8.14 is http://wp.me/P3YUcF-k. The Get Shortlink button is available in the Editor with or without Jetpack. Without Jetpack, the post on my site above has a shortlink of http://www.trishussey.com/?p=4593, which is really the post's unique ID number assigned to it when it was created (all posts, pages, categories, and tags have to have a unique id number within the database or things get broken). With Jetpack, the URL is passed through WordPress.com (if you just enter wp.me in your browser's address bar, that's where you end up) and is given a unique URL only associated with that post—forever.

Shortcodes

If you frequently embed videos, images, or other media from other sites into your posts or pages, shortcodes will make your life much easier. In Chapter 12, "Using WordPress: Images, Videos, and Other Media," I'll talk more about inserting media and the magic of oEmbed, but for right now, this is what you need to know. WordPress will automatically insert and correctly embed videos, images, and many other types of media natively. For many sites, you only need to have to put the URL of the media on its own line in a post or page. This will put that media there and format it according to your site's theme style. However, if you'd like more control over how the media is embedded, shortcodes will let you control many aspects of the final result. Figure 8.16 shows you all the currently supported media services you can use shortcodes for.

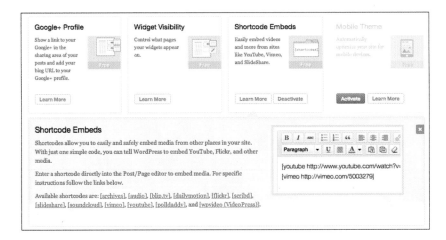

FIGURE 8.16

Shortcodes screen within Jetpack.

That's a lot of services! Some of them you might not have even heard of, but you've probably heard of YouTube, and when you click the link within the Jetpack screen, you come to a page on WordPress.com (http://en.support.wordpress.com/videos/youtube/) that tells you all you need to know about shortcode embeds for YouTube. Following is a quick reference list from the page with some of the common things people like to do with YouTube videos:

- To embed the video with default width and height adapted to your theme: [youtube=http://www.youtube.com/watch?v=JaNH56Vpg-A]

- To specify the width and height explicitly: [youtube=http://www.youtube.com/watch?v=JaNH56Vpg-A&w=320&h=240]

- To specify the width only: [youtube=http://www.youtube.com/watch?v=JaNH56Vpg-A&w=320]

- To hide the related videos from appearing after the video is done: [youtube=http://www.youtube.com/watch?v=JaNH56Vpg-A&rel=0]

- To start at a certain point in the video, convert the time of that point from minutes and seconds to all seconds, then add that number as shown (using an example start point of 1 minute 15 seconds): [youtube=http://www.youtube.com/watch?v=JaNH56Vpg-A&start=75]

- To specify a start and end time for a video, do the same as the above but add the end time as shown: [youtube=http://www.youtube.com/watch?v=JaNH56Vpg-A&start=75&end=85]

There are similar support pages for each of the supported services. More sites are being added all the time, so by the time you are reading this, there are probably several more services that you can use shortcodes with.

 NOTE   Just because a service doesn't have a shortcode, it doesn't mean you can't embed its media into your posts or pages. Many sites without shortcodes support oEmbed (more on that in Chapter 12) or have their own way to embed media.

 NOTE   What if I don't want to use Jetpack? Will I still be able to insert media?

Yes, absolutely! Jetpack just makes the embedding functions a little easier. WordPress has extensive support for media embedding even without Jetpack installed.

Shortcodes can be very convenient for people who embed a lot of media. For folks who don't, it's not a big deal, except that this is another of the Jetpack features that is turned on by default and you can't turn off.

Custom CSS

Cascading Style Sheets (CSS) are what give themes their look and feel (colors, fonts, font sizes, how links look, how images are placed). Changing the style of your theme isn't terribly hard, and I'll cover some of the easier ways to do this in Chapter 16, "Customizations Without (Much) Coding." What this Jetpack module does is help you make changes to your theme without editing the files themselves. Why is this a big deal? Because if your theme is updated, and you've edited the actual files for the theme (again, Chapter 16), when you run the update, *you will likely lose all your customizations*. Royal pain doesn't even scratch the surface of the headache this causes. The Custom CSS module solves this problem by storing your customizations separately from your theme. When the theme is updated, your changes are preserved. Figure 8.17 shows you the Edit CSS screen (which you find under Appearance settings). We discuss what to do here and all the options in Chapter 9, "How WordPress Themes Work," and Chapter 16.

FIGURE 8.17

Custom CSS screen under Appearance.

If you don't think you'll need or want to use Custom CSS, you can disable it by clicking the Learn More button under Custom CSS in the Jetpack settings screen.

Extra Sidebar Widgets

In Chapter 10, we talk all about widgets, how to use them, and what they are good for (and not so good for). This Jetpack module, which can be disabled, adds four additional sidebar widgets to the default ones WordPress enables for all themes (and any widgets your theme might include, as well):

- The RSS Links widget lets you easily add post and comment RSS feeds to a sidebar on your theme.

- The Twitter widget shows your latest tweets within a sidebar on your theme.

- The Facebook Like Box widget shows your Facebook Like Box within a sidebar on your theme.

- The Image widget lets you easily add images to a sidebar on your theme.

These are all very handy widgets and ones that a lot of people want to have on their sites. There are ways to add all these widgets without using Jetpack, although it is certainly handy that they are bundled together in one plugin.

Photon

Everyone who has a site wants it to load quickly. It's just a fact of being on the Internet. If a site doesn't start loading in a couple seconds, you might not bother waiting around for it. In addition to the caching settings we covered in Chapter 7, "Setting Up Your WordPress Site the Right Way: SEO, Social Media, and More," what Photon does is make copies of your uploaded images and use the massive network of servers that power WordPress.com to serve them to your site visitors. This is called a Content Delivery Network (CDN) where servers located around the world attempt to send your content to your visitor from a server *physically* closest to them. So Photon would serve a visitor in New York City your images from a server there (or close to there) and a visitor from San Francisco from a server there. The closer the server is to you, the faster it should load for you because Photon makes copies of your images and serves them instead of the ones from your server. There can be issues if you upload an image and then edit it. Photon wouldn't have the latest version of the image on its servers.

Will this cause most people grief? No. Can Photon make your site faster? Yes. Noticeably? Maybe, it depends on if your site has a lot of images already. It can't hurt to try, test, and see what (if any) improvement you see.

Conclusion

This section touched on only a *fraction* of the features and modules that Jetpack provides. If you look at the Jetpack screen and the list of all the modules from earlier, you can see this is a *massive* plugin. As we talked about in Chapter 4, "Installing WordPress Plugins," you can have too many plugins. You can easily have plugins that conflict with each other and cause issues. You can add so many plugins that your site crashes or loads like molasses in February. Because Jetpack is such a massive plugin and has so many features that are turned on by default and can't easily be disabled, it is a controversial plugin. Some folks love it. Some folks hate it. Some folks have a love-hate relationship with it. In the past, I've insisted that it be turned on for all the sites I manage. Now I'm more discerning about which sites need to run Jetpack and which ones don't. For sites that absolutely must have the fastest load times possible, Jetpack is out of the question.

The weight far outweighs the benefits. I don't need many of the Jetpacks features on my personal site—at the moment—so I've deactivated it. Could I change my mind in the future? Very likely. It all depends on the new features added and if I can turn off the things I don't need.

IN THIS CHAPTER

- Parts of a WordPress theme
- How themes work
- Basic theme settings
- Using the default WordPress themes

HOW WORDPRESS THEMES WORK

The first part of this book was about setting the stage for your website. These were the foundational lessons and steps—getting a domain, getting a host, installing WordPress, installing plugins, and installing themes. Now in Part 3 of the book, we move into making your website come alive with all the customizations that we can throw at it—without you having to learn coding. Before we move on to Chapter 10, "Tweaking, Tuning, and Customizing Your WordPress Site," and Chapter 16, "Customizations Without (Much) Coding," I thought it would be a good idea to *really* explain what WordPress themes are all about. As you know from Chapter 5, "Installing WordPress Themes," themes are a piece of cake. Finding and activating a new look for your website can take just moments, but often when I'm teaching WordPress classes, I find that it can be confusing for new WordPress users to understand what a theme will do, what a plugin will do, and what WordPress does in determining the look and feel of your website.

Frankly, it's a little confusing to me at times, as well. Themes can include features that are often managed with a plugin (such as social media links to your Twitter, Facebook, and other profiles), and plugins can do things that themes often do (such as changing layouts). However, there are some general guidelines for how themes and plugins are supposed to behave. This is what we're going to talk about in this chapter—how themes work and interact with WordPress, your content, and plugins.

WordPress Themes Explained

In Chapter 2, "What WordPress Is and How it Works," I talked about how CMS tools like WordPress separate content and functions from the presentation of the content. So changing your theme doesn't alter your content, and adding new content won't change your theme. Yes, there are exceptions to both these points, but for the moment, let's keep "don't" and "won't" in mind. A good way to imagine a WordPress theme is to think about a suit or dress. When you buy a suit, dress, or any other piece of clothing, a body doesn't come with the clothes; you supply the body (you) to make the clothes "work." And like clothes, when you change from jeans and a t-shirt for working in the garden into a suit or ball gown, you're not changing you—you're just changing a wrapper for your body. You're changing how you look to the world.

In WordPress, there is no option to "go naked"; you always need a theme activated for the site to work. There is always a default theme included with WordPress so that there is some way to display your content when WordPress is "turned on." If for some reason, you delete all the themes from wp-content/themes, your website will be a blank page. Nothing. Zip. Why? Here's why.

WordPress themes are the instructions for how WordPress should lay out your website. The theme defines the headers, sidebars, footers, menus, and creates the HTML code for the site to be "a site" as well as pull your content from your database. Your theme—through the style sheet—sets the colors, fonts, how big the text is, and where text will and won't appear on the site. Themes even go so far as to tell WordPress how to organize the structure of your content (from the presentation standpoint). Without all that information, WordPress has no idea what to do with your website. It can't even create the website itself because it doesn't have the instructions to do so! So, yes, your theme is more than just a wrapper for your website. It's more than just a suit of clothes that makes your website look smokin'. Your theme has the code to make your website *exist*.

All WordPress themes need two things to work. They need files to describe, define, and create the web pages (the HTML code itself) and a style sheet that defines how things should look and be laid out on the site. In truth, the simplest

WordPress theme needs only two files, index.php and style.css, to work. The index.php file includes all the HTML required, as well as the special code (called The Loop) to pull the content from your WordPress database, and style.css defines how things should look. In practice, no one has a theme that simple, but it's possible. In reality, WordPress themes have all the pieces and parts of the layout as separate files (such as header.php., footer.php, sidebar.php) just to make coding and editing the theme easier and the site load faster.

That's WordPress themes in a nutshell—a set of files that define how a website looks and that pulls information from the WordPress database to put the content there. Now let's talk about what you're actually doing when you are customizing your site/theme in Chapter 10.

Working with WordPress Themes

In Chapter 10, we talk about customizing your theme to make the site your own. Chapter 10 doesn't, and can't, cover every possible thing WordPress themes can do to make a site unique. That chapter covers the basic things that all WordPress themes should be able to customize. So let's talk about that for a moment; what are you actually doing? Truth be told, unless you actually download a copy of the theme, edit the files associated with it, and upload those back up to your website, you aren't *really* customizing the theme. What you're doing is using built-in options and settings to change a few things around. When we cover changing the header or background for your website, those changes aren't permanent. You can always revert back to the default settings at any time. So you might have your own custom header for the site, but what is really happening is the theme has been coded to allow you to use a feature to swap out one header for another without having to edit the theme files (that function is built in to WordPress, by the way).

Chapter 10 can't cover everything themes can do because themes can do so much now. To cover all the custom post types, post formats, dynamic home pages, and other new theme options, I could write a book just about those and I'd still end up leaving things out.

Theme Settings

When you're customizing your theme, settings/choices, such as your header, background, which widgets are where, and menus, are stored as preferences *for that one theme only*. If you switch between Twenty Twelve and Twenty Thirteen, you'll have to pick your header, background, and reassign menus all over again. For menus, you generally only need to tell the new theme which menu(s) you want where, and often some widget settings will carry over, but expect that whenever you switch themes, you'll have to spend a few minutes setting it back up again.

Some themes (both free and commercial) have more extensive settings available, such as custom logo areas, social media settings, default layout settings, and color choices. When themes have that many options and settings, often there is an option to save/export those settings and then restore/import the settings as well. This is a very handy feature if you need to start fresh at some point or are a developer and need to move a site from one server to another.

A newer feature of WordPress is that a theme's settings aren't lost when you switch to another theme. So if you have Twenty Eleven (still one of my favorite of the default themes) all tricked out the way you like it, then you try Twenty Thirteen and change your mind, when you reactivate Twenty Eleven your settings will still be there. It is still a good idea to double-check things, but you shouldn't have too much work ahead of you.

This brings us to how you know what is a theme setting versus a plugin or WordPress setting. That answer is pretty simple. If you are changing a setting on an option under the Appearance setting, it's for just the theme; if you're using an option that's under the Settings section, it's sitewide regardless of what theme is active. This can get confusing when themes and plugins have their own buttons on the sidebar (if you look at Figure 6.1 with the menu bar from my site versus our demonstration site, you'll see these buttons), but generally, if a theme has a button, you'll know it (and will clearly affect only that theme), and plugins with their own buttons are still sitewide changes. Confused? Don't worry, as you work with your site, it will make sense in context. Remember the discussion in Chapter 7, "Setting Up Your WordPress Site the Right Way: SEO, Social Media, and More," when we discussed Google Analytics code? This is exactly one of those times when you could have the setting in a plugin or the theme.

Default WordPress Themes Explained

I think one of the reasons the theme repository at WordPress.org took off was that the default themes included with WordPress prior to version 3.0 were bland, boring, and pretty dreadful. Essentially the only people who were using one of the default themes (like the eponymous Kubrick), were people who didn't know how to switch themes or were testing something on default installs of WordPress.

Yes, they really were that bad. Things changed with WordPress 3.0. Big things. Version 3.0 wasn't just a huge leap forward for WordPress as software (menus and a host of other improvements were launched), but it was the version when the Twenty Ten theme was introduced. Twenty Ten changed everything about the default theme packaged with WordPress. It was elegant. It had solid design and typography behind it. Twenty Ten included support for *all* the new features in WordPress 3.0 (custom headers, custom backgrounds, menus, and more). Maybe most important, Twenty Ten was designed as a *parent theme*, but that meant that developers and designers could make new themes based off of Twenty Ten without changing the original theme. If new features were added to Twenty Ten (which happens with every new version of WordPress), those new features would be included in the child theme automatically.

Since then, each year has brought a new default theme. Each theme tries to take a slightly different design direction, giving new users some real choice for their sites before they even need to start looking through the Theme Repository. Personally, I really liked Twenty Eleven. I made a child theme for it (mostly as practice for teaching and writing my second book, *Using WordPress*) and used that as the theme for my personal blog for a year or two (that's a long time for a person like me). At the time I'm writing this, Twenty Twelve, Twenty Thirteen, and Twenty Fourteen are the themes included with every new WordPress install. You can download Twenty Ten and Twenty Eleven from the theme repository, and both themes are still maintained and updated by the theme team at WordPress.org. (Yes, there is a team dedicated to just theme design, development, and maintenance.)

Twenty Twelve

Twenty Twelve was released with WordPress 3.5 ("Elvin" for Elvin Jones), and in addition to including all the features and functions you'd expect (custom headers, custom backgrounds, and the like), it was the first default theme to be *responsive*. This means that the theme will automatically adapt and change to the screen size of the device viewing the page. Figure 9.1 shows what the site would look like on a computer screen.

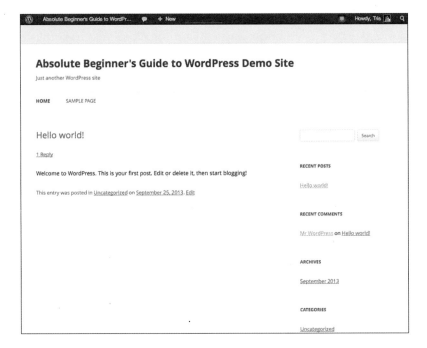

FIGURE 9.1

How the Twenty Twelve theme looks in your browser.

The same theme, now on a tablet in landscape orientation, is shown in Figure 9.2.

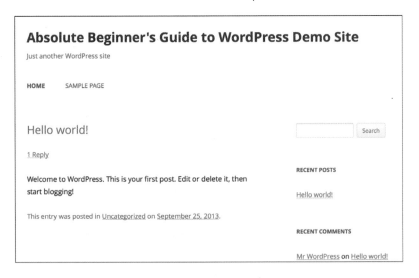

FIGURE 9.2

The same theme, on an iPad in landscape orientation.

And in portrait (Figure 9.3).

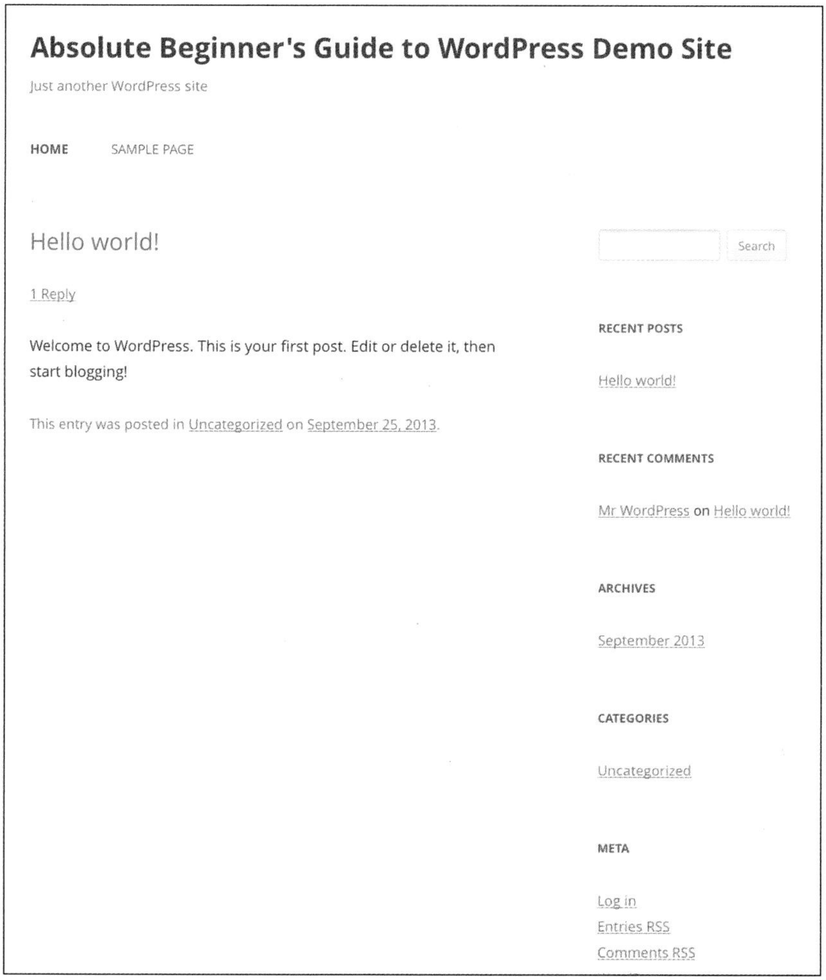

FIGURE 9.3

The 2012 theme on an iPad in portrait orientation.

And finally, an iPhone. Note that the Menu is now behind the Menu button (Figure 9.4).

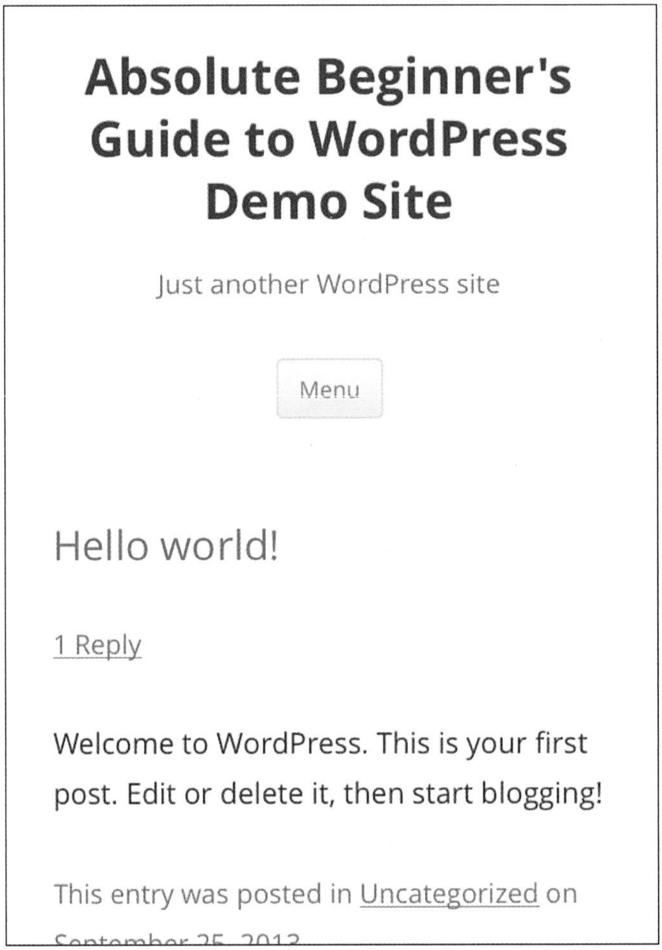

FIGURE 9.4

The 2012 theme on an iPhone.

All this is built in, ready to go from computer to tablet to mobile device. Twenty Twelve was the first default theme to do this and recognized that people need to have an out-of-the-box solution for supporting mobile devices. Yes, there are great plugins to do this (Jetpack and WPTouch are my favorites), but if you don't *need* a plugin for a feature or layout, that's much better. Remember, you should use the fewest number of plugins to do the job required—extra plugins can slow down your website. I've found Twenty Twelve (and Twenty Eleven) to be solid themes for both websites and blogs. Although I like the design of Twenty Eleven better, Twenty Twelve is a solid theme.

Twenty Thirteen

Twenty Thirteen was released with WordPress 3.6 ("Oscar" for Oscar Peterson) and brought a completely new look to the default theme choices. Twenty Thirteen was designed to focus on blogging with bold colors, post formats that really stood out from content, and a single column layout with footer widgets instead of sidebars. Figure 9.5 gives you a look at it.

FIGURE 9.5

Theme Twenty Thirteen.

Twenty Thirteen was built to give WordPress users a choice between themes that could work great with blogs (but were even better at creating websites) and a theme that is intended to be a blogging theme. The focus is on the words on the page, not putting things in sidebars and such. Like Twenty Twelve (and all the themes now), Twenty Thirteen is responsive and written in HTML 5. If you want to blog away and write great words, Twenty Thirteen is a solid theme to start with.

Twenty Fourteen

Twenty Fourteen is described as a theme to return WordPress to its roots as a blogging engine, but with modern touches. While some of the *early* looks didn't thrill me, the final released version is very polished, sophisticated, and modern. It has great typography and options that make it a great choice many different kinds of blogs (Figure 9.6).

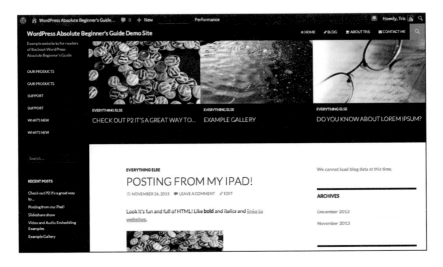

FIGURE 9.6

The demo site using Twenty Fourteen.

One of the cooler features of Twenty Fourteen is how it can highlight featured posts. Through the Customize section (we'll talk more about it in Chapter 10), you can have posts with a specific tag (featured is the default, but you can change it) displayed at the top of the home page as a grid (as you see in Figure 9.6) or a slider (as you see in Figure 9.7).

FIGURE 9.7

Featured posts as a slider.

The Grid setting is the easiest to "get right"; picking the right size featured image to display is much simpler. For the Slider option, you should have images at least 1038 pixels wide (or bigger). In either case, you quickly stop using the featured section by not having any Posts with "featured" as one of the tags. Twenty Fourteen highlights an esthetic of focus on the content, not on bells and whistles on the page.

Conclusion

This has been a pretty heavy chapter. I know it's not everyone's cup of tea, but understanding how themes and WordPress interact with each other will help you use WordPress more easily and efficiently. Often, new WordPress users are confused at how one person can do one thing on a site, but they can't. Sometimes it's a plugin, but sometimes it's the theme. Understanding how themes, plugins, and WordPress work together is the first step in being able to pick through those questions.

IN THIS CHAPTER

- Adding a custom header to your site
- Adding a custom background to your site
- Creating and managing menus
- Using WordPress widgets

10

TWEAKING, TUNING, AND CUSTOMIZING YOUR WORDPRESS SITE

Now that we understand, in general, how themes work, let's get down to making your site more your own and less looking like everyone else's. A crucial part of this chapter—and everything we do in it—is that all the customizations we cover are theme dependent and theme specific. Here's what this means for you. Whether a theme allows you to change the header image or the background or how many widget areas or menus there are depends on the theme. For example, Twenty Thirteen doesn't allow for custom backgrounds. You can have a custom header image of nearly any size, but you can't change the background color (without editing the theme or creating a child theme—which we'll cover in Chapter 16, "Customizations Without (Much) Coding"). Similarly, how many widgets and where they fall on the page are all tied to the theme. It goes beyond what is available from the theme, too. When you set a custom header image using one theme, if you switch to a different theme, your custom image won't be there—you'll see the default header image *for that theme* instead. Same goes for widgets, menus, and backgrounds. Those images aren't lost. You can easily choose your header again from your media library (assuming the image falls within the theme's header image dimensions); you just have to set it again.

Yes, this can be quite disconcerting when you're trying out new themes, especially if you spent a lot of time getting your theme "just right." Then you switch to a new one only to feel like all your work was for naught. However, the things you did on the first theme are kept in settings if you switch back to it. Because every theme handles these features differently, I needed to pick one single theme as the "example theme" for this chapter. I picked my favorite of the recent themes made by the WordPress Team: Twenty Eleven. Twenty Eleven sports some really interesting (and powerful features) that make it a great example theme. You can learn more about Twenty Eleven on the WordPress.com page for it: http://theme.wordpress.com/themes/twentyeleven/. In Chapter 17, "Advanced WordPress Settings and Uses," I'll use Twenty Twelve as the example for using WordPress as a website. Twenty Eleven works just fine for websites, but Twenty Twelve is a lot better, and you'll read why in Chapter 17. We're going to be spending this entire chapter under the Appearance menu, so go ahead and click it, activate Twenty Eleven (download and install it if you need to), and let's get to it.

 TIP In this chapter, we're going to be spending a lot of time flipping between changing something and then looking at the result on the site. My tip for you is to open the home page of the site in a new browser tab or window and keep it open. This way you just need to switch to that tab or window and refresh to see the changes.

Using Custom Headers

Within the Appearance settings section, click Header, and you'll see something like Figure 10.1.

FIGURE 10.1

Header settings.

The top half of the page shows the current header and, more importantly, what the recommended dimensions for header images should be. Since WordPress 3.5, theme authors could specify *minimum and maximum* header dimensions. For Twenty Eleven, the *suggested* dimensions are 1000 pixels wide and 288 pixels high. What happens if you pick an image larger or smaller than those sizes? We'll get there. First, scroll down a bit and look at the default images. Notice how awesome they are and that you can let WordPress choose one randomly for you (Figure 10.2).

FIGURE 10.2

Whoa random!

Why pick this option? First, pick it if you can't decide among any of the default options, and second, this feature *also* applies to headers you upload. So you upload two or more headers you can have WordPress pick them at random for you. This is a really easy way to make your site more interactive and dynamic—and also requires very little work on your part. Just work up a few headers and, ta da, you can have people in awe of your site. Sweet.

Below the random section are some other options we'll get to in a moment. First, let's change this header image. There are several ways to approach a new header image, but two of the ways are by chance and by design. By chance, I mean picking an image (say a photo you took), uploading it, and seeing what you get when you crop it to the right dimensions. By design, I mean using an image editing program (Paint.net is one of my favorites for Windows, and Preview on the Mac does a good job at basic scaling and cropping) to create a header with the exact dimensions you need. How you approach it is up to you. For the example, I'm going to upload an image I *know* is bigger than the dimensions so you can see cropping in action. Uploading a header with the exact dimensions is going to turn out exactly as you think it would.

I clicked the Choose File button, picked the image I wanted to upload, clicked OK, and then clicked the Upload button. Figure 10.3 shows you the result. You can see the whole image, but in the middle are the "marching ants" of the area that when I click Crop and Publish will become the header image.

FIGURE 10.3

Cropping an uploaded image.

When I first came to this screen, the default cropping encompassed the entire width of the photo I wanted, but not the height. Lucky for me, Twenty Eleven allows headers of at least 1000 pixels wide by 288 pixels high. This meant I could expand the height of the cropped area to include all the 2010 Olympic flame torches. After I saved the changes, my new header will be in place. Figure 10.4 shows you the before with one of the default header images.

FIGURE 10.4

Before with a default header image.

And Figure 10.5 is the result after.

FIGURE 10.5

After with a custom image.

Just like with the default images, if I upload more than one header image of my own, I can have WordPress choose from those as random headers as well. I love to do this to add an extra bit of flair to my site and make the site more creative.

It also lets me pick more than one image that I like and not have to decide! For a business site, you can use this to have a header with your logo and more than one sales message or slogan or any other kind of imagery. Notice the bit below the upload section to be able to choose an image from your Media Library? This lets you use any image you've already uploaded into your site as a header (or a background for that matter—the same option is available on the Custom Background settings). Very handy if you want to use different headers at different times and rotate among them (but have only one at a time, instead of several randomly chosen).

The last option on the page is whether you'd like to display the header text as well. By default, this is usually the site name and tag line. Sometimes (as is the case in Twenty Eleven) the text is above the header image, so removing the text brings the image to the top of the page. In other themes, the text is overlaid on top of the image. When the header text is on top of the image, you have to consider the text color (which you can usually change with most themes) and the image so the text is still readable over the image. Even if the text is a contrasting color from the image itself, the business of the image might make it hard to read the text. One option for overcoming this issue is to incorporate the text you want into the header image itself (again with an image editor) so you can get everything just right. Headers are one thing, but what about changing the background of your site? That's possible as well—if the theme allows it. Let's go through those steps now.

Using Custom Backgrounds

The Custom Background screen works very much like the Custom Header screen, except without the cropping or randomness. Figure 10.6 shows the Custom Background settings screen. The top shows you a preview of the background—in this case, a solid gray. First, let's change the background color of the site. By clicking the Select Color button, I can move the circle in the color box and the slider on the right to get to the color I'd like. I picked something like a deep purple (Figure 10.7). After I click Save Changes, I can see what the new background color looks like (Figure 10.8).

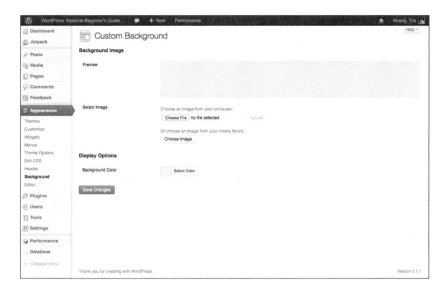

FIGURE 10.6

Custom background settings.

FIGURE 10.7

Choosing a new background color.

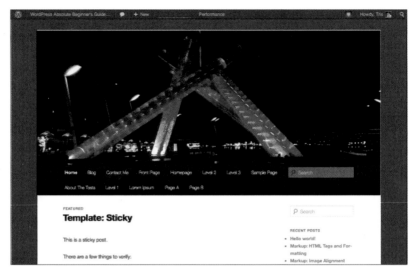

FIGURE 10.8

The result—a purple background.

Now that we have tried a different background color, let's move onto a different background image. Background images are tricky. It can be hard to find a nice, subtle background that tiles appealingly without making viewers want to gouge their eyes out. Just like uploading a custom header, you click Choose File, find the file you want, and then click upload. Figure 10.9 shows you what the setting looks like after uploading a texture.

FIGURE 10.9

Uploading a texture for a background.

Notice that we now have a bunch of other options for how the background image behaves. I'm using an image that tiles nicely, but if I turned off the tiling, I could have the image repeat horizontally or vertically. I could have the image start on the left, middle, or right side of the page. I can also decide if the image is fixed in place or if it scrolls with the rest of the page. If the image is fixed and the image is smaller than the height or width of the page, the background color chosen will show through. In my example, the tiled image covers the entire page to give the page a nice linen texture (Figure 10.10). An important bit to know: The background color loads first—if only for a moment—before a background image loads. So, make sure that your background color is as pleasant as the image and goes with the background. In the examples here, the brief jarring explosion of purple before the linen texture loads is offputting. Changing to something like a nice subtle gray (or white) would be better.

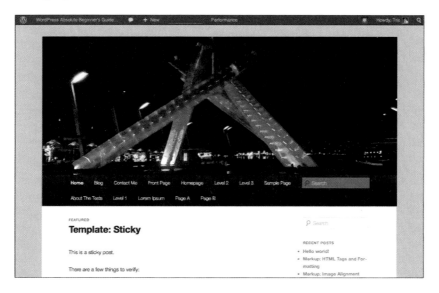

FIGURE 10.10

A linen background for the site.

That's all there is to setting a custom background, but as you can imagine, there is a lot more to backgrounds—and headers—than just these settings. You have to consider how everything looks together, and that can be really hard. Thus far, everything we've done has involved making changes on the live site. We click Save Changes, and it is so. What if you could play around with backgrounds, headers, colors, and other settings to see how the changes look on your site and *not* have the changes be set in stone? You can with the Customize option.

Clicking Customize under appearance loads a window with your current theme and site on one site and a series of options on the left. You can see what your site would look like with or without the header text. You can try different headers and backgrounds—even upload new ones—and see if they "work" for your site. All this is possible, and if you like the changes, you can click Save & Publish to make all the changes live *all at once*, or click Cancel and not make any changes at all. Figure 10.11 shows what this looks like for the site as we have it right now.

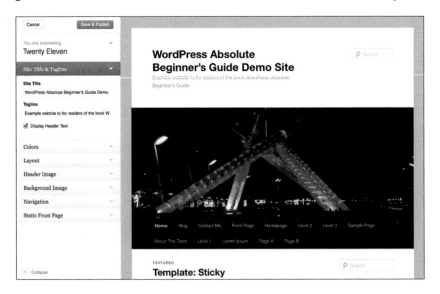

FIGURE 10.11

The Customize options. Play around with your site's settings without people seeing them.

This is very handy when you're trying out new ideas, but you don't want the whole world seeing the most ghastly header on the face of the Earth. Keeping the header and background we have, let's move on to working with the next thing people want to change pretty quickly on their site—the menu bar and navigation.

Using WordPress Menus

One of the most important parts of any website is clear and logical navigation. Making sure visitors to your site can find the pages you want them to (without having to use search) is absolutely important. This is why when WordPress Menus were introduced in WordPress 3.0, we all rejoiced. Before WordPress Menus, most menus were made up of Pages, and getting the order right could be really difficult. And if you wanted to mix in Posts or Categories, that required not just editing your theme files, but understanding some coding as well. Those were the Dark

Ages of WordPress menus. Today you have complete control over your menus and have any content you'd like on them, in any order; it's as simple as clicking, dragging, and dropping.

There is a gotcha here—you need *content* to make menus.

TIP   Yikes! We have no content to make menus! What do we do? There's an easy fix for that: import some demo content! WordPress.org offers theme developers standardized demo content to test their themes against, and you can download it for testing. Visit http://codex.wordpress.org/Theme_Unit_Test and right-click the link https://wpcom-themes.svn.automattic.com/demo/theme-unit-test-data.xml to download the content to your computer. Then follow the instructions in Chapter 11, "Using WordPress: Content," for importing content. If you're just playing around with WordPress, this is great content to start with. Just make sure you delete all the posts and pages before you set your site free on the world!

TIP   What if I don't want to add all that fake content (that I have to delete later)? You can fake it. You can use empty Links with the names you'd like as placeholders for the Posts, Pages, or Categories that haven't been created yet. Just remember to replace the placeholders with the real items later!

However you handle the content issue at this point (you could even jump ahead to Chapter 11, create some real content, and come back), the first thing we need to do is create a Menu. Before we do that, I want to frame Menus for you. Don't think of Menus only as things to help people navigate your site from the main menu bar in the header (where we expect menus to be now); think of them more broadly as containers to hold links to areas you'd like people to navigate to on your site. You see, Menus can be used in widgets for sidebars and footers as well! You can have one menu that serves as the main navigation of your site and other menus that appear in the sidebars of other pages to help people navigate more deeply into your site without cluttering up your main navigation. Combined with Jetpack, which allows you to control where widgets are visible your site, you can have menus that are connected to the context of the page the people are on. Figure 10.12 shows you the basic Menus screen before you've created any menus. WordPress assumes that you'll want your pages as menu items, so they are there as placeholders for the moment. In the Menu Name box, type in a name for your menu and click Create Menu to create your first menu. I like to use names that connect to what function the menu will have (main navigation, sidebar, footer navigation), but it doesn't really matter what you call the menu (you can name it

Bob for all WordPress cares). For the examples here, we'll be creating two menus: one for the main (or Primary, as Twenty Twelve calls it) menu and one for a sidebar. Let's create the main navigation first, so I'll call it Nav. Before we start adding items to the menu, I'm going to click Screen Options to allow us to see the Posts option (Figure 10.13). This will let us add individual Posts to the menu just like any other content item. Although it's not on by default, this option is handy to have active if you are building a website with WordPress and use Posts as one of the ways to organize your content. We'll cover this in more depth in Chapter 17.

FIGURE 10.12

Creating the first menu.

FIGURE 10.13

Making Posts visible to add to menus.

Now with our first menu created, let's customize it a little. By default, WordPress creates a link called Home to the home page of your site, and it is just a link to your site. Clicking the triangle on the item opens the properties of the menu item

(Figure 10.14). I don't want to make any changes to this item, so I'll click the triangle to close it. Looking at the default menu—which is all of the Pages in the site right now—I want to remove Blog, Front Page, and Home Page from the menu. To do that, I click the triangle and then the Remove link for each one; then I click Save Menu to save the changes. Figure 10.15 shows what the menu looks like after I'm done.

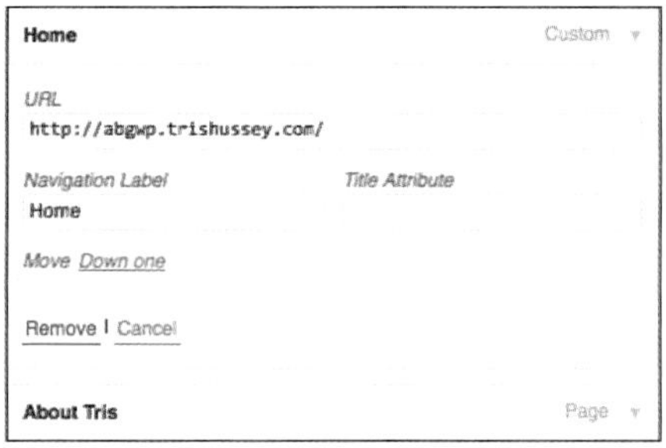

FIGURE 10.14

The Home menu item properties.

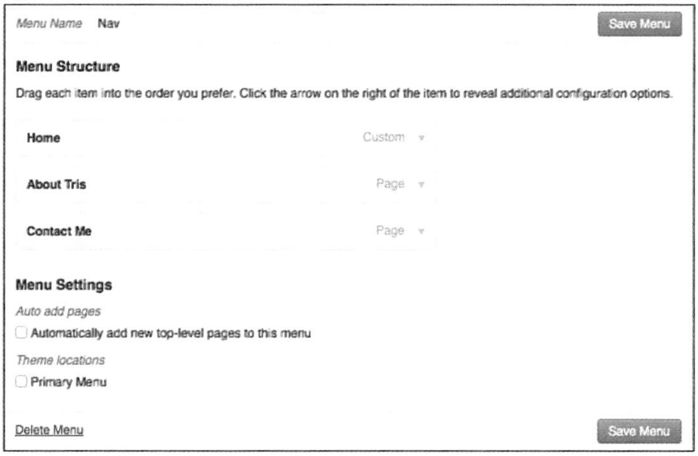

FIGURE 10.15

Down to three menu items.

I'd like Contact Me to be under About Tris, and I can do that one of two ways. One is to click and drag that menu item until the dotted lines indent below the item above (Figure 10.16), or you can click the triangle and click the link to move the item where you'd like it: up one, under the item above, or to the top of the menu (Figure 10.17). Either way works, so click Save Menu when you're done.

To add items to a menu, click the sections on the left (Pages, Posts, Links, or Categories), click the check box next to what you'd like to add, and then click Add to Menu. I'm going to add the Hello World post to the bottom of the menu just like this (Figure 10.18). New items are always added to the bottom of the menu. You can move them where you'd like either by clicking and dragging or using those same links in the menu item properties to move them.

FIGURE 10.16

Moving a menu item by dragging.

FIGURE 10.17

Moving a menu item with properties.

FIGURE 10.18

Adding a new menu item.

Although we've created this menu, moved items around in it, and added an item to it, we haven't actually added it to the site. Because menus can be used as widgets, and themes can have several menus areas, you need to tell WordPress where you'd like this menu to appear (if at all). Adding the menu to the site is as simple as clicking the check box next to the menu location under Theme Location where you'd like it to appear. For Twenty Eleven, there is only one location: Primary Menu (Figure 10.19). You can also manage where menus appear under the Manage Locations tab where, if you had several locations and several menus created, you could assign them all at once (Figure 10.20). You probably noticed the check box would let you automatically add new Pages (not Posts!) to the currently selected menu. This is a handy option if you're creating new sections that you'd either like to reorder in the menu later or just want on your site's navigation automatically. I tend to leave this off, as do most people, so you can choose what appears on each menu without having to worry that a test page (or a Private Page) isn't broadcast to the whole world automatically.

FIGURE 10.19

Setting the menu location in the menu area.

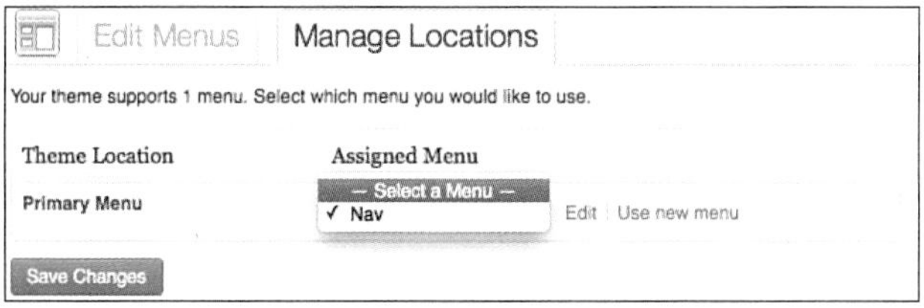

FIGURE 10.20

Setting the location under Manage Locations.

Picking either option works. Now that the menu is located, saving the menu settings and refreshing the site shows the new menu in place (I've hovered my mouse over About Tris so you can see the submenu; see Figure 10.21).

FIGURE 10.21

The new menu in place!

With a "regular" menu done, let's create another menu we'll use as a widget later in this chapter. To make this even more interesting, we'll create the menu with Links that will serve as placeholders for Posts, Pages, and Categories that don't exist yet. The first step is from the Edit Menus tab to click Create a New Menu, give the menu a name, and click Create Menu. Instead of adding Posts, Pages, or Categories, click the triangle next to Links. Putting a pound sign (#) in the URL field will make sure if you do happen to click the menu item, you'll stay on the same page. Figure 10.22 shows one Custom link for Products added to the new menu I've called Sidebar and a Link called Support ready to be added.

FIGURE 10.22

Adding items to a new menu for a sidebar widget.

These menu items don't go anywhere, but they serve as placeholders for sections of the site to come later. After you create the post or page that will take the placeholder's place, click Remove, get rid of that one, and add the correct one in its place. Notice that when you expand a menu item, there is a box with Navigation Label that looks like you can edit the name of the menu. That's exactly what you can do in that spot. I decided that Our Products sounded better than Products, so Figure 10.23 shows editing the name in the Navigation Label box. If you change the navigation label of a Post, Page, or Category, the menu item info will show the original name in case you ever want to change it back (or can't remember what the original was).

FIGURE 10.23

Changing a menu item's label.

After you have created more than one menu, you can quickly jump between editing them with the pull-down menu at the top of the Menu screen (Figure 10.24).

FIGURE 10.24

Changing menus to edit.

That's all there is to menus. Some themes have several menu areas (for example, two at the top and one in the footer); others have only one. Regardless of how many menu areas there are, creating, editing, and managing them is all the same: click, select, drag-and-drop, and save. Always save. In the next section, we'll talk about widgets and put this Sidebar menu to good use.

Using WordPress Widgets

Now that you've had practice with menus, widgets are going to be a breeze. Like menus, widgets are objects that you drag and drop into place to have them appear somewhere on your site. Theme authors can—and do—have widget areas in sidebars, headers, footers, even in the middle of posts and pages. Widgets are merely little containers of HTML code that "does something" on your site. That "something" can be really broad. Widgets can display your latest posts, your latest comments, the posts from another site (through RSS), custom menus, videos, Twitter feeds, Facebook-like boxes—the sky is the limit with widgets. Figure 10.25 shows the Widgets screen for the demo site.

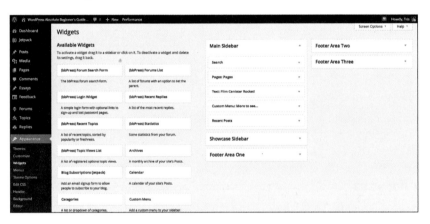

FIGURE 10.25

Widgets screen on the demo site.

It's important to recognize that both themes and plugins can provide extra widgets that you can use on your site. So what you see in the figure includes widgets from Jetpack and Twenty Eleven. If you aren't using Twenty Eleven as your theme or don't have Jetpack turned on, you won't see the same widgets. In fact, the widgets on my own site look very different, as well (beyond my site looking entirely different).

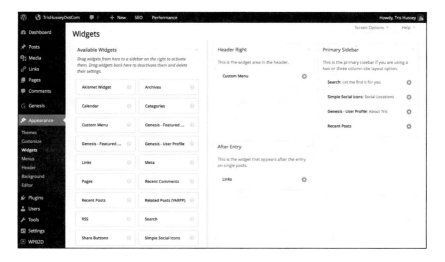

FIGURE 10.26

Widget area on my site.

Don't get caught up in whether you see a particular widget on your site or not; adding a widget to a widget area always works the same, regardless of the widget. Because there is such a tremendous range of widgets, I can't cover how to configure all possible widgets. By and large, configuring a widget *should* be self-explanatory. This section is designed to explain how widgets work and what some of the possibilities are, not to explain the entirety of the widget world.

The Widgets screen is divided into two parts. The left side is where available widgets are located—widgets that can be added to the widget areas of your site. The right side shows all the widget areas for your site. In this example, Twenty Eleven has Main sidebar, Showcase sidebar, Footer One, Footer Two, and Footer Three areas. Some theme developers do a great job at providing enough information to know where, why, and how each of the widget areas are used. Other theme developers don't, so you might wind up doing a little trial and error dropping a widget into an area and seeing what happens on the site. Back to the available widgets side, Figure 10.25 didn't show the entire screen; there was an important widget section offscreen that you need to scroll down (or in my case, collapse the Available Widget pane by clicking the triangle) to see: Inactive Widgets (Figure 10.27).

▣ Widgets

Available Widgets ▾

Inactive Widgets ▾

Drag widgets here to remove them from the sidebar but keep their settings.

Meta ▾   Gravatar Profile (Jetpack) ▾

FIGURE 10.27

Inactive Widgets section.

This section is crucial to being able to experiment with widgets and be able to quickly switch between them. Why? As the text says, widgets dropped there *don't lose their settings.* So to show why this is so important, let's start off with how to add widgets to widget areas.

Adding a Widget to a Widget Area

First, decide which widget area you want to put your widget into and click the triangle next to its name to open the area. (In Figures 10.25 and 10.27, the Main Sidebar area is open.) Then click and drag a widget from the Available or Inactive widgets section into the widget area. When you let go, the widget opens to reveal its settings. In this case, I used Recent Posts as an example (Figure 10.28). You can see a space for a title (if you'd like to change the default title), the number of posts to display, and the option to display the date the post was published. Click Save (even if you don't make changes, clicking Save ensures that the widget's default settings are saved) and then you can close that widget area, go to your site, refresh the page, and see your new widget in place.

FIGURE 10.28

Settings for the Recent Posts widget.

What if you have lots of widgets, not much room on the screen, and can't see where to drag it to? You can add a widget directly to any widget area right from the Available Widgets or Inactive Widgets areas by clicking the little triangle to reveal a widget placement menu. Just pick the widget area you want to place the widget in and click "Add Widget" (Figure 10.29). Simple as that, and you're done. When you click "Add Widget," the widget will be added there and the widget settings will open up just like in Figure 10.28.

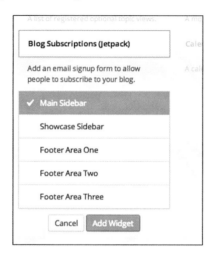

FIGURE 10.29

Easy widget placement menu.

Moving Widgets Around in Widget Areas

When a widget is in place in one widget area, that doesn't mean it's stuck there. If you'd like to move a widget from one area or another, just open the widget area you'd like to move it to and drag the widget from one area to another. The widget's settings will be preserved, so don't worry about that. You should check how the widget looks on your site, however, to see if you need to make any changes in the settings. For example, having five posts in a sidebar might look fine, but in a footer, you may only want one or two.

Removing Widgets from Widget Areas

Removing a widget is just as easy as adding them—except, what happens after you drag and drop determines what happens if you want to use that widget again. If you drag the widget to the Available Widgets section of the screen, all the settings for that widget will be lost. So if you decide later to use the widget again and drag it back into a widget area, you'll have to redo the settings. That isn't too bad for simple widgets like Recent Posts or Recent Comments, but some widgets (like the Jetpack Twitter Timeline widget) have more involved settings, and you *don't* want to lose those. If you want to keep the settings for a widget when you remove it from a widget area, drag it to the Inactive Widgets section. Then if you want to use the widget again, the settings will be preserved, and you will be good to go. Even for the most complicated widget settings, if you have to start from scratch, that isn't so bad, but there is one widget that you really don't want to lose the settings for—the most powerful and flexible widget of them all: the Text widget.

 TIP If you have been configuring a widget and feel like you need to start fresh with it, dragging it from the widget area to Available Widgets and then back will give you a clean start. Because you lose the settings, the widget will open with all the default settings again.

 TIP The Available Widget area can be collapsed to make it easier for you to drop widgets into the Inactive widgets section. In the title bar of "Available Widgets," look for the little triangle, click it, and the area will close and bring the Inactive Widget section higher up on the screen.

Text Widget: The Most Powerful of Them All

How can a text widget be the most powerful and flexible of all the widgets? "Text" is a bit of a misnomer. Sure, you can use it to type in whatever text you'd like—maybe a little welcome message, a legal disclaimer, a copyright statement, or a privacy message—but you can also paste in HTML or JavaScript code to add just about anything into your widget areas. Want a YouTube video in your sidebar? Sure. Code for banner ads from Google or other advertisers? Absolutely. Code for a cool-looking widget from a new social network? Not a problem. It's all as simple as copy and paste. Let's do a quick example embedding a YouTube video into the sidebar of our demo site.

 CAUTION If you're using WordPress.com, you will be limited to basic HTML and other simple text entries for text widgets. I'll talk more about this in Chapter 14, "All About WordPress.com."

The first step is to find the video you want to use and click the Share link below the video; then the Embed link to see the embed code (Figure 10.30). For this example, we're going to use my video for how to make a film canister rocket with baking soda and vinegar (a very fun thing to do, by the way). Because we're going to use this in a sidebar, the default 560 pixel width will be too big for our needs. In the menu next to Video Size, choose Custom and enter 249 in the first box (the second box will automatically fill in with the correct number to keep the video in the correct proportions). You'll notice the code changes above with the correct dimensions (Figure 10.31).

FIGURE 10.30

Embed settings for the video.

FIGURE 10.31

Getting the custom code for the video.

Select the code in the box and copy it to the clipboard (Edit menu, Copy or Command-c or Ctrl+c). Now switch back to the widget area of your site and drag a text widget from the Available Widgets to a sidebar (or wherever you want). In the open text area, paste the code and click Save (Figure 10.32). It's important *not* to click the check box to automatically add paragraphs when pasting code into text widgets. That check box can cause WordPress to alter the code, and it won't work on your site. Now go to your site, refresh, and see the video in place on the sidebar (Figure 10.33).

FIGURE 10.32

Pasting the video embed code into the text widget.

FIGURE 10.33

Ta da! A video in the sidebar.

That's all there is to it! If you can copy and paste, you can add just about anything to your sidebar that you want!

TIP   If you want to add some text into a text widget that includes pictures, links, and formatting—and you don't want to learn HTML to code it—just start a Post or Page, get the text to look how you'd like it, and click the Text tab. That will give you the HTML you can copy and paste into the text widget. You don't even need to save the Post! We'll learn all about Posts, Pages, and the Text view in Chapter 11.

Now you can see that if you go to the trouble of getting that code (and getting the size and settings just right), if you lose the work, it's a pain. If I decide to remove the video in the future, I can keep the settings all safe and sound in the Inactive Widgets area. Then if I'd like to use the widget again in the future, it's all ready to go.

Custom Menu Widgets

In the previous section on menus, I created a menu called Sidebar that I wanted to use as a Custom Menu Widget for the sidebar of the site. Here's how to do it. Drag the Custom Menu widget from the Available Widget section to where you want the menu to appear (I put it in the Main Sidebar again). Choose the menu to display, give the widget a title (optional), and click Save (Figure 10.34).

FIGURE 10.34

Custom Menu widget.

After it is saved, switch back to your site and refresh. Click Done (Figure 10.35).

FIGURE 10.35

The custom menu in place.

Tapping into the power of custom menus and widgets gives you a new way to help guide visitors around your site. Combine that with Jetpack visibility, and you can have menus (and other objects) appear on only some sections of your site and not others. We'll delve into visibility in Chapter 16, "Customizations Without (Much) Coding." For now, just enjoy and play with custom menus (and all the other widgets).

Cautions

You are probably wondering right now, "Can I have too many widgets?" That answer is simple: Yes. Okay, so how many widgets are too many widgets? Well, that depends. Like plugins, widgets are bits of code that have to run when your site loads. Although caching will help if you're loading content from other websites (like YouTube, Facebook, or Twitter), you are at the mercy of *their servers* to make sure what's in your widget loads. If one of the external sites is having a problem (it happens), then that *might* cause your site to load more slowly as well. Even if the widget isn't loading external content, it's still loading something, and that can slow things down. So, the more widgets you have, the more you risk slowing down your site. Next is clutter. If you fill up your sidebars, footers, and whatever else with lots of widgets, your site might start looking cluttered—even if it still loads quickly and is otherwise fine. You should think about whether all the widgets add value to your readers. Do you really need all the widgets for your visitors to get the most out of your site?

It's a tough conversation to have with yourself, but it's important. I look at the widgets on my site often and do a cull of widgets to make sure my site loads fast and doesn't look cluttered. It's a good habit to have, and your visitors will appreciate the effort.

Conclusion

As chapters go, this one packs in a lot of cool stuff that you can start using right now to help your site stand out. The right theme with the right header, background, menus, and widgets gives you a very powerful site for whatever you'd like to do online. So far we haven't had to dig into HTML (much), and all these tasks can be handled with just a lot of drag and drop and click and save. If you jumped from here to Chapters 11 and 12 and stopped, you'd be able to have a great site that looks and works well. The other chapters put the icing on the cake, but they are *extras* to the main function of the website: to look good and present content to people.

In Chapter 16, we step into a bit of deeper customization. Some tasks require a little coding; most don't. These are customizations I've found over the years that people want to do. There are tasks that can't be done with the options in this chapter.

11

USING WORDPRESS: CONTENT

This chapter is all about words—specifically, putting words onscreen that will become the content for your website. We'll cover how the Post and Page editors are the same—and how they're different. We'll cover what Posts and Pages are, and why I keep referring to them separately (and why I also talk about pages with a lowercase "p"). We'll talk about categories, tags, and how to use them to organize your content throughout your site. If you need to move your content to another site, or bring another site's content into yours, we'll get to that, too. Finally, we'll wrap up with managing comments, because although not specifically content-related, comments are tied to the content, so it makes sense to talk about them. Before we get to how to create content in WordPress, let's talk about the main types of content: Posts and Pages.

Posts, Pages, Custom Post Types, and Post Formats Explained

There are two basic types of content in WordPress: Posts and Pages. All other kinds of content are derived from one of those two types (generally Posts). So what are Posts and Pages (and why do I keep capitalizing them!)? Let's start with Posts.

Posts: Also Known as the Blog Post, But More

When WordPress first came out, the only content type was a Post. That was the way a lot of blogging tools worked back in 2003 when WordPress 0.75 came out. A post was, essentially, a blog post. A piece of content that was intended to be a part of a much larger whole—a blog. It's that sense of connectedness that is essential to understand posts. Posts are *always* connected to each other. All posts are connected to each other by time, and we can see this through the time-based archives within WordPress (day, month, year). You can go back and page through all the posts you've written (and published), based on when they were published. Posts are also connected by author, category, and tag. However, if more than one person is writing on a site, each post could have different authors, categories, or tags from any other post; you can't say that *all* posts are connected to each other this way. Just to make things a little more confusing, all posts must be in at least one category. Remember in Chapter 6, "Setting Up your WordPress Site Right the First Time," that when we looked at the Writing settings, there was the Default Category, and it was set to Uncategorized. That's it. If you don't assign a post to a category when you publish it, it will be assigned to the default category. This is, by the way, why we'll edit the name of the default category to something (anything) other than Uncategorized. If you forget to assign a post to a category, the default category should at least be something meaningful.

Okay, let's recap. Posts are content that are connected to each other through time (all posts), category, tags, and author. That's the key. Posts are *pieces of content that have a relationship to other pieces of content*. You can always look at the "Archive" page for an author, category, tag, or date and see all the Posts that match those conditions. "Archive" is in quotes because it isn't so much an "archive" as storage as it is "archive" as a list. Being able to list all the posts of one particular type is very, very powerful and allows you to do some very clever things with your content. Later in the chapter, I'll talk about these clever ways to organize your content using posts and pages (and other content types). This is very important to think about if you're using WordPress to build a website. Now let's talk about pages.

Pages: Standing Alone with Purpose

Pages are what people tend to think of as "regular web pages." They are intended to be (relatively) static and can stand alone and still have context and meaning. The best examples of pages are the About Me and Contact pages. If you get to those pages on a site, they make sense all on their own. They don't need any other pieces of content for context or to make sense. Pages can't be assigned to a category or tag, and although pages do have published dates and authors, you can't look at all pages in a list (easily) using either of those. Pages aren't just boring old content, though. They have tricks of their own—page templates. Page templates are used to do things like have content without sidebars, have a Page that displays Posts, and many other cool things we'll see throughout this chapter and book. The catch is that Page templates are defined by the theme you're using. Some themes have lots of Page templates; others only one (the default one). Pages were developed as a response to WordPress users who wanted content that could stand alone outside of the stream of blog posts and maintain a place in the site. We all wanted Contact and About pages that we could keep outside of the flow of posts and be used for content that didn't match up nicely with what a blog post was or is. Pages were also the first things to be pulled into the early ways we handled menus. The reasoning is that we wanted people to read our posts, but the pages were the extra information (About, Contact, Downloads, Hiring) that visitors wanted to know as well. Then people wanted to use WordPress to make "traditional websites" and things got *really* interesting, but that's a story for Chapter 17, "Advanced WordPress Settings and Uses." Now what if you'd like content that looks, works, and behaves like a post, but *not* in the stream of blog posts? Content that is contextually linked, but as you create more content, it doesn't clutter up your stream of carefully crafted blog posts? That is why and how Custom Post Types were developed and added to WordPress.

Custom Post Types: Pulling Posts Out of the Blog Stream

WordPress 3.0 (Thelonious) didn't just bring in menus, new admin interfaces, and other changes; WordPress 3.0 also introduced Custom Post Types to the WordPress community. Custom Post Types are pieces of content that work and behave like posts, but they don't appear in your "regular" stream of posts. For example, you want to add testimonials, happy customers gushing about you and your company, to your site. It makes sense to have those as posts because you can easily put all testimonials in a Testimonials category and point visitors to something like http://abgwp.trishusseyc.om/archive/testimontials (or just /testimonials if you use WordPress SEO and set it up to do that—see Chapter 7, "Setting Up Your WordPress Site the Right Way: SEO, Social Media, and More") to read all the testimonials. However, you also have a blog, and if you created each testimonial as a Post—even under a single category like Testimonials that blog posts never used—visitors (and search engines) could see the testimonials mixed in with blog posts. Not terrible, but it makes for a messy content listing. Also, you can't just point visitors to a menu or link to all your posts without doing something like making sure all posts are *always* in one particular category (as well as others) that you can use for navigation. But this approach, relying on people to remember to always set a specific category, is doomed to fail at some point. Someone will forget to set the right category (even if it's the default one) and will wonder why their post isn't listed on the blog, and you'll have to look to see they missed the check box.

Right—messy and annoying. By using Custom Post Types, this isn't an issue at all. Blog posts are created as posts and you can use any of the ways—including the default ones—to list the posts for people to read. Testimonials have their own, separate way of being displayed and listed. Nice, neat, and simple. Some of the original explanations of Custom Post Types talked more about needing specific types of posts and how to organize them (with their own category and tag tools), but in the three years since WordPress 3.0 came out, the most popular use to Custom Post Types I've seen is being able to pull postlike content (content that is connected to each other) out of the regular blog stream. We'll talk more about setting up Custom Post Types and how to incorporate them into your blog in Chapter 16, "Customizations Without (Much) Coding." You'll find themes and plugins create Custom Post Types to work their magic (like Testimonials and Slideshow plugins), so you're likely to come across Custom Post Types and not even know it!

Post Formats: Styling Posts in New Ways

WordPress 3.1 (Reinhardt) brought in a new way to style posts: Post Formats. Post Formats are designed to allow theme designers to provide ways to offer quick, styled ways of presenting content. Formats such as asides, quotes, images (where the entire Post is a single image), and image galleries are some of the default Post Formats WordPress starts with (themes and plugins can create their own, as well). You can read the (somewhat geeky) explanation on the WordPress Codex (http://codex.wordpress.org/Post_Formats), but essentially, Post Formats created a standardized way to let WordPress users have a similar experience as Tumblr (www.Tumblr.com), which is a hosted blogging service that focuses on the idea of post formats as a way to style content in different ways. So if you have a quote you'd like to share, it might have a nice big quote mark image at the top; maybe the text is in a nice italic font, and there is space at the bottom for who said the sage words. Photo galleries, asides, even Twitterlike status updates—each has a style that reflects and displays that content in the best way possible. The important thing to understand is that Post Formats are not a separate kind of post, just a different way to *style* it. You can even have Post Formats for Custom Post Types! Remember that Post Formats are just and only that—formatting, style, and layout for regular posts.

These are the basic types and kinds of content in WordPress. They *sound* a lot more complicated than they really are. Just remember: Pages stand alone, posts are connected, Custom Post Types are a special kind of post separate from your blog posts, and Post Formats make posts look cool. Now that we have that straight, let's look at how content is created: the Editor.

The Post and Page Editor Explained

The first thing to know is that the Post, Page, and Custom Post Type editors are *functionally the same.* The only differences between them come down to Posts and Custom Post Types having sections to add Categories and Tags, whereas Pages have Page Templates instead (not that the functions are the same). Just like with Menus in Chapter 10, "Tweaking, Tuning, and Customizing Your WordPress Site," checking out the Screen Options is a good idea here, too. Figure 11.1 shows the options I like to see. I tend to write for sites that have more than one author, so I like to be able to switch authors if I need to. I also like to be able to see the check marks to enable or disable comments or trackbacks on that post (or page) as well. If these bug you, hide them from view. Many plugins (like WordPress SEO and All In One SEO Pack) add sections to the Editor as well, so things can get cluttered at times. Hide the sections you don't want to see (or don't need to see), and you'll be happier for it. You can also collapse sections by clicking the triangle in the corner of the title bar. Heck, you can even move the sections around to the order you want by clicking and dragging them. The Post and Page editors are very flexible to match how you like to work.

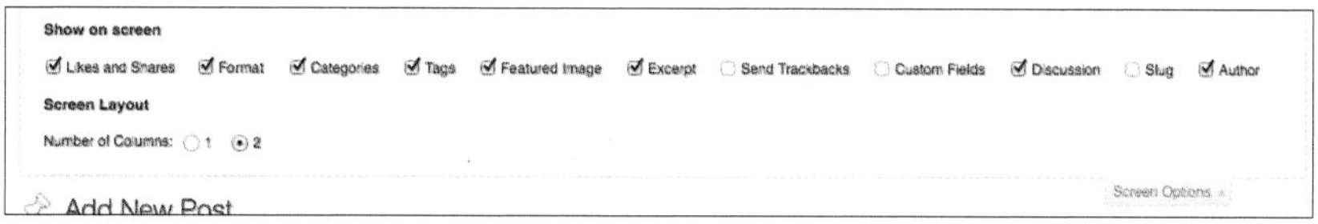

FIGURE 11.1

Screen options for the Editor window.

Now let's get down to the Editor itself. Regardless of whether you mouse over the Posts button in the admin area and select Add New, hover over the Pages button and select Add New, or use the +New menu at the top and select Post or Page (Figure 11.2), you'll get to the Editor screen (for Posts or Pages).

FIGURE 11.2

+New menu.

Figure 11.3 shows the Post Editor, and Figure 11.4 shows the Page Editor. They look pretty much the same, don't they? This is good. You don't have to learn different editors for the different kinds of WordPress content. Even Custom Post Types use the same Editor, making learning those easy as well. Besides the top of the page that says Add New Post/Page, the only difference you'll see is in Figure 11.5—the Tags, Categories, and Post Formats on the Post Editor and Page Templates in the Page Editor.

FIGURE 11.3

Post Editor.

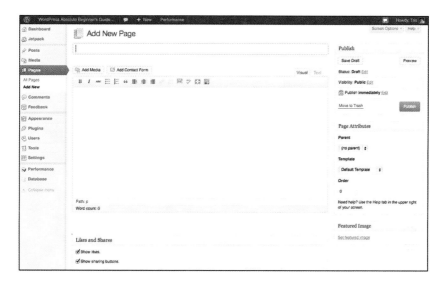

FIGURE 11.4

Page Editor.

FIGURE 11.5

Post versus Page Editor.

Before we continue the tour of the Editor, we need to click one wee but important button; we need to open the Kitchen Sink. This little button in the editing toolbar reveals a second row of buttons that are packed with handy features. We'll talk about them shortly, but for now click the button and check out the fancy new buttons (Figure 11.6).

FIGURE 11.6

Opening the Kitchen Sink.

Because we have Jetpack enabled, we have an extra button next to Add Media: Add Contact Form. As you add other plugins or themes, more buttons might appear in your editing area. Some themes help you with quick shortcodes for buttons, multicolumn layouts, and other tools, but for now we're going to stick to the basics.

Most of the icons on the toolbar should be pretty familiar to you if you've used a word processor, but some might leave you a bit stumped, so let's cover those. Figure 11.7 has the annotated image and the descriptions follow.

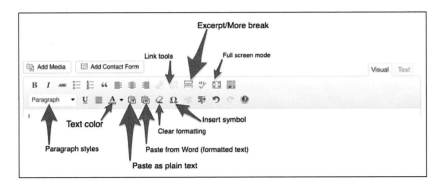

FIGURE 11.7

A few tools you might not recognize.

Let's start at the top and work our way down through the buttons. The pair of icons that look like links in a chain are the tools for creating (the whole links) and removing (the broken links) links in your content. They don't "light up" until there is text selected. Next is an odd-looking button that inserts the <!-- more --> HTML tag in your post at the insertion point. The "more tag" is what gives you the break in your content where you'd see the Read More... link. If your theme shows just excerpts on your home page or archive page, you might not ever need this. However, if you have a really long post that you don't want taking up a lot of real estate on the home page, you can use this tag to split the post into two parts so readers can finish the post on its own page. This makes for less clutter on your home page but lets people continue reading if they want. The button with the arrows pointing out to the corners is the full-screen, distraction-free writing mode. A common practice for many writers (including this one) is to block out all other distractions while writing to focus at the task at hand—writing. If you click the button, you get a screen that looks like Figure 11.8.

FIGURE 11.8

Distraction-free writing.

When you start typing, even the toolbar at the top disappears. Talk about focus! You already know what the Kitchen Sink is, so let's move down to the next row. The Paragraph Styles menu (Figure 11.9) lets you quickly switch between different built-in styles for your text. These aren't definable styles; these are HTML styles that are important for creating structure for documents. Paragraph is normal text, Address is for addresses, Preformatted is typically used for code, but the headings are probably the most important ones in the list. Heading 1 is usually the title of the post or page, but consider Headings 2 through 6 as sections and subsections of your content. Breaking up the content with headings does several things: First, it makes the content easier to read. There are breaks in the flow of the text for people's eyes to stop on. Second, it gives your readers an idea of the structure of your content. H2 is a major heading after the title, H3 is a subsection of the H2 above it, and so on. Again, a structure makes it easier for people to read and follow your content. Third, headings give search engines an idea of the big sections of the document as well so they can characterize and index the content more fully and accurately. Headings are a simple thing you can do to make your content so much better for readers and search engines. The styles menu is one of my favorite tools in the Kitchen Sink, but my real favorites are still to come!

FIGURE 11.9

Paragraph styles.

The "A" with the gray bar is a menu that lets you change your text's color (Figure 11.10). This is something that I tend to caution against. It is very easy to get carried away with colors in your text and have things get out of control. I've had to fix more than my share of posts and pages that went sideways from over-exuberant color application. Use it like hot sauce on your food; use a little to try, and use a lot only if you know what you're doing.

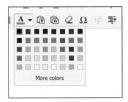

FIGURE 11.10

Text color menu.

The next two buttons, Paste as Text and Paste from Word, go hand in hand with each other. They handle the same task or problem in slightly different ways. Suppose you have some text from a Word document (or web page) that you'd like to put into your post or page. However, when you copy and paste the text, everything seems messed up on your site or the text just looks different from the rest of the site—and just wrong. These buttons fix this. After you copy the text, but before you paste it into your post or page, you can click the Paste as Text button (Figure 11.11) and paste the text into the window. Then when you click

OK, WordPress will put the text into your post as plain text. All formatting, links, and such will be gone. Now, if you'd like to keep some of the formatting (bold, italic, bullet lists) and the links, you click the Paste from Word button and do the same steps (Figure 11.12). Now when you click OK, WordPress keeps some of the formatting and discards the rest. Paste from Word is like "Paste and Match Style" functions in word processors. Use this for times when you want the basic formatting, but not things like fonts, font sizes, or colors. Believe me, this is a very handy button indeed!

FIGURE 11.11

Paste as Text window.

FIGURE 11.12

Paste from Word window.

NOTE   In the newest version of the code that makes the editor work, the need for Paste from Word has been diminished. The basic function handles pasting rich content (the term for formatted text) much more smoothly. As good as the Editor is, it's better to be safe than sorry in my book. I use Paste as Text and Paste from Word myself.

The little eraser icon is a Clear Formatting button. It's for those cases when the formatting of the text has gotten out of hand and you need to start from scratch. It happens. It's easy to get formatting a little wonky if you've been working on a post or page for a while and maybe copying and pasting sections of text around. This will get you out of a jam in a click.

The last button on the tour is the Insert Special Character/Symbol button. When you click that button, you'll get a table of special characters and symbols you might need in your text (Figure 11.13). If you know how to type en dashes, em dashes, or ü, the Editor will handle those just fine, but if you don't, this is the tool you need.

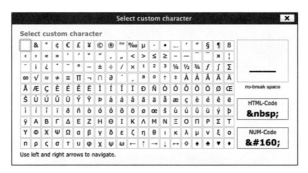

FIGURE 11.13

Insert special characters.

Now that we've discussed some of the key buttons, let's start creating content.

Writing and Posting Content

Because the Editor works the same when you write a post or page, we'll cover the mechanics of writing and posting content first: the basic tasks for typing content in, formatting it, adding links, and clicking the Publish button (and what happens after that). For the examples, I'll switch between creating a post and a page just to illustrate the *similarity* between the two, but later in the chapter, I'll create posts and pages focusing on the special features in each of them. For now, let's start typing.

Regardless of how you get to a blank Editor window, the first thing is the title at the top of the screen. I typically have a snappy title in mind before I start my posts, but that's just my process. You can put a title in whenever you want, and change it anytime you want, but after you save to Draft or Publish, the URL for the post is automatically set based on the title you have at the moment. Yes, you can change the URL later, but it's not a good idea to do that after the post or page has been *published*. After you've published content, changing the URL can cause people to get a 404 Page Not Found error. So, from a fresh Editor screen, type in a title (remember from Chapter 7 about how to write for search engines), and then click down into the content area (Figure 11.14).

FIGURE 11.14

Post with title, ready to accept content.

 NOTE   What's the deal with the weird text? I'm using some handy *lorem ipsum* text as fake text for these posts. Yes, it's Latin. No I'm not making this up. You can learn more about *lorem ipsum* from lipsum.org.

Formatting text works exactly like you'd expect. Select some text; click the I to format the text with italic. Select some text; click B to format the text as bold. So let's get to things that *aren't* so straightforward, like links, headings, and blockquotes.

Creating Links

To create a link within your text, first select the text to be the link (remember the lessons from Chapter 7 on writing for SEO); then click the Link tool button (the whole links icon) and you get to a window like Figure 11.15.

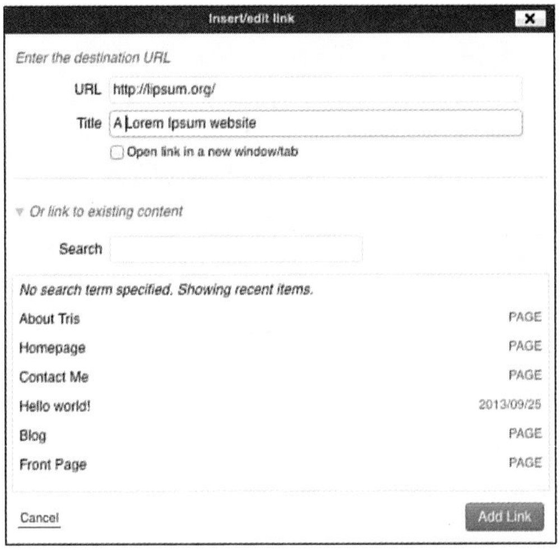

FIGURE 11.15

Inserting a link.

The URL for where you'd like the link to go to goes in the top box (where I have a URL) and the Title is what readers see if they pass their mouse pointer over the link *without* clicking on it. The Title is optional, but a nice thing to do for visitors and search engines. Below that section is one that is closed when you first come to the Insert Link screen—Link to Existing Content. This lets you quickly look for past posts (they have dates beside them) or pages (they just say PAGE) to link to within your content. This is a fast and easy way to link to content within your site without having to go to your site, find the post or page, copy the URL, and come back to the editor to insert the link. When you click Add Link, you return to the Editor with the link all set and done. Simple as that.

Inserting Images

I'm going to spend a lot more time talking about images and other media in Chapter 12, "Using WordPress: Images, Videos, and Other Media," but if I don't talk about how to insert images, at least briefly, parts of Post Formats won't make sense. Inserting an image (or other kinds of "media") all starts with clicking the Add Media button above the main editing toolbar (Figure 11.16).

FIGURE 11.16

Media button in the Editor.

Technically, you need to click in your post where you'd like have the image inserted, and *then* click the Add Media button. I'm going to insert an image in the second paragraph of the text and have the image float to the right and the text wrap around it to the left. Clicking the Add Media button brings you to a window where you can upload your pictures, videos, PDF files, and podcasts. You can drag and drop as many images as you want onto this window for them to upload. If that doesn't work for your browser, you can click the Upload button to see the regular file chooser window. I'm going to drag two images onto the window. We're only going to use one for this example (Figure 11.17).

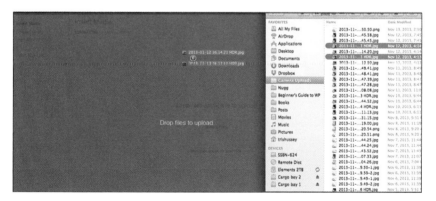

FIGURE 11.17

Dragging and uploading images.

If you don't have any images uploaded yet, you'll just see a blank window to upload, like in Figure 11.17. But if you already have images uploaded, you see the other images. You can still drag new images to upload into this window and the images will upload. No need to click the Upload tab; WordPress figures it out.

NOTE How big an image can I upload? If by "big" you mean dimensions, there isn't a limit. However, the real limit is file size, which tends to be 7MB for most hosts. If you have files larger than that to upload (videos and podcasts can often be far, far more than 7MB), you'll need to use FTP to upload them. The downside is that media files that you upload via FTP *aren't listed in the Media Library.* More about managing media in Chapter 12.

After uploading my two images, both have check marks in the upper-left corner of the image (Figure 11.18), so I click the check for one of the images to deselect. This makes sure I'm putting only one image in right now. In Figure 11.19, you can see the options I've set for this image. I've given it a caption, set the alignment to Right, and if someone clicks the image in the post, it will show the image on its own page (Media file option). And I've set the medium-size image (300×225). When I click Insert into Post, I get Figure 11.20.

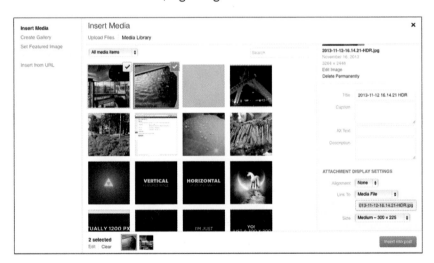

FIGURE 11.18

Images uploaded and selected.

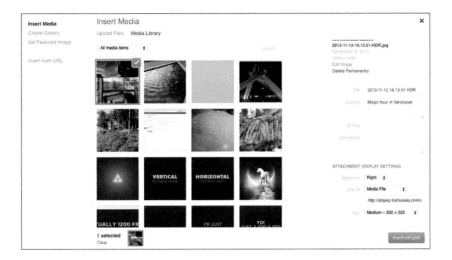

FIGURE 11.19

Setting the options for the image.

FIGURE 11.20

Image in the post.

Looks pretty spiffy. Now let's insert another image with a few different settings. I put a blank line between a couple of the paragraphs and clicked the Add Media button again. Using the second image I uploaded, I'm opting for no caption, no alignment, and the large size (Figure 11.21), which in the post gives me what you see in Figure 11.22.

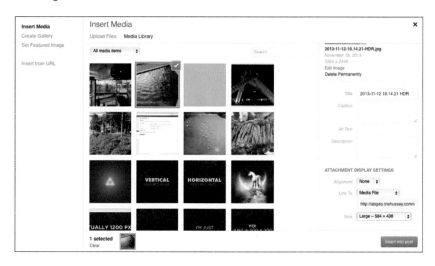

FIGURE 11.21

Inserting a second image.

FIGURE 11.22

Second, larger image in place.

Before I publish this post, I'd like the image to be centered on the page. All you need to do is to click the image and then the center text button on the editing toolbar. Images behave just like paragraphs or any other text in that respect.

If you want to change something about the image after you insert it, click the image once in the Editor, and two icons appear in the upper-left corner. The picture icon lets you edit the properties of the image; use the other icon to remove the image from the post (Figure 11.23). I'm going to switch the first image from floating right to floating left. After clicking the picture icon, I see this edit screen (Figure 11.24).

FIGURE 11.23

Editing image properties and settings.

FIGURE 11.24

The editing window with float left set.

There is a lot more to that screen than what we just did. Don't worry, we'll cover all of that in Chapter 12. For now I'm going to hit Publish, and you can see the post with the images in Figure 11.25.

FIGURE 11.25

Yes, those are pretty pictures.

That's all there is for images—for now. In Chapter 12, we'll get more into galleries, featured images, slideshows, and all other media-related topics.

Headings and Paragraph Styles

Inserting headings (or using any of the styles from the pull-down menu) is as simple as clicking in the paragraph you'd like for the heading and picking the heading level from the menu. The same process goes for any of the other styles. The default style is the Paragraph style. For clarity, a "paragraph," when you're editing text like this, is a chunk of text that you separated from text above and below with a return. This is important because even though a heading (like Headings and Paragraph Styles above) isn't a paragraph in the grammar world, for formatting content, it is. It's a distinct and discrete block of text that has formatting distinct from above it and below it, and the formatting will carry throughout the entire block of text. Like a blockquote, for example.

Blockquotes

If you have some text you'd like to stand out from the rest of the text, especially if it's a quote from someone else, you can use the Blockquote button. Just click in the section of text and click the button with the big quotation mark (") icon. You'll see something in the Editor that looks like Figure 11.26, where the text in italic is the text with blockquote applied (the bold text above is a Heading level 2).

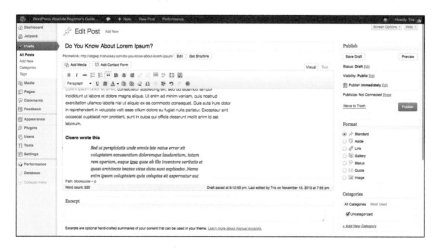

FIGURE 11.26

Blockquoted text and a heading.

Clicking the Preview button gives you a look at what the post looks like thus far (Figure 11.27).

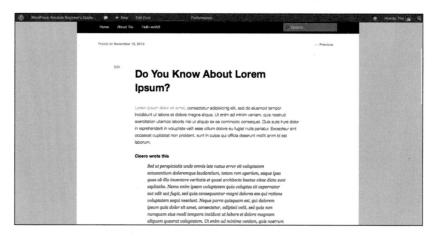

FIGURE 11.27

A preview of our post.

Editing Published Posts

Notice the little Edit Post in the menu bar at the top of the window and the little Edit in the gray box on the page? If you click those, you'll be tossed back into the Editor to be able to edit the post some more. This post isn't published yet, but even if it were, as long as you're logged in to your site, you'll see those. No, your visitors can't see them (I know you're wondering that), just you, and only when you're logged in (which will probably be most of the time). I went ahead and clicked Publish back in the Editor, and after WordPress works its magic, the post is live and ready for the world to see (Figure 11.28). You'll notice that Publish from Figure 11.14 is now Update, as in Figure 11.28. If you make changes to the content, you click Update to make those changes live. Don't worry, you don't have to publish a post before you leave the Editor. In Figure 11.14, you'll notice a Save Draft button. You can at any point click that button, leave the Editor, and come back later to finish the content. You can get back to any post or page you have on the go (or have already published) by clicking the Posts or Pages button on the left. The default behavior for those buttons is to show you a list of all the posts and pages. (You can also get to that page from the All Posts or All Pages fly-out menu as you pass your mouse over those buttons.) From that list, clicking the title of a post or page will bring you to the Editor. We'll talk more about the All Posts and All Pages list and how to use it later in the chapter.

FIGURE 11.28

Post published.

Autosaving: Save Your Work and Your Sanity

If you've been trying this as you read, you might have noticed that WordPress automatically saves your work as you go. Your content is automatically saved every few minutes, so if you accidentally close the window or lose your Internet connection, or whatever, you won't lose all your work between clicking Save Draft or Publish/Update. This is a handy feature that everyone uses from time to time. I certainly do. Even while writing this section, I accidentally hit the Back button between creating Figures 11.14 and 11.15, and the text I pasted in was there when I came back to edit. The link was gone, but the bulk of the text was there. Now what if you're working on a longer post or working on a post with a few people? What about going back to a previous version or seeing who made what changes? WordPress has you covered there with Revisions. We'll come back to it later in the chapter and show you what a great tool it is.

Believe it or not, that's the basics of editing content. I encourage you to experiment with the full-screen Distraction-Free Writing Mode, inserting symbols, the Paste as Text, and Paste from Word tools, but as far as the basics of writing and posting content in *general*, that's it. I'll cover inserting and managing images, videos, and other media in Chapter 12. I'll cover Categories, Tags, Page Templates, and all the rest in their own sections later in this chapter. This section is about the general writing. We're not all done with the Editor, though—we still have a lot of nifty features to go through.

Scheduling Posts and Pages

What if you have some content that you don't want to appear until sometime in the future? Maybe you have an announcement that can't be live until 8:00 a.m. on a Monday, but you want to finish writing on Friday and have it "be live" Monday morning without needing to do anything else. That is as simple as a few clicks from the Editor (Post or Page).

Start with whatever content you're working on, and *before* you hit Publish, click the Edit link next to Publish Immediately. You'll see something like Figure 11.29 with options for changing *when* the page (or post) will be published.

FIGURE 11.29

Scheduling a post.

When you click OK, Publish becomes Schedule, so when you're done with the content, clicking Schedule will tell WordPress to publish that post at that date and time (Figure 11.30). Until that time, the only people who can see the post or page are the author of the content, an Editor, or an Administrator of the site.

FIGURE 11.30

Post ready to be scheduled.

NOTE   Can I backdate content? Yes, you can, and there aren't any rules against doing that, but the real question is *why* are you doing it. If it's making sure your content has a certain flow or order, that makes sense, but you might want to think of using Pages instead of Posts if time and order are that important.

Post/Page Status

Even after content is published, you can change its status from the Editor using the Status menu. Clicking Edit next to the status gives you a menu where you can change content from Draft, Pending Review, or Published/Scheduled (Figure 11.31). So content that is live (or due to be live) can be pulled back to Draft (unpublished) status at any time. Functionally, Draft and Pending Review are the same (the content isn't live), but in an All Posts or Pages list, Drafts and Pending Review can easily distinguished from each other (Figure 11.32).

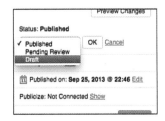

FIGURE 11.31

Published, Draft, or Pending menu.

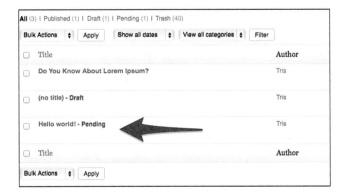

FIGURE 11.32

Draft and Pending posts.

What Pending Review means to Editors is that there is content ready for their review and approval before it goes live. For sites where the Editor has final say, especially where you use the Contributor role, which can't publish content live, this feature is handy to be able to tell what is ready and what is still being worked on.

Controlling Who Sees Your Content

Although most of the time you want people to be able to read everything on the site, there are times when you might like to hide some content from most visitors, or even behind a password. This is what the Visibility options are all about (Figure 11.33). Public is the default; anyone and everyone can read the content on the site. Password protected will see that the post or page exists, but unless you have the password, you can't read the content. Private means that no one except the author, Editor, or Administrator can even see that the content exists. It doesn't appear on post or page lists within the Dashboard, or on any public part of the site—even if you know the URL to the content, it doesn't exist for you to view (if you're not logged in to the site *and* have the required privileges to see it). This is more than just hiding a page in plain sight by publishing it and not directly linking to it (there are always ways to find that kind of content). This is a complete "need to know basis" kind of hiding content.

FIGURE 11.33

Public, Private, or Password Protected posts.

If you're setting the Visibility on a post, you'll also see an option below Public to "Stick this item on the Front page" (aka a Sticky Post). This pulls that post out of the timeline and puts it at the top of the Post stream—regardless of how old the post is. As newer posts gather below it, this Sticky Post will remain at the top. This is a great way to make sure certain posts (think in general content terms) are more likely to be seen. It will also come into play later when we talk about the special Showcase Page Template in Twenty Eleven.

Visual Versus Text Views

The last part about working with content is the difference between the visual (or rich text or WYSIWYG editor) and the text (or source or HTML) views of the content. The visual view in the Editor lets you see what the content looks like (for the most part) when it's published. You can always click Preview to see what the content will look like on your site within the template, but you have a general idea of how things will be. The key here is that while you *see* bold, italic, links, and images, in the background, WordPress and the Editor components are writing HTML (the language of websites) for the content. Most people rarely (if ever) need the Text view, but sometimes….

First, let's look at one of the posts on my personal blog in the visual editor (Figure 11.34).

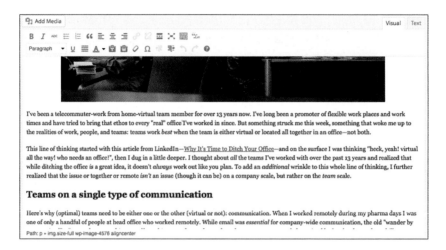

FIGURE 11.34

A post in the visual editor.

Now the same post in the text view (Figure 11.35).

FIGURE 11.35

Same post, but all HTML.

Yep, that's HTML. If you look closely, you might make out some of the text and formatting that makes the things you see. Those of us who learned to create web pages back in the 1990s remember this code well. It's all we saw of our pages before the world saw them as websites. Today—not so much. Why would you ever need to switch into text view? A few reasons. One (and most common) is if there is something on the page that just doesn't look right, you can see if looking at the source view helps. Clicking the Close Tags button sometimes helps to fix strange formatting problems that might have crept in. Generally this isn't something you want to mess about with. It's pretty easy to wind up with a real mess if you aren't careful. The other reason is if you need to paste in HTML code to embed a video, slideshow, or some other interesting piece of web content. If you paste HTML into the visual editor, WordPress will convert the code into…well…words. It will make sure that the code isn't code anymore so it won't do anything on the page. Sometimes we *want* this to happen when we're showing off samples of our code (there are better ways to do it, though), so this isn't a bad thing that WordPress does, but it's not what most people want to happen when they are pasting code into the Editor.

For the code to "work," you need to flip to text view, make space for the code, and paste it in. It will *generally* be okay to switch back to the visual side to continue working on the content, but be ready for it not to work. Pasting the code into Notepad or TextEdit wouldn't be a bad idea just until you're sure it works.

More About Posts

Now that we have all the basics of the Editor down, it's time to look at things specific to Posts and Pages. First up are Posts. In Chapter 17, when we talk about using WordPress to make a "website," we'll *really* tap into clever ways to use Posts to get content grouped and gathered how you'd like them to be. And when combined with Custom Post Types, things get really interesting and fun. For now, let's stick with standard posts as blog posts and start off with Post Formats.

Post Formats

When Tumblr came onto the scene in 2007, it turned the blogging world on its head. Instead of focusing on posts as posts, Tumblr looked at each type of content and developed styles to match and reflect the content. So, yes, Text (a post in the WordPress world) is pretty straightforward, but the way Tumblr styled quotes, pictures, updates (like Twitter tweets), and other content was quite interesting and appealing to people. In 2011, WordPress 3.1 first included Post Formats as a way to appeal and keep up with the Tumblr phenomenon. By officially codifying Post Formats into the WordPress core, it made it easier for theme developers to take advantage of, making certain kinds of posts look different from others just by letting users click an option button in the Post Editor. The standard Post Formats are as follows:

- Aside
- Gallery
- Link
- Image
- Quote
- Status
- Video
- Audio
- Chat

Asides and Status are designed to be like Facebook updates (Asides) or tweets (Status). Chat is designed to look like a conversation through instant messaging or any other back and forth with people. Gallery and Image are for multiple (Gallery) or single (Image) images to show them off. Video is for showing a video as the sole piece of content. Likewise, Audio is for embedded audio files (like for podcasting). Finally, Link is for sharing just a single link to another website.

How each of these Post Formats look for your theme—and even which ones are supported—is truly dependent on the theme developer herself. For example, Twenty Eleven doesn't have Chat, Audio, or Video Post Formats included, and Figure 11.36 shows you what a few of the Post Formats look like in Twenty Eleven (not terribly fancy).

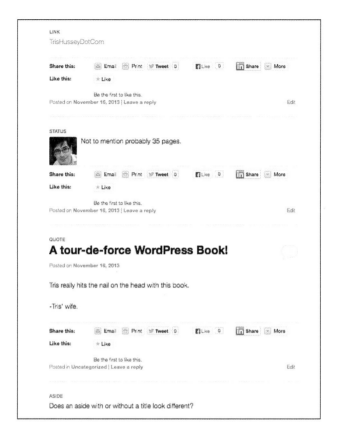

FIGURE 11.36

Some Post Formats in Twenty Eleven.

For the most part, using Post Formats is like creating any other post. The only trick is seeing how they *look* when the post is published. For example, Asides and Statuses in Twenty Eleven don't show the title of the Post on the home page. However, if you have a listing of Recent Posts (by using the Recent Post widget), if you skip the title entirely, there will be an entry with the post's ID number (such as 204). So you might need to put a title in so the rest of the site (and regular post) looks logical. The best way to learn about Post Formats is to try them and use them. If you don't like how they look, just click the option button from whatever the format was to Standard, and it's a "regular post." One of the longer-term projects within the WordPress development community is to work on how you set and use Post Formats. Right now, the debate is still going on about how to handle Post Formats in the Editor. I'm pretty confident that by the time this book is in your hands, Post Formats in the Post Editor will look different than they do now.

How to Use Categories

Categories are one of the key underpinnings of Posts in WordPress. Because all posts must belong to at least one category (and if you don't set one, one will be set for you), categories are the main way to organize your posts in WordPress. Pages, remember, can't be assigned to Categories (pages stand alone). So, what are categories anyway? Categories are big buckets to group content together. If you have a site about crafts, you might have categories for knitting, crocheting, pottery, and card making. If you have a site about cars, you might have categories for makes (Ford, Chevy, Toyota) or models (sport, SUV, trucks) or whatever your niche is. Categories are the large groups that you can use to put posts together. Categories can have subcategories, as well, so if you have a knitting category, you might have subcategories for hats, sweaters, or scarves. A category about Ford cars could have subcategories for the various Ford models (Mustang, F-150, Focus, Model-A, Model-T). Categories are all about organizing your content.

Before you can assign posts to categories, you need to create them first. There are two ways to do that. One is within the Post Editor and the other is in the Category manager. Let's look at the Post Editor first. Opening the post from Figure 11.25, I'm going to create a category of Photography to file it under (right now, it's just Uncategorized).

After reopening the post in the Editor, on the right side I click +Add New Category, and there is a form field I can fill in. I put in Photography (Figure 11.37) and then click Add New Category. The Category is created, and now I uncheck Uncategorized (because I don't want that to be one of the post's categories anymore) (Figure 11.38). When I click Update post, the new category will be set for the post.

FIGURE 11.37

Creating a new category.

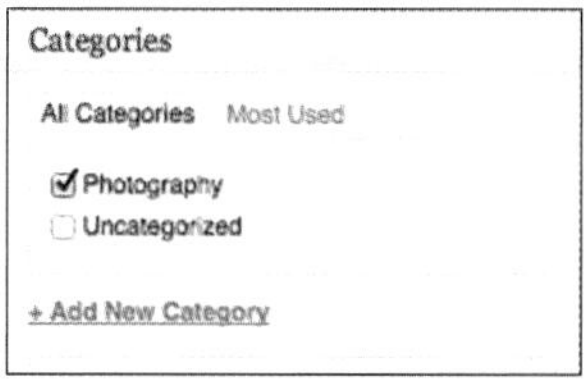

FIGURE 11.38

Category created.

Now if wanted a subcategory for Photography, I would click +Add New Category again, and after Enter the New Category (I'm using Magic Hour), I use the pull-down menu to select Photography from the list (Figure 11.39) and then click Add New Category. I now have a subcategory of Photography in the list above indented from its parent (Figure 11.40).

FIGURE 11.39

Creating a subcategory.

FIGURE 11.40

Subcategory created.

That's creating Categories within the Post Editor. If you click the link in the main Admin menu bar below Posts, labeled Categories, you come to the Category management screen (Figure 11.41). From here, you can see all the categories for the site and how many posts are in that category. You can see on the left side the area to create categories, and it works the same as within the Post Editor. The Description field is optional, but some themes use it to add information to the top of Category archive pages (all the posts within that Category). To find out if your theme supports it, put a description in for one of your categories, and go to the Category archive. You can jump to the Category archive for any of your categories by passing your mouse over the name of a category and clicking the View link. This brings us to editing existing categories. Let's fix that Uncategorized category once and for all. Passing my mouse under Uncategorized, I click Edit and get to a screen where I can edit everything about the category. In Figure 11.42, you can see I've changed the name to Everything Else and added a description. Notice that the field Slug is blank? It used to have Uncategorized in it, and I deleted it so when I changed the name of the category, the slug would be updated as well. The Slug is what is used for the URL of the Category archive. Figure 11.43 shows the new category listing with the updated category name, slug, and description. You might have noticed that unlike the other two categories, I can't delete Everything Else. That's because it's the default category. If I switched to a different category under Writing settings, then I could delete the category.

FIGURE 11.41

Main category management screen.

FIGURE 11.42

Editing Uncategorized.

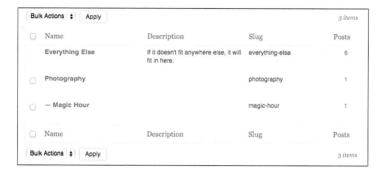

FIGURE 11.43

Category editing complete.

NOTE What happens when I delete a category? Do those posts disappear? No. If you delete a category that posts are assigned to, one of two things will happen. If a post was assigned only to that single category, it would be put into the default category (from Writing Settings). If it has more than one category, then essentially nothing happens. The deleted category disappears, and that's that.

The topic of Categories and Tags can get pretty confusing, but remember that Categories are big topics that many posts could fall under. Even subcategories are "big" topics, just not as big as their parents. Now Tags are something slightly different.

What Are Tags?

Tags in WordPress are essentially keywords specific to that particular post. Although you can use the same tag on different posts (meaning they are all about that specific topic), Tags are meant to be specific. The line between what makes a good tag and what makes a good category is pretty blurry. After a while if you've tagged a lot of posts with the same tag, you might want to promote it to a Category. Likewise, if you think you're going to have a lot of posts about a certain category and it turns out you don't, you might want to make it a tag. There are plugins to help you make this switch as well as a manual way I'll talk about later in this chapter.

Just like Categories, you can add Tags in the Post Editor or through a special Tag management page. Back to the Pretty Pictures post, below Categories is the space for Tags. You can enter as many Tags at once as you like, separated by commas. Click Add when you're done (Figure 11.44). You can always keep adding tags; you don't have to add them all at once. When you click Update, the tags will be set. Notice that tags don't have a hierarchy. There are no parent or child tags. Tags are all equal and are all keywords.

FIGURE 11.44

Adding tags within a post.

Click the Tags link from the Admin button area and you'll come to the Tag management screen (Figure 11.45). Just like categories, you can create and edit tags in the same way. Because there is no "default" tag (tags are completely optional for posts), you can delete any tag you want. Editing works the same way as Categories (with the exception of setting a Parent).

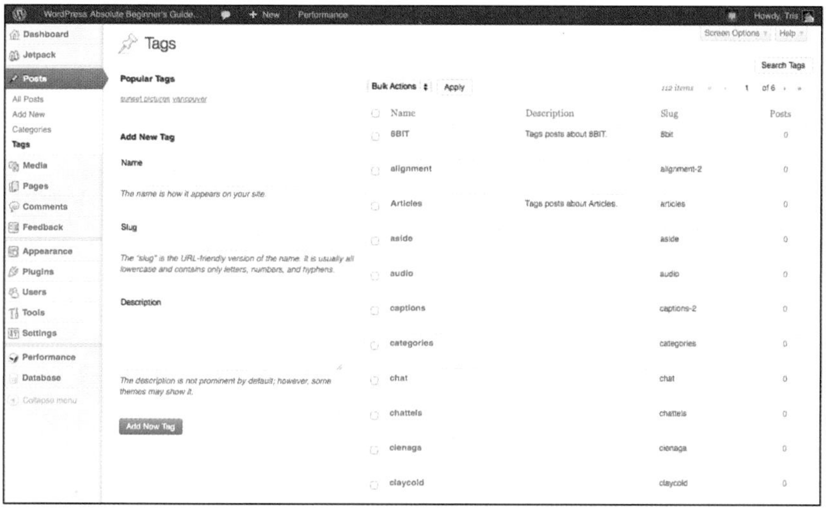

FIGURE 11.45

Tag management screen.

In the examples I've been using, we're been adding tags and categories to *exist-ing* posts; typically, you add tags and categories to posts before they are pub-lished. This makes sure that readers and search engines all know the context of a post when they first see it. And as you've seen, you can always add and remove categories from any post after it's been published.

> **TIP**   How many Categories and Tags should I have? This is a
> common question people ask. I like to keep my sites to 10, maxi-
> mum 15, categories. More than 15 categories (often even more
> than 10), I find that only a single post is in a category. That's fine
> when you're just starting out, but as your site matures, if you still
> have a lot of categories with only one or two posts, you should
> think about demoting those to tags. As for tags, I think the sky is
> the limit. Because tags are designed to be post-specific keywords,
> it's natural to have lots and lots of tags. Don't go crazy per post
> (I'd say no more than 5 to 8 tags per post), but in general don't
> worry about how many tags you have.

That does it for the special powers that Posts have. Now it's Pages' turn, and although Pages might seem pretty boring, standing alone and all, Page templates are so interesting and powerful that they make Pages a superhero in a league of its own.

Taking Advantage of Pages

Pages might not seem like they have the sexy versatility of Posts, but believe me, Pages have lots of tricks up their sleeves. Depending on your theme, the pages in your site can be just plain old content or super flexible content containers. How? Through Page Templates, but we'll save those for the end of this section. First let's recap what pages are and aren't.

Remember that pages are content designed to be able to stand alone. They don't have the inherent connection to each other like posts do. While pages do have a sense of time in terms of when they were published, you can't (by default) go to a Page archive that lists all the pages in a site, ordered by time. Pages fill a need for content that is outside of the stream of posts (or Custom Post Types) that has its own sense of meaning. Before WordPress Menus were introduced in version 3.0, we used Pages to determine and drive the navigation for the site. Today, Menus allow us to have much more flexible navigation, but Pages still have their own organizational structure that you can leverage in your site to organize content: Page Order and Parent-Child Pages. All the settings for these features are on the right side of the Page Editor (Figure 11.46).

FIGURE 11.46

Page Attributes.

Parent-Child Pages

Using categories (and subcategories), you can get a an idea of a hierarchy of content, but really it's more a hierarchy of topic. The posts themselves are all at the same hierarchical level. With Pages, you can create a page that is a Parent Page to another, and this defines a clear hierarchy that is reflected in the URLs of the two pages. I created a page called "Hire me" and set its Parent to be "About Tris" (Figure 11.47). When I publish the page, the URL for the new page becomes http://abgwp.trishussey.com/about-tris/hire-me/, and you can see a sense of hierarchy between the two pages (Figure 11.48). But that's as far as the hierarchy goes for the pages at this point. Unless you manually delete /hire-me/ from the address bar, there isn't a built-in connection to About Tris. Nor is there any indication on About Tris (not automatically, at least) that there are child pages connected to it. Yes, there is a hierarchy, but it isn't one that is discernible by default on Pages. Advanced WordPress theme developers can make these connections in the templates for Pages and use them; in practice, though, few people do. There is one way that we look at a list of all the pages on a site, and that is the Pages widget for the sidebar. This is a handy tool and gives us a chance to talk about Page Order.

FIGURE 11.47

Setting Page parent-child relationships.

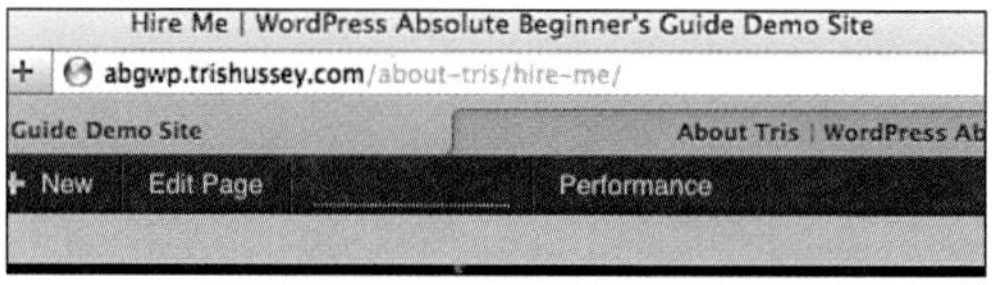

FIGURE 11.48

Page hierarchy (ish).

Page Order

Page Order is a simple way to list pages in an order you'd like other than by the date. First let's look at the Page widget and how it works. By putting the Page widget in the sidebar, you can choose to have the pages sorted by Title, Page Order, or Page ID (Figure 11.49). Page ID is essentially order by date, because the ID number of a page (or anything in WordPress) increases by increments. I set the Widget to Page Order and in Figure 11.50, you can see how the Pages are ordered. You can see that Hire Me is a child of About Tris because it is indented below it. Beyond that, this looks like sorting by title. Essentially it is, because all the pages in the list have the same Page Order, 0. I'd like the order to be About, Contact, Blog, Homepage, Front Page; the way to do that is to set the Page Order for the Pages (respectively) 0, 1, 2, 3, 4. I'm going to use the Quick Edit function to set this instead of opening each page in the Editor. This is just a teaser for talking more about managing posts and pages later.

FIGURE 11.49

Looking at Page Order in a widget.

FIGURE 11.50

How the widget looks on the site.

From the listing of All Pages, I pass my mouse over the title of the page and click Quick Edit. The area that opens up lets me adjust several things about the page, but not its content. Figure 11.51 shows editing "Blog" and making its page order 2. Page Order counts up from zero, and if pages have the same order number, it then orders them alphabetically. If you have lots of pages, you could have all the ones together, all the twos together, and so on. The result of changing the order of all these pages is in Figure 11.52.

FIGURE 11.51

Setting the page order for the Blog page.

FIGURE 11.52

The Page widget on the site with the new order.

Page Order can be applied in several ways by template designers, but for day-to-day WordPress users, this is going to be the most common way they run into them. This leaves the best of the Page tricks for last: Page Templates.

Page Templates

Page Templates is where Pages really get cool. Page Templates can take several parts of WordPress and pull them into one interesting package. Most of the time theme designers include a default Page Template and maybe one that is full width (no sidebars, or in Twenty Eleven's case, one *with* sidebars). Some themes include Templates that can list all Posts (in cases where the home page is technically a blog page, but doesn't display all posts), or like Twenty Eleven, a special home page style that includes a featured Post slider.

Using Page Templates is simple; in the Editor, choose which Template you'd like the page to use (Figure 11.53) and go from there. It's at this point that I can't tell you all the various options. I could tell you how to use the Showcase Template in Twenty Eleven, but that won't help you with the FrontPage Template in Twenty Twelve. Because Page Templates are up to the theme designer, the sky is the limit. I've created page templates that have different headers, sidebars, and footers from other posts and pages. I've make page templates to load only some posts. You can also create a page template that will list all that page's child pages (or when on a child page, its parent). There is lots you can do, and it all depends on the theme.

So—just explore!

FIGURE 11.53

Choosing a Page Template.

Using Revisions

As you're working on your posts and pages, you are editing, tuning, tweaking, adding images, adding links, and all the rest. If you have a multi-author blog, you might also have other people doing the same. So, how do you see what someone else has done and "roll back" their changes if you don't like them? Just like Word, WordPress has a track changes feature called Revisions—and it's always turned on. Although not as powerful as Word's Track Changes function (being able to approve or reject individual changes), you can see what's been done between each Save or Autosave, compare between the two, and roll back to an earlier version if you need to. Figure 11.54 shows the revision history for my About Me page on my own site (yes, the earliest entry is really 5 years ago), and Figure 11.55 shows you what it looks like to compare the current with the previous version. The check box at the top lets you compare two revisions (so a day ago versus two days ago, for example) against each other. Clicking to restore will take the current post or page and return it to the point of the last revision.

FIGURE 11.54

Revisions on my About page.

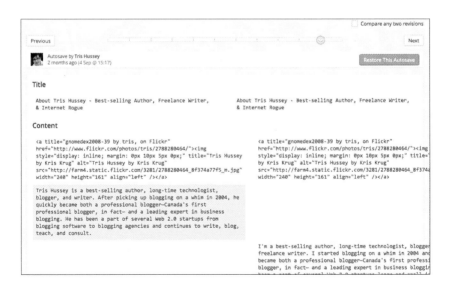

FIGURE 11.55

Comparing two revisions.

Perfect? Not really. It's getting there, though. WordPress 3.6 made a big step forward for revisions, but right now if you need to fix one part of a post or page and keep all your other changes, you can't do that. Yet. That feature is sure to be coming, but not in the near future.

Managing Posts and Pages

Throughout this chapter, you've seen figures with the All Posts or All Pages list, and now I'm going to spend a little time explaining how it works. Beyond the obvious (listing all the posts or pages you have, ordered with the most recent at the top), there are lots of other features that you can use to manage your site.

You can look at posts from a certain month and year, category, drafts, sticky, pending, or ones that you've deleted. You can even see your posts with an excerpt of the content with the click of a button (noted with an arrow in Figure 11.56). For pages, there are fewer options for looking at the list (Figure 11.57), but they both share the capability to quickly view, edit in the full editor, use the Quick Edit (you saw that for Pages when you set the page order), and best of all—bulk editing.

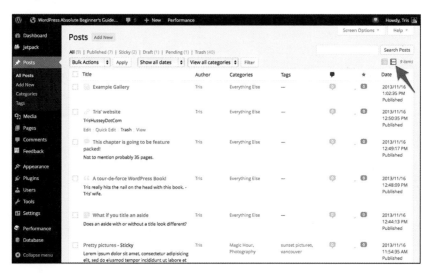

FIGURE 11.56

All Posts listing.

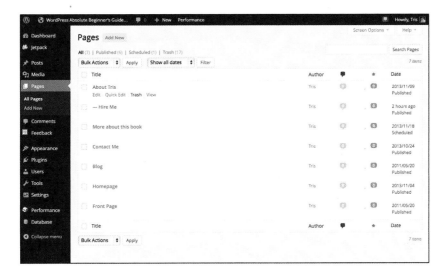

FIGURE 11.57

All Pages listing.

Bulk editing allows you to change things like the Published status, Author, Categories (Posts), Tags (Posts), Template (Pages), and other properties in one fell swoop. It works like this: Click the check marks next to the posts or pages that you'd like to edit (I'm going to use posts as the example to make two posts unsticky), select Edit from the Bulk Actions menu, and click Apply (Figure 11.58). Then select the option I'd like to change in both posts (in this case, to unstick them from the front page), and click Update (Figure 11.59). That's it.

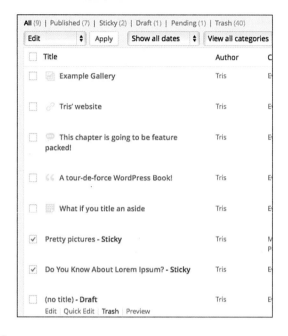

FIGURE 11.58

Selecting two posts to bulk edit.

FIGURE 11.59

Changing the posts.

If you need to turn off the comments on a large number of posts or pages, this is *the* fastest way to get the job done. Remember, if you turn off comments on posts or pages, the change isn't retroactive, so this is the best option to take care of that. The All Posts and All Pages screen is pretty powerful. Sometimes—in fact, most of the time—it's the fastest way to add a tag or two to a post, change a post or page back to Draft if it needs to be pulled, or lots of other changes. Take advantage of this tool! It's there, it's powerful, and it will get more powerful as WordPress becomes more sophisticated.

Importing and Exporting Content

Suppose you want to move your content to a new site or make a backup of your posts and pages. Or you have content from another site that you'd like to add to this site. Is it possible? Absolutely, just use the Import and Export functions. We'll start with Export for this example. Go to Tools from the side menu, then Export (or click Tools, then choose Export), and you'll see a screen like Figure 11.60.

FIGURE 11.60

Export screen.

Choose what you'd like to export (I'm going to choose all the content for this example), and click Download Export File. In a minute or two (depends on how much content needs to be exported), WordPress will tell your browser to download the file (Figure 11.61), and if you want to open it, you can. It's just a text file in XML, but it isn't intended for people to read. WordPress export files are designed for WordPress or other CMS systems to read on import.

FIGURE 11.61

Exported and downloaded file.

What if you wanted to *import* that content? Simple, just use the Import tool. Now there is a trick. The first time you use Import, WordPress needs to install and activate the Importer plugin. Here's how that works.

First, click Import under Tools, and then click WordPress (assuming you're importing WordPress content; for another CMS, choose that one) (Figure 11.62). You'll see the Install plugin screen (Figure 11.63); click Install. After it is installed, click Activate and Run Importer (Figure 11.64), and you'll come to the screen where you can click to pick a file (Figure 11.65). I'm using the file we just exported, in case you're wondering. After you click Choose, and then Upload file, you'll come to a screen that will let you match the content to an existing user or create a new one (Figure 11.66). I chose to map to the existing user (me), but if you're importing a lot of content, it's a good idea to let WordPress create a new user. Then you can sort the content by user in the All Post or All Page views and go through it. You already know you can use Quick Edit and Bulk Edit to quickly change a piece of content's author, so the content you keep you can transfer to yourself or another user. The last screen shows the results of the import (only the bottom). In this case, because I was just importing the same content I just exported, WordPress didn't import duplicates (which is helpful) (Figure 11.67).

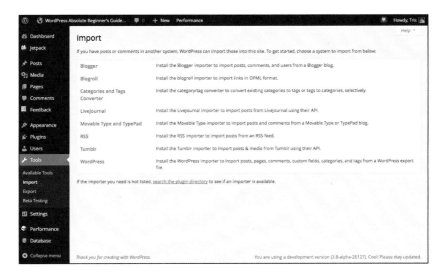

FIGURE 11.62

Import screen.

FIGURE 11.63

Installing the import plugin.

FIGURE 11.64

Activate and run the importer.

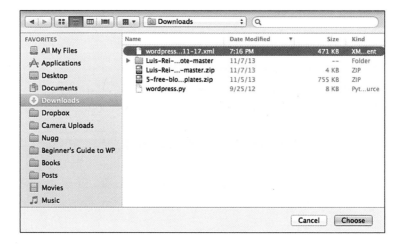

FIGURE 11.65

Choosing the file to import.

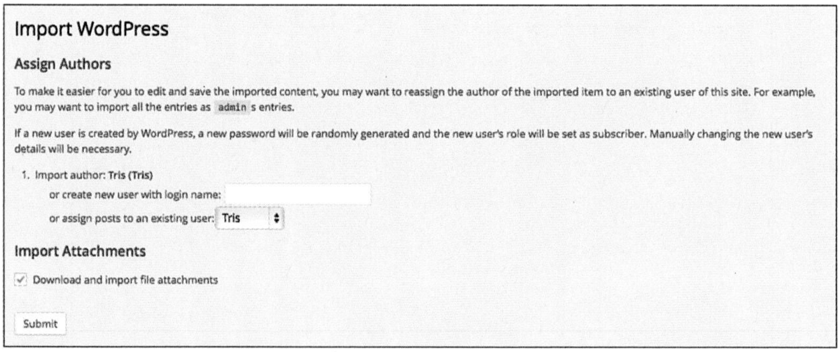

Import WordPress

Assign Authors

To make it easier for you to edit and save the imported content, you may want to reassign the author of the imported item to an existing user of this site. For example, you may want to import all the entries as `admin`'s entries.

If a new user is created by WordPress, a new password will be randomly generated and the new user's role will be set as subscriber. Manually changing the new user's details will be necessary.

  1. Import author: **Tris (Tris)**

    or create new user with login name:

    or assign posts to an existing user: Tris ▼

Import Attachments

☑ Download and import file attachments

[Submit]

FIGURE 11.66

Mapping the imported content to a user.

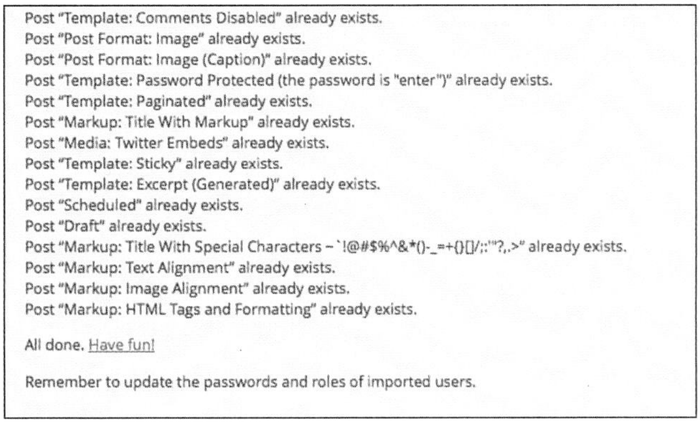

```
Post "Template: Comments Disabled" already exists.
Post "Post Format: Image" already exists.
Post "Post Format: Image (Caption)" already exists.
Post "Template: Password Protected (the password is "enter")" already exists.
Post "Template: Paginated" already exists.
Post "Markup: Title With Markup" already exists.
Post "Media: Twitter Embeds" already exists.
Post "Template: Sticky" already exists.
Post "Template: Excerpt (Generated)" already exists.
Post "Scheduled" already exists.
Post "Draft" already exists.
Post "Markup: Title With Special Characters – `!@#$%^&*()-_=+{}[]/;:'"?,.>" already exists.
Post "Markup: Text Alignment" already exists.
Post "Markup: Image Alignment" already exists.
Post "Markup: HTML Tags and Formatting" already exists.

All done. Have fun!

Remember to update the passwords and roles of imported users.
```

FIGURE 11.67

Import complete!

WordPress is designed so that you aren't locked into using it forever. You can always export your content to move it to another CMS. This is especially important when we talk about WordPress.com. If you start with WordPress.com and decide later to switch to hosting your own site using WordPress.org, you can quickly and easily move all your content from one to the other with just a few clicks—including all the images!

Managing Comments

The final part of this content chapter covers Comments. As I talked about in Chapter 6, "Setting Up Your WordPress Site Right the First Time," setting up Akismet is essential to keeping your site free of spam comments and links (and keeping your sanity intact, as well). Most comment management can be done in the Comments screen (Figure 11.68) or from the main screen of the Dashboard. When you have a new comment from someone who hasn't commented before (and Akismet didn't flag as spam already and didn't bother you with), you'll receive an email that there is a comment in moderation. From the Comments screen or the Dashboard, you'll see the comment highlighted, and you can approve, delete, or edit the comment. After you approve it, you can even reply to the comment right there by clicking the reply link. Simple as that. As more people comment, you'll see all the comments in the Comments screen.

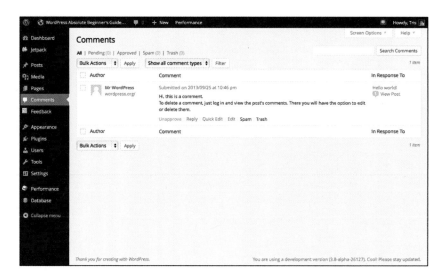

FIGURE 11.68

Main comments management screen.

NOTE Editing comments? Isn't that bad? Yes and no. Sometimes people leave a great comment, but maybe include a swear word or two. Instead of just trashing the comment and asking the commenter to resubmit it, you can (essentially) bleep out the swearing. Once in a while I've seen people leave things like their address, phone number, or email address in a comment. Because those are public, that's not always a great idea, so I edit those out, too. If I do end up editing a comment, I always put a note within the comment that I made an edit and why.

Conclusion

Whew. Now that was a chapter rich in content about Content. The lifeblood of a site is its content, so it makes sense that this might be the longest chapter in the book. We've covered the different types of content, how to create content, and specific things about each content type (except for Custom Post Type, which we'll cover in Chapter 16). There is much more I could write about (like the art of writing great blog posts), but for now the best advice I have is to try all the things in this chapter and then explore more to find the goodies that I didn't have space to mention! We'll come back to talking about content on and off throughout the rest of the book. Now it's time to move onto media!

USING WORDPRESS: IMAGES, VIDEOS, AND OTHER MEDIA

In Chapter 11, "Using WordPress: Content," we talked a lot about *words*. Sure there was one short section on how to add an image to a post, but that was about it. Why? Simply because there is so much more to talk about around images, videos, audio files, and other files that I knew that topic needed a chapter on its own. And here it is.

This chapter is, essentially, about everything that *isn't* words for posts and pages. All about dealing with images, videos, podcasts, and other files that people want to have in their sites. We'll cover all the important parts of pulling multimedia into your content.

Managing Media

Before getting back to working with images and such, let's talk about managing all the media for your site. We first talked about organizing media in Chapter 6, "Setting Up Your WordPress Site Right the First Time," with the media settings. The focus there was what should WordPress do with the files you upload (and I recommended keeping the setting to organize uploads by year and month). Now let's talk about how you look at all those images you upload.

Clicking the Media button on the admin sidebar (or using the fly-out menu and clicking Library) brings you to the Media Library (Figure 12.1). From here you can manage just about everything having to do with your media. You can rename media, delete them, and even do basic edits to many kinds of images. Like the Post and Page lists, if you select multiple images at once using the check boxes, you can apply an action to all of them at once. In the case of media, that action is just to delete them (for now). Passing your mouse over an image (or other media) reveals Edit, Delete Permanently, and View. The Edit Media screen (Figure 12.2) gives you the chance to change the item's name and other data about it. We'll get to what happens when you click the Edit link *here* shortly.

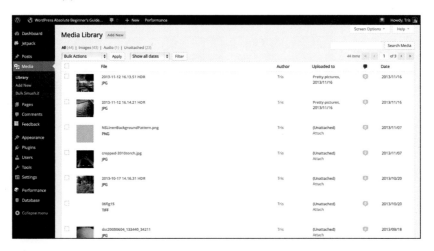

FIGURE 12.1

Media Library.

FIGURE 12.2

Edit Media screen.

TIP As you can see from Figure 12.1, *most* of the images don't have meaningful filenames. This isn't bad right now, but soon there will be lots of images, and if you ever need to search for an image you used before and would like to use again, what will you search for? Exactly. It takes only a second (and I often forget when I'm uploading things), but naming images with a name that makes sense will help you find and search for images later.

If you're trying to figure out what images you have on hand, the Media Library is the place. You probably noticed when we were inserting the images in Chapter 11 that you saw something that looked an awful lot like this screen. There's a good reason for that—functionally they *are* the same. So when you're inserting an image into a post, you can search for images (assuming you know what to search for) and edit images, as well as upload them, from that screen.

NOTE It's important to know, and remember, that if you've uploaded some media to WordPress using FTP—even if it's in wp-content/uploads/—it *will not* appear in this media list. This is one of those frustrating parts of working with videos, podcasts, and other large files in WordPress. After you upload a file through FTP, you have to know how to get the URL for that file to use in posts, pages, widgets, and so on. Don't worry, I'll cover that in this chapter.

But wait a second—when I upload images to WordPress, *you said* that the images are organized into folders by month and year. I don't see any folders here. I want some folders! I know you're thinking that right now. Heck, I wish I could create folders, or at least tag images, to have "logos," "screenshots," "photos," and any other organization scheme for media, too. But we don't. At least not yet. When? I don't know, but it's something I'm pretty sure WordPress developers are looking at. The Media Library and all the aspects of managing media are well overdue for an overhaul. Just like WordPress 3.8 has focused on making the admin screens better, more useful, and just better, Media and the Media Library will get attention in the future.

Working with Images

Chapter 11 covered the basics of how to upload and insert an image into a post or page. Now we're going to take things a little further with galleries, featured images, and editing images *after* you upload them. We'll start with the easiest of the set: Featured Images.

Using Featured Images

Many themes, though not all, use Featured Images to give Posts and Pages a little extra visual boost. Think of a featured image as the singular image that defines what your post is about. If you would say it with a picture, you would use…; that's the question to ask yourself when picking a featured image (it's usually pretty obvious). How themes use Featured Images varies widely. Some display them on the home page or in archive listings. Others also put the featured image at the top of the post or page. What you get just depends on what the theme designer had in mind.

If your theme supports Featured Images, the place to start will be in the Editor down the screen and on the right (Figure 12.3). Clicking Set Featured Image brings you to the now familiar media screen. You can pick from one of your existing images or upload a new one. When you have the image selected, the button on the right will activate to Set Featured Image (Figure 12.4). After you click the button, you are returned to your post and will see something like Figure 12.5. The Set Featured Image becomes Remove Featured Image, if you want to remove or change the featured image for the content. You need to remove and then reset a featured image if you need a different image than the one you originally chose. When you click Publish or Update, your new featured image will be in place. What will it look like? That's anyone's guess. It depends on the theme.

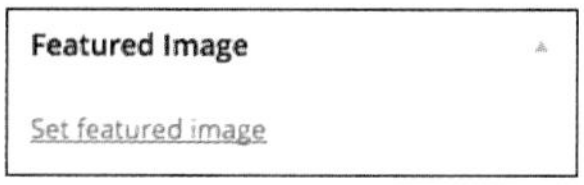

Featured Image   ▲

Set featured image

FIGURE 12.3

Step one, clicking the Set Featured Image link.

FIGURE 12.4

Choosing a Featured Image.

FIGURE 12.5

Featured Image selected.

TIP One of the keys to using Featured Images well is learning what the right image dimensions are for your theme. Some themes will use the image as is as the featured image. Others will crop or scale the image to fit specific dimensions. Figure out what the right size is for your theme and make sure you stick to it for consistent-looking content.

What about when you need more than a featured image, or more than a few images in a post, and you have lots of images to show—and putting them all in a post would just be too much. Then you need a gallery or slideshow!

Using Galleries and Slideshows

Out of the box, WordPress has a very basic gallery function built in. It's not great, but it will do in a pinch. To get more advanced galleries and slideshows, you need to install a plugin (or two) to get the job done. There are lots of slideshow and gallery plugins out there. I've used NextGEN gallery (http://wordpress.org/plugins/nextgen-gallery/ free), "Genesis Responsive Slider (http://wordpress.org/plugins/genesis-responsive-slider/ free, but it only works on Genesis child themes), and WooSlider (http://www.woothemes.com/products/wooslider/, paid) in the past with great results, but for sake of clarity and simplicity, I'm going to use a plugin we've already talked a lot about: Jetpack.

First, let's insert a gallery with Jetpack turned *off* so you can see what creating a plain-old-basic WordPress gallery is like. For this example, I'm going to create a gallery in a new page, and the end result will be in the new default theme Twenty Fourteen, but this works the same way in posts or pages and *any* theme.

Now start a new (or open an existing) post or page. You can start writing the text and put in the title, if you want, but the magic starts when you click Add Media. From the Add Media screen, click Create Gallery. You should see something like Figure 12.6 (except *without the check marks*).

This is where you determine the images that will make up your gallery. If you drag and drop several images onto the window, they will be the images for the gallery. In this example, I'm going to use some existing images. To select multiple images, click the images while holding down the Ctrl key (Windows) or command key (Mac). You'll see a blue check appear in the corner of each image selected (Figure 12.6). Don't worry if the images aren't in the order you want them; we'll take care of that in the next step.

FIGURE 12.6

First step to create a gallery.

When you have all the images selected, click Create Gallery, and you'll see Figure 12.7. Now you can caption the images if you want, set the number of columns, and drag the images into the order you prefer. When you're done, click Insert Gallery, and you'll see the placeholder image in your post or page where the gallery will be in relation to the rest of the content (Figure 12.8).

FIGURE 12.7

Images selected.

FIGURE 12.8

Gallery inserted and placeholder image in the content.

When the post or page is done, click Publish and you're done! Figure 12.9 shows the final product. Not stunning, but functional.

FIGURE 12.9

Gallery live!

That's the basics. For plugins like NextGEN gallery, WooSlider, or Genesis Responsive Slider, they work *outside* of the Insert Media screens. They have their own ways of managing the images in the sliders. However, if you use Jetpack, everything is integrated with the Insert Media tool. It's handy, to say the least. After you activate Jetpack, you have access to several great gallery features. From the Jetpack screen, activate the Tiled Galleries (Figure 12.10) and Carousel (Figure 12.11). You don't have to have both active, you can choose one or the other if you want. Tiled galleries give you new options for the galleries beyond just square. The Carousel option lets visitors click from your pictures into an immersive slide-show of your images. After you turn these options on, there will be new options under the Media Settings that you can check out. Let's edit that gallery from Figure 12.10 first. Going back to that page, I click the gallery and then the Edit Image button (Figure 12.12); this brings up the Gallery Editor again. From the pull-down menu, I'm going to choose Tiled Mosaic and click Update Gallery to return to the editor. Nope, it doesn't look different yet; this is just a placeholder image, remember. We have to click Update and refresh the page to see what's new (Figure 12.14).

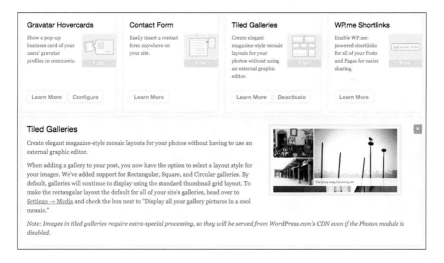

FIGURE 12.10

Tiled galleries option.

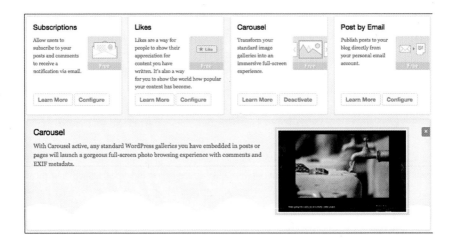

FIGURE 12.11

Carousel option.

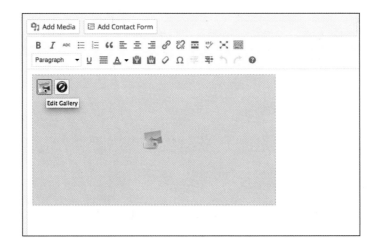

FIGURE 12.12

Edit Gallery button.

FIGURE 12.13

Changing the gallery style.

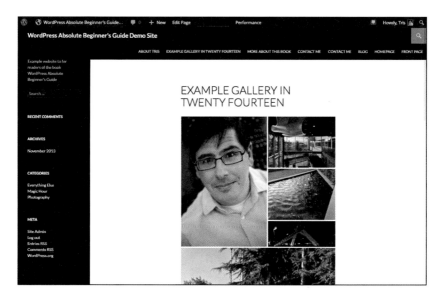

FIGURE 12.14

New tiled gallery.

When you pass your mouse over each image, the caption slides up from the bottom of the image, and when you click the image, you automatically get a slideshow of the entire gallery (Figure 12.15).

FIGURE 12.15

Jetpack Carousel slideshow.

Pretty spiffy and certainly easy. You can read up on these gallery styles on the official Jetpack page—http://jetpack.me/support/tiled-galleries/—which is handy because I'm sure there will be even cooler galleries in the future.

If you want to move beyond these basics, or have a slider that automatically changes images on a page, you will need to find a plugin or theme that supports that. Twenty Eleven has a built-in Featured Post slider that uses a static page with a specific template and setting certain posts as Sticky to make it happen. Other tools use shortcodes or integration with the theme (like WooSlider and Genesis Responsive Slider), which is very handy and ensures that the integration between theme and slideshow is as seamlessly as possible.

Using the Image Editor

Sometimes you upload an image and realize that it needs to be a touch smaller or would look better cropped. Or, oops, you need to rotate the image for it to make sense. It happens, and WordPress can help you out of those quick jams (and this is very handy when you're working with Featured Images). The built-in Image Editor in WordPress isn't intended to replace an image editor on your computer (although the online ones *are* getting better). The built-in editor is for quick fixes, like resizing and such. It takes just a couple clicks to get to the editor, and it starts with either clicking Edit below the image via the Media Library, *or* if you're inserting an image through Add Media, you can edit the image there. Figures 12.16 and 12.17 show you what I'm talking about.

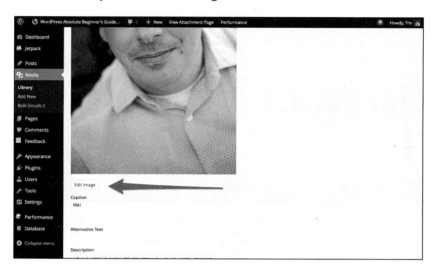

FIGURE 12.16

Edit Image button on image detail through Media Library.

FIGURE 12.17

Edit Image link within the Insert Media screen.

Regardless of how you get there, it looks like Figure 12.18 when you arrive.

FIGURE 12.18

WordPress Image Editor.

By clicking and dragging in the image, I bring up the "marching ants" selection area that will let me crop the image. In this case, I'd like to crop the image so it's shorter but the same width. Clicking the crop icon (Figure 12.19) will set it, and the result is Figure 12.20.

FIGURE 12.19

Cropping an image.

FIGURE 12.20

Image cropped.

Make sure you click Save, or you'll lose the changes you just made. Let's make the image's dimensions smaller with the scale tool. Clicking Scale Image opens up an area to set the new dimensions. WordPress will make sure that the image will stay in proportion (so it won't look stretched or squished) and won't let you make the image larger than you originally uploaded (so it will still look good). I'm shrinking this image by half to set the width from 500 pixels to 250 (Figure 12.21).

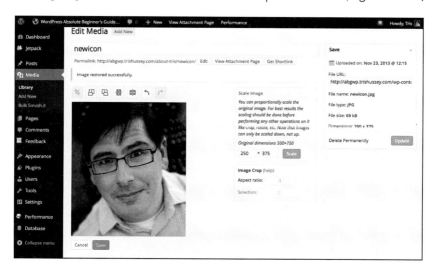

FIGURE 12.21

Cropped and scaled.

When everything is done, click the Update button to save all the changes to WordPress *and* update all the instances of the image in the site. Did you notice the box for choosing to update the thumbnail only or all sizes except the thumbnail? This lets you make changes to only the areas of the site you want. Often the thumbnail image has the wrong cropping, so you want to fix that—or the thumbnail is fine, but you really want to change the rest of the images. This is how you can have that kind of fine-grained control. The buttons for rotating the image clockwise or counterclockwise as well as vertical or horizontal flipping work just as you'd expect. Just remember to click Save *and* Update to make sure the changes "stick."

Remember the Image Editor is really intended for quick fixes. You can't add text to images, apply effects, or that sort of thing.

Now for some honesty.

The WordPress Image Editor can be a great lifesaver, but it's wonky. It doesn't always work like you expect or update images the way you want them. Myself, when I'm trying to get an image right for a post, I use the image editor on my laptop. Even Preview (on the Mac) can be better than what the WordPress Image Editor is (or should be).

Optimizing Images

Over the years, with better digital cameras and faster Internet connections, we've gotten used to uploading images right from our devices to Facebook, Twitter, and our websites. However, Facebook and Twitter and many other sites show you a scaled-down and *compressed* version of the image for the world to see. Maybe the full image is hiding around in their servers somewhere—Facebook and Flickr let you download full-size copies of your images—but what you look at on the pages aren't the full-sized images. They aren't even just *visually* reduced by 50 or 25%; they are *physically smaller files* in dimension, resolution, and file size. WordPress does a similar thing with creating thumbnails, small, medium, and large sizes of the images while keeping the full-sized image available as well. Now let's talk about taking this a step further. Let's ensure that images load quickly for everyone all the time. The first thing to do is on you, but there are a couple automagic things that will make your efforts really shine.

First, don't upload the full-sized, right-off-your-camera image. It's huge. I'm just as guilty of doing this as anyone else, but for *most* people's needs, the full-size 2.5 megabyte 3200×2400 pixel image is overkill. So if you take a moment, open the image in Preview or Paint.Net (Windows) or any other image editor *before* you upload it; reduce the dimensions by half, and export the JPEG (for photos) to 80% quality. Your visitors probably won't be able to tell the difference, and the file size will be much smaller. How much? Doing this on one of my images from my iPhone, the 1.3 megabyte image became a 348KB image. Half the size. Less time needed for you to upload it, less time needed for your visitors to download it to view it. You don't have to go to the extreme of this example (reducing the dimensions by half) to get much smaller images, but before you upload, it's a good idea to make sure you're only uploading the largest size you *really* need to get the job done. However, most hosts and WordPress put a limit on how big a file you can upload (for me, it's 7 megabytes), which really comes into play when we talk about podcasts and videos, but even here it sets an upper limit to think about. You can, however, do even more. You can even compress and optimize images automatically as you upload them. How? WP Smush.it.

WP Smush.it

WP Smush.it uses a Yahoo! Service to compress and optimize PNG, JPEG, and GIF images automatically for you when you upload. The results can be pretty amazing and lead to significantly smaller files—which means your site loads faster for everyone. Figure 12.22 gives you an idea of the savings I'm talking about.

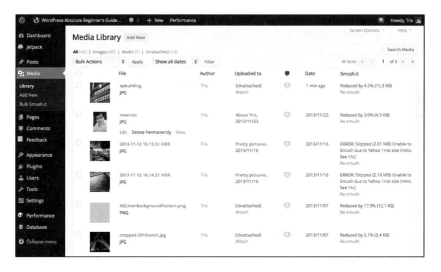

FIGURE 12.22

Media library with Smush.it compressed images.

Oh, you noticed that some of the images have error messages in the Smush.it column? Yes, the Yahoo! Service allows images only 1MB or less to be processed. So my full-sized photos are too big to smush. The others? Just fine. The plugin WP Smush.it is a newly reinvigorated effort from the original WP Smush.it effort that languished. This plugin adds a little extra time to the upload process because it has to upload the image to WordPress, then send to Yahoo!, then back to WordPress for all the final image size creating. I think the extra time is worth it, however. Saving even a few KB across an entire page adds up fast. Combining Smush.it with caching leads to some pretty awesome load times. Of course, we can make things even faster thanks to Jetpack, Automattic, and WordPress.com.

Photon

Part of the Jetpack plugin suite is a module called Photon, which, after you activate it, takes your images and hosts them *literally* on servers around the world so they load faster for everyone. Photon takes the load off your server to serve the images to visitors by using the servers that host WordPress.com and all its millions of users. You can learn more about Photon on the official page: http://jetpack.me/support/photon/.

There is a catch, though. For Photon to work, Jetpack changes how your site serves images. Although there is a copy on your server in case there is a delay from the Photon servers, if you, for example, *edit* the image the way described earlier, it won't take effect with Photon. To make changes to an image, you need to upload a new version of that image with a different name for the image to be replaced. I've seen an issue where a site owner wanted to replace the featured image with a better cropped version, and cropping a new image and using FTP to "replace" it didn't actually work. The Photon copy was still the master copy for the site.

So can Photon help you? Sure. Is it for everyone? Mostly. I think for a lot of sites with pretty normal and basic image use, Photon will give the site a little load time boost. Here's the thing, though, as we've talked about with Jetpack before; Jetpack loads a lot of code to go with it. So using Photon might really only bring your site to a level that is on par with a non-Jetpack-enabled site, so the speed improvements might be a wash.

I recommend that you try it, see if Photon (and Jetpack for that matter) are more of a help than an hindrance, and see what works for your site.

Video and Audio Files

Videos and audio files are where things start to get tricky. Remember that "uploads limited to 7 MB" thing I mentioned just a bit ago. Right. So I'll show you why this is an issue with video. A simple 58-second video, rendered through iMovie as standard definition, is about 38MB (Figure 12.23).

FIGURE 12.23

Short video, but still a big file.

There is no way to upload that video through WordPress out of the box. The only way to do it is through FTP, and that means the video won't show up in the Media Library. You'll have to *remember* the filename and where you uploaded the video to use it. So if I upload that video to my demo site, the URL is going to be something like http://abgwp.trishussey.com/wp-content/uploads/c6video.mp4 (assuming that's what I name the video). Hard to remember? No. A little inconvenient? Yes. However, that's it. Audio files (like podcasts) are generally smaller, so my one-minute WordPress podcast episode is well under the limit for uploading. Here's the question: Why would you upload videos to your own site instead of YouTube? The reality is that unless you're planning on *selling* the videos or need to restrict access to them for some reason, you should take advantage of YouTube's breadth and reach. Because you can upload a video up to 15 minutes long (imagine the file size!), it's a real bonus. Audio files are a different beast. There just aren't the same options available for free audio/podcast storage. Services like Soundcloud are great to start with, but will cost you money to keep using. So for the case of audio files, I think uploading them to your own server is the best course of action.

 NOTE Okay, there actually is a way to upload larger videos within WordPress, but it isn't free. You do it by subscribing to the paid VideoPress service. More information is on the VideoPress site: http://store.wordpress.com/premium-upgrades/videopress/.

To recap, uploading videos can be a little tedious, and YouTube is a better choice. With audio files, uploading them through the media uploader is probably going to work for short segments. Great, but how do I *use* them?

Let's get to that right now.

Embedding Content in Posts and Pages

Getting your media *into* a post or page has gotten so easy now that it almost seems like magic. First, here is a post that I created that will have a video I uploaded, a podcast, and a YouTube video (Figure 12.24).

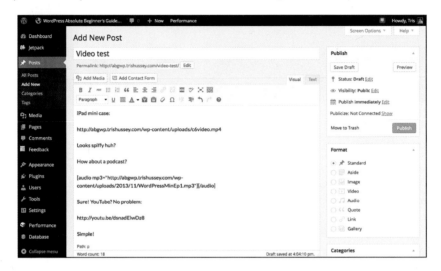

FIGURE 12.24

Inserting media into a post.

Notice the distinct lack of strange or fancy code? Right, that's because we don't need fancy codes or plugins for *most* media that you're going to come across. For the video, I just pasted in the URL to where I uploaded it. Notice that it is *not* a link. It's just text. This is important. Flipping to the text/HTML side of the editor just to be sure it's not a link is a good idea if you're not sure. The podcast? I uploaded it just like I would an image and clicked to Insert it into the post, and the shortcodes were written for me (Figure 12.25).

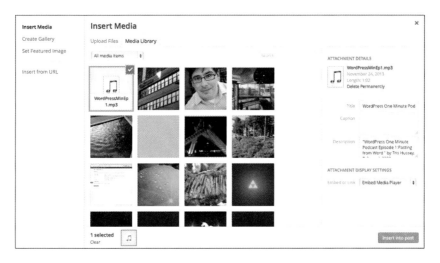

FIGURE 12.25

Adding an audio file.

For my YouTube video, I went to my channel, copied the Share link for the video, and pasted it in (Figure 12.26). Again, pasted as *text*, not a link.

FIGURE 12.26

Share link from YouTube.

When I published the post, the result is in Figure 12.27.

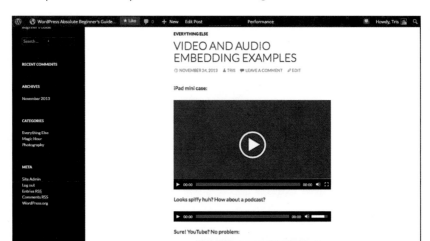

FIGURE 12.27

Video and audio galore!

Yes, it's really that simple. WordPress has built-in HTML5 players for video and audio files (which means they also work for mobile devices) and uses a system called oEmbed to pull in the players from YouTube, Flickr, Vimeo, and other services automatically. The end result is that putting multimedia into your posts and pages is painless. No worrying about media plugins or pasting special embed codes that sometimes don't work. Most of the time, this is all you need. For the increasingly rare occasion when you do need to paste in embed codes, here's what you need to do.

Slideshare, for example, uses an iframe embed code for its slideshows (Figure 12.28), and after you copy the code, you need to paste it into your new post in text. Start your post and click the Text tab and *then* paste (Figure 12.29). You can switch back to the Visual site if you want, and you'll see a big yellow placeholder box where the slideshow will be in relation to the rest of the content. When you publish, the slideshow (or whatever you embedded) should be there.

FIGURE 12.28

Copying the SlideShare embed code.

FIGURE 12.29

Pasting in text mode.

A little more complicated, but still not too hard. Now what about *other* kinds of files? Just as easy.

Other Files

You can upload text, PDF, Word, ZIP archives, and most other files to your site through the Media Uploader (keeping under the 7MB limit of course), and then like any other kind of media, insert it into a post—for example, a PDF version of a post (Figure 12.30) to be included at the end of the text version (Figure 12.31). There are some file types that you can't upload through the Media Uploader (such as epub for books and scripting files), but FTP will work fine in those cases.

WordPress is really media made easy.

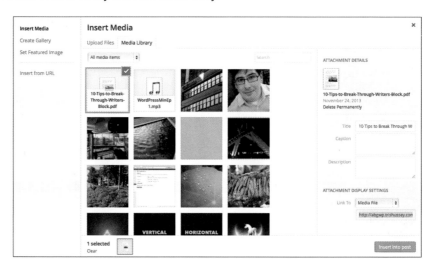

FIGURE 12.30

Picking a PDF file to put into a post.

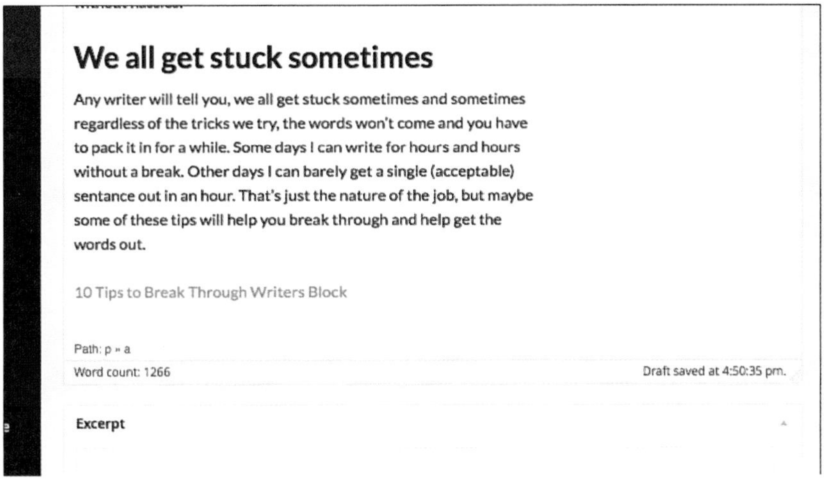

FIGURE 12.31

PDF file in a post.

Conclusion

If there is one thing WordPress has made really easy—besides publishing content—it's including media with your content. Just about everything is drag and drop, click and publish. It's very satisfying to be able to go from taking photos, uploading them, and having a slideshow and gallery of the pictures in just a few minutes. It's awesome. This chapter wraps up the part of the book about content. These early chapters should be enough for most users to get their site going and humming along. In the next chapters, we get into some cool and advanced stuff. Hold on, this is where it gets good.

IN THIS CHAPTER

- Making your site "mobile ready" for smartphones and tablets
- Managing your site from your smartphone or tablet
- Posting content to your site from your smartphone or tablet

13

WORDPRESS AND MOBILE USERS

Mobile Internet users, people using smartphones or tablets to browse the web, are one of the *fastest growing segments online*. In the next couple of years, mobile users and mobile devices will be the single dominant category online. So, how does your website look on an iPhone or tablet? Don't know? You should. Using WordPress? Well at least you're a good way there, if not all set. Curious? Journey on with me.

Making Your WordPress Site Mobile Ready

When people talk about making a website "mobile ready," the first thing to understand is that people aren't talking about whether the website will *load* on a smartphone or tablet—they are talking about how it *looks* and if mobile users can navigate the site. For the most part (there are some exceptions), any website will load on a smartphone or tablet. There aren't special mobile-activating HTML codes people need to use. The issue is that a non-mobile-friendly website can be hard to read and even harder to navigate on the smaller screens where you use touch controls to do things. If you have a smartphone or tablet, you've probably visited lots of sites like this—sites where the text was really small and you had to zoom in (a lot) to read what was on the page, and it had navigation menus that you couldn't use with fingers and touch. It's not a great experience. Let's not do that to our site visitors, shall we? Good.

There are two ways to fix this problem in WordPress: One is using plugins; the other is picking the right theme. Both have their pros and cons. In the end, both can work very well. You just have to decide which is right for you.

Themes

Starting with the right theme is probably the easiest way to go. Pick a theme that works on all devices and you can stop right there. If you're using any of the newer WordPress.org themes (2010 through 2014), all of these are "mobile ready" or "responsive" themes. A responsive theme has additional stylesheets and code that allows it to adjust and change the layout of the theme, depending on the width of the window. So, in reality, a responsive theme isn't changing for a mobile device; it's just assuming that if the screen is a certain size or smaller, it is a mobile device. It's clever and it works pretty much all the time. So if you look at the demo site on my desktop browser (Figure 13.1), an iPad (Figure 13.2), an iPad mini (Figure 13.3), and an iPhone (Figure 13.4), you see how the site has adjusted so the content looks its best. Menus? The three bars in the corner of the iPad mini and iPhone screens are the menu. Tapping those bars reveals the menu that you see on the desktop and iPad (Figures 13.5 and 13.6). A responsive theme "knows" the space it has to work with and adjusts accordingly.

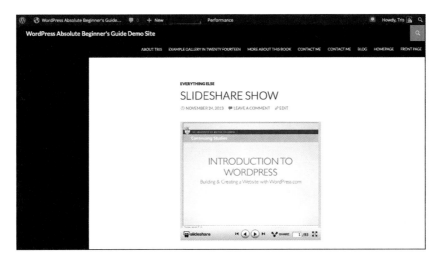

FIGURE 13.1

Demo site on a desktop browser.

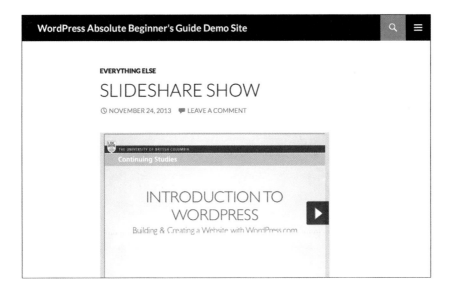

FIGURE 13.2

Demo site on an iPad.

FIGURE 13.3

Demo site on an iPad mini.

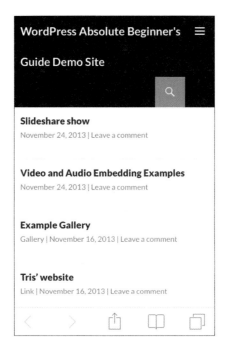

FIGURE 13.4

Demo site on an iPhone.

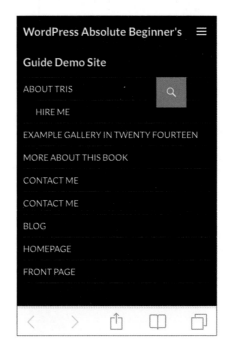

FIGURE 13.5

Menu on an iPad mini.

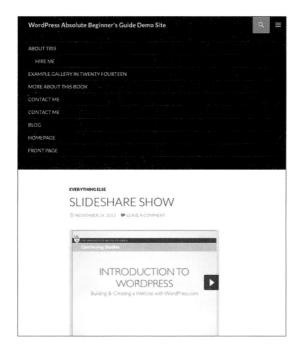

FIGURE 13.6

Menu on an iPhone.

Are responsive themes perfect? No. Even with responsive themes, your content might not look exactly as you intend. Some gallery and slideshow plugins don't work on mobile browsers. The Jetpack, Genesis, and WooThemes ones do, but not all do. Sometimes text is still small or the images don't scale properly. Responsive themes also can't account for how plugins will—or won't—behave on mobile devices. Responsive themes just change the layout; they don't prevent things from loading that don't work on mobile devices. To pull off that kind of magic, you need a plugin.

Plugins

Using a plugin to handle mobile visitors takes a step beyond a theme adapting to a different screen size. Plugins work by determining whether the user is on a mobile device and serving up a completely different theme to mobile users, a theme that is specifically designed only for mobile devices and overrides all the other parts of your theme. Although a responsive theme will look like your "regular" theme, but smaller, a plugin-driven solution will look very different. In my opinion, there are only two options worth talking about: Jetpack and WPTouch Mobile (http://wordpress.org/plugins/wptouch/). For Jetpack, you just need to turn on the mobile theme (Figure 13.7), and when you reload the page on your iPhone (or similar-sized device), you'll get a layout like Figure 13.8. (This example shows the About Tris page.)

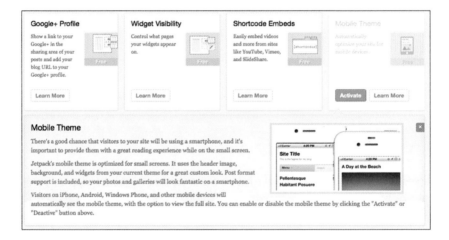

FIGURE 13.7

Turning on the mobile theme in Jetpack.

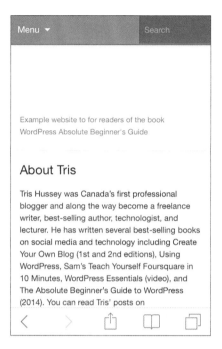

FIGURE 13.8

Jetpack mobile theme on the iPhone.

There aren't too many settings for the Jetpack mobile theme (accessed from the Configure button in the mobile theme section) (Figure 13.9), and the theme works very well out of the box. It's pretty basic. It works, it's simple, but it's also not very customizable. WPTouch Mobile on the other hand, has a raft of possibilities—not to mention that the mobile theme for Jetpack and WordPress.com uses code contributed by the WPTouch Mobile team. When you download and install WPTouch Mobile, *their* settings screen immediately lets you know they mean business (Figure 13.10).

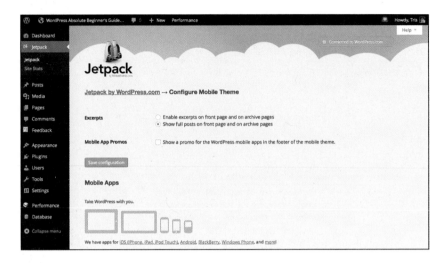

FIGURE 13.9

Jetpack Mobile Theme settings.

FIGURE 13.10

WPTouch mobile settings.

The figure doesn't even show *half* the options you have with this awesomely powerful plugin, but that's okay. Because even just turning it on gives mobile users a great experience (Figure 13.11).

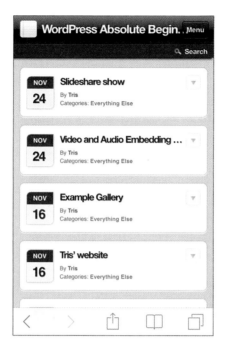

FIGURE 13.11

WPTouch mobile on the iPhone.

Notice the completely different look and feel, and there is a lot you can change about it. I recommend making sure the menus are all set correctly, but beyond that, chances are you're good to go. The Pro version of the plugin (paid) offers more customization and features, but the free version is powerful enough for most people. As you can see, though, there is a downside to using a plugin like either of these. For smartphones, you lose the branding and such that you might have added to your theme. For tablet owners, if you have a responsive theme, that version will show. If you don't have a responsive theme, these plugins cover you only for smartphones, not tablets.

NOTE   It nearly goes without saying—since Adobe has abandoned the project—but any site that uses Flash won't work on Apple mobile devices (iPads and iPhones). Because Apple devices still dominate the mobile browsing world, seeing Flash on a website is pretty rare. However, if you're working on fixing up an older website, make sure all the Flash you might have been using is replaced with a mobile-friendly alternative.

How to Decide What's Right for You

You might be pretty confused at this point. Plugin or responsive theme, what's the right choice? What will cover my bases the best? First, it doesn't hurt to have a theme that is responsive. Consider it your safety net. I've opted for only responsive themes, and recently, I'm using plugin-based solutions less and less because I like having a consistent branding and look across *all* devices. That might not be the right choice for you and your visitors, though. You might need the features, especially if you have a large smartphone audience, that a plugin brings that a simple responsive theme can't. My advice is to start with a responsive theme and then add a plugin to the mix if you need to.

Writing, Posting, and Managing Your Site from a Mobile Device

Not that long ago, although you *could* work with your WordPress site through the browser on your smartphone or tablet, it wasn't something I would have suggested for most people. If I did, it was only if you needed to do something in a pinch. Today, between the mobile apps and improvements to the Dashboard in WordPress 3.8, you *can* do a lot from your mobile device. Maybe not everything, but all the really important things, such as posting, approving comments, and even updates to WordPress. Don't believe me? Here is how the demo site looks on my iPad (Figure 13.12) and iPhone (Figure 13.13).

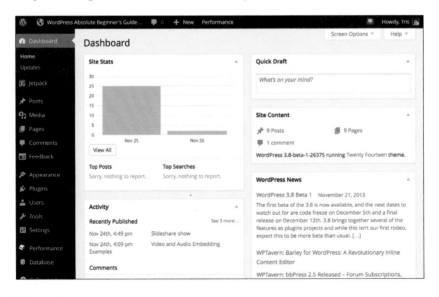

FIGURE 13.12

WordPress Dashboard on iPad.

FIGURE 13.13

WordPress Dashboard on an iPhone.

As you can see, this is certainly workable. A few taps will get you to most tasks. Now, for *writing*, that's a task best left for the WordPress Mobile app (iOS, Android, Blackberry, Windows Phone, and more: http://wordpress.org/mobile/). The mobile app focuses the posting process down to key steps and uses an interface much better designed for mobile use than the website probably ever could be. How do I know? I spent the better part of two years doing the majority of my writing (articles, blog posts, even some book chapters) on my iPad and gave a presentation to WordCamp Vancouver 2013 (http://www.slideshare.net/trishussey/wordpress-your-ipad-doing-it-right) on the topic of this chapter. I'm a huge and enthusiastic supporter of light, mobile workflows. For this chapter, I'll be using the WordPress app for iOS—specifically on the iPad—for screenshots and examples.

WordPress Mobile App

The WordPress mobile app hasn't been, honestly, my favorite way to publish to my blogs from my iPad. It is, however, the app that is most consistent and is most likely to work well now and in the future with your WordPress blog. Do I recommend you download it? Absolutely. Are there better apps out there? Maybe. However, because the WordPress Mobile app is free, you can't argue with the price. You can find the WordPress mobile app on the app store for your device or start at http://wordpress.org/mobile/ and follow the direct links to download the app version you need. After you have the app downloaded and installed, it's time to add your site.

Adding Your Sites

Tap the Settings icon in the app and then tap to Add a Site. You can sign in to WordPress.com now if you want, but you can hold off and do that later (Figure 13.14). Choose whether you're adding a self-hosted site or a WordPress.com site (Figure 13.15) and log in to the site (Figure 13.16). If you log in to WordPress.com, you'll be offered a list of your blogs to choose from (Figure 13.17). Because I have Jetpack turned on for the demo site, I was prompted to log in to WordPress.com so I could check my Jetpack stats (Figure 13.18) from within the app (which is a great feature, by the way). That's it! When the app works through the process of logging you in and getting your Post and Page list, you'll see something like Figure 13.19 with your posts and other parts of your site.

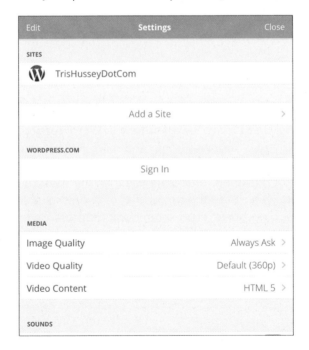

FIGURE 13.14

Settings for the mobile app.

FIGURE 13.15

Which kind of site to add.

FIGURE 13.16

Logging in to my site.

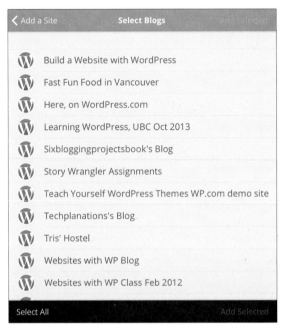

FIGURE 13.17

Sites in my WordPress.com account.

FIGURE 13.18

Ooh! Jetpack!

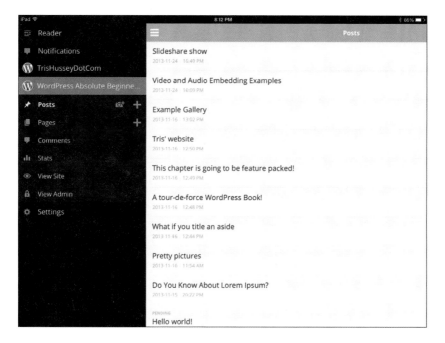

FIGURE 13.19

Done!

Posting Through the Mobile App

When you tap to create a post or page, you'll see a screen like Figure 13.20. The title goes at the top and the text goes below. Here's the thing about the text—for formatting, it's all in HTML. If you want to type a long post and format it later in your browser on your laptop or desktop, that's great. Figure 13.21 shows a little example of the text for the post with bold, italic, and a link inserted. You can use the quick buttons at the bottom of the screen to do this basic formatting. It might not look pretty, but it works. If you hide the keyboard, you can tap the Settings icon to get to the Post/Page properties, like setting a category or tags (Figure 13.22). If you want to write and save this as a draft to finish later, tap on Status to change from Published to Draft. This setting determines what the post's status will be when you send the post up to your site, not what the post's status is at this moment (a touch confusing for me as well). When you're all done, tap Publish in the corner of the screen (you might have to hide the keyboard first). Adding images you say? Let me tell you all about that.

FIGURE 13.20

Blank post.

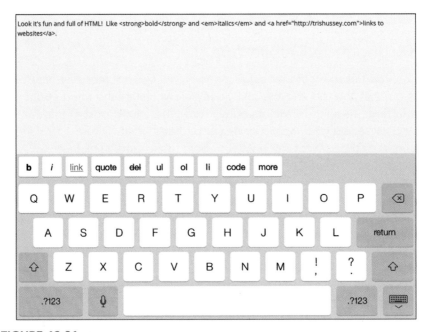

FIGURE 13.21

A little HTML.

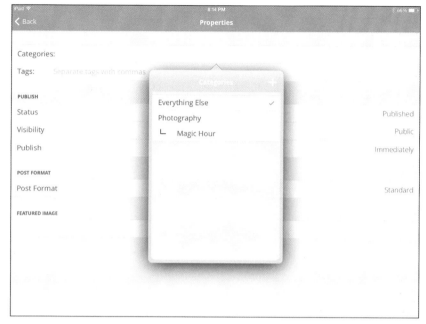

FIGURE 13.22

Properties screen.

OTHER WAYS AND APPS TO WRITE CONTENT

For most people, working and writing in HTML isn't fun. Heck, even for those of us who know *how* to, we don't generally *like it* for extended writing sessions. So here's the question: How do you write plain old text, and still have formatting, but not in Markdown (and the offshoot Multimarkdown) is a short form for writing and formatting text. It uses sets of symbols like * and ** to mark sections of italics (*) and bold (**) or # to denote a heading. Even links can be set with using brackets ([ ]) and parentheses. Here's the best part—learning Markdown is easy. It will take you just a few minutes to get all the basics you need to know. Plus all the Markdown-aware writing programs also let you copy HTML code from your Markdown text. This is exactly how I *really* write on my iPad. I write in a Markdown-aware editor, with all my formatting, links, and headings I'd like, then I have the app copy HTML to the clipboard that I paste into the WordPress Mobile app. It sounds like a lot more work than it really is. At some point soon, I expect that the WordPress Mobile app will support Markdown as well, which will make things even easier.

There are a lot of Markdown tools for iOS, Android, Mac, and PC. A quick search will give you lots of options to try.

Handling Images

Working with images on mobile devices can be challenging. On iPads and iPhones, it's especially limiting. You can work only with images that are on your device, not any of the images already uploaded to the Media Library on your site. Adding an image to your post starts with tapping the image icon and allowing the app access to your photos. Then you pick the photo you want and the size you want and it's inserted. Unfortunately it's inserted at the bottom of the post, and you can't edit the information about the image (Figures 13.23, 13.24, and 13.25). You can add in a Feature Image through the Post/Page properties, but again—limitations.

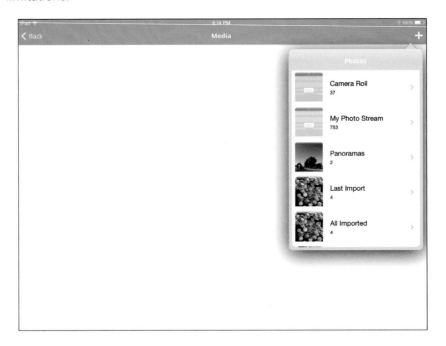

FIGURE 13.23

Picking an image.

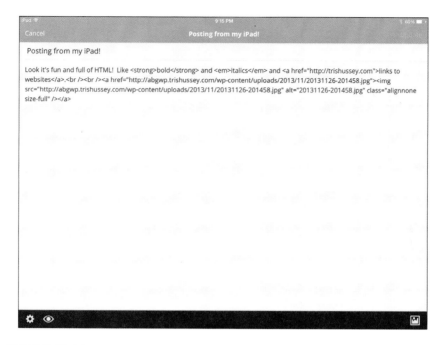

FIGURE 13.24

The post with the image added. More HTML.

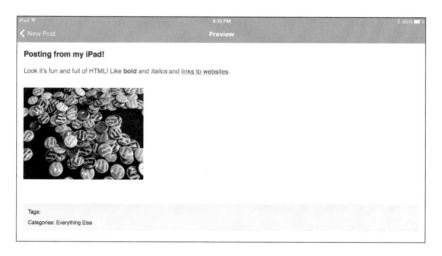

FIGURE 13.25

Previewing the post.

My advice, and experience, is that the mobile apps are pretty good at getting text up to your site, but they still have a long way to go before working with images is easy. Generally, I would write my posts, send them up as drafts, and then add the images I needed (unless the post didn't need an image).

Managing Comments

Of all the site management tasks that the WordPress mobile app can do, I think it's managing comments where it shines. Really. You can check through the mobile app when you have a comment waiting (with Jetpack installed, these notifications can be pushed automatically to you from the mobile app), check the comment, approve (or mark as spam), and even reply. Sometimes I think the whole process is faster and easier on my mobile devices—even my iPhone—than on the desktop. Tap, tap, tap. Reply. Done. If you use the mobile app for nothing else, that alone will be worth it.

Administering Your Site

Administering your site through your browser or the mobile app is not worth it for more than the occasional task. Yes, it works just like the desktop version, but it's a lot trickier to tap and read everything. Check boxes and menus might not always work the way you'd like them to, and little pop-up screens—sometimes they just don't work at all. I've installed and updated plugins in a pinch, but I don't do much more than that—certainly not any serious troubleshooting. Go ahead and log in to your site on your mobile device. Try it. You'll find it workable, but not something to use all the time.

Conclusion

When the World Wide Web as we know it now was born in 1991, we couldn't have imagined the devices we have today. I have more computing power in my iPhone than I did in the Mac I used back then. (If nothing else, it didn't even have a color screen!) The mobile world has dramatically changed how we approach publishing online content. Lucky for us, the WordPress world is keeping up. We have great themes, plugins, and apps to make sure our content is accessible and available to all. And while you're at it, you can even do a little writing on your tablet if you want. It's a great focused experience, I can tell you that for sure (and it's one of my favorite ways to write).

ALL ABOUT WORDPRESS.COM

In Chapter 2, "What WordPress Is and How it Works," I introduced WordPress.com and said I'd talk more about it in this chapter. If you jumped ahead and skipped Parts 3 and 4 (so how WordPress generally *works*), you might want to go back shortly and read them. As I said in Chapter 2, WordPress.org (self-installed/self-hosted sites) and WordPress.com sites (essentially) run the exact same code, and they work pretty much the same way. Creating posts, creating pages, picking themes, using widgets, working with media—nearly everything in Parts 3 and 4 are the same with either system. No, you can't install your own theme or install plugins using WordPress.com, but nearly all the features of the Jetpack plugin are built in to WordPress.com. That's why Jetpack was created, to make more of the features available to WordPress.com users accessible to self-hosted WordPress users (in one easy plugin).

After a little housekeeping, about setting up and managing your WordPress.com account, the rest of the chapter covers the similarities and differences between WordPress.com and self-hosted WordPress. This is less of a doing things chapter and more of a learning things chapter. But first, let's get that WordPress.com account.

Creating a WordPress.com Account

As you can imagine, we start at WordPress.com and sign up for an account. If you already have a WordPress.com account, skip this section and go to the next one. Click Get Started (Figure 14.1) to get to the sign-up page (Figure 14.2). Enter your email, check your username (if you need to edit it), pick the URL for your blog (we're going for the just free option using wordpress.com right now), set your password (I use a random one), and click Create Blog.

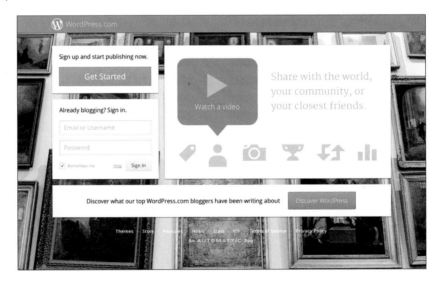

FIGURE 14.1

WordPress.com home page.

FIGURE 14.2

Sign-up page.

NOTE Why would I need or want a WordPress.com account if I use self-hosted WordPress? As you saw in the chapters that talk about Jetpack, you need a WordPress.com account to use Jetpack. A WordPress.com account is also handy for tapping into all the other Automattic services like Akismet, PollDaddy, and Gravatar. It's free and sometimes handy to have a blog/website to experiment with a little.

Then you'll see a screen like Figure 14.3 to go check your email. The email you receive should look like Figure 14.4. Click the Active Blog button to continue. Now WordPress takes you through a few steps to help you hit the ground running on WordPress.com. Don't worry if you can't decide right now on all the steps; you can change any of these later if you want. First, you set the name and tagline for your site (Figure 14.5). Then pick a theme that appeals to you right now. There will be lots to choose from later, so taking the default offering is fine (Figure 14.6). On the next screen, you can see what that theme has to offer (Figure 14.7). You can click the Previous button to go back and choose again, but you can also just click

Next and look at themes later when you're done (and have more content). Next, you have the option to connect your social media accounts to this site (Figure 14.8). If you don't want to do this now, you can do it later under the Sharing settings. Finally, you have the option of creating a post here (Figure 14.9), but I'd suggest just clicking Finish right now. Finish brings you to the "Dashboard," which is a little confusing because this isn't the Dashboard we think of when talking about WordPress. That's the area we've been working in for most of this book. In fact, if you click the little ghost head in the corner and choose the name of your blog from the list (Figure 14.10), you'll also come to a "Dashboard" (Figure 14.11). No, no, this isn't confusing at all for people! For the sake of all our sanity, what you see in Figure 14.11 is what I'm going to call the Dashboard.

FIGURE 14.3

Next step—activating your site and account.

FIGURE 14.4

Activation email.

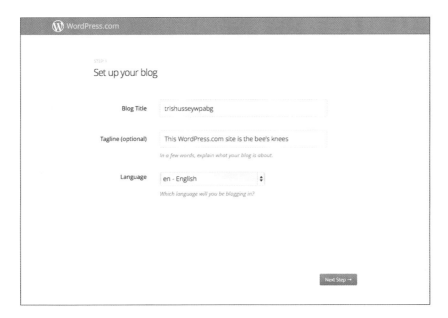

FIGURE 14.5

Site name and tagline settings.

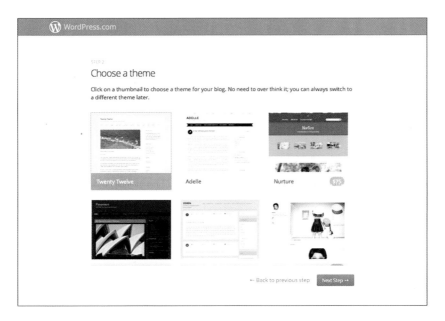

FIGURE 14.6

Picking a theme.

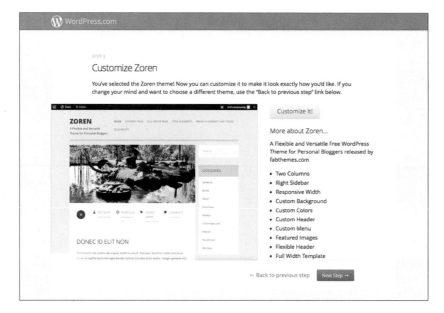

FIGURE 14.7

Theme features.

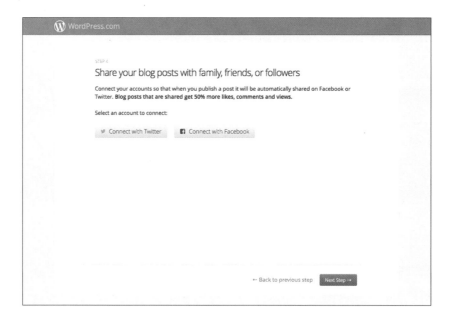

FIGURE 14.8

Connect your social media accounts.

FIGURE 14.9

Create a post if you want.

FIGURE 14.10

Going to the "real" Dashboard.

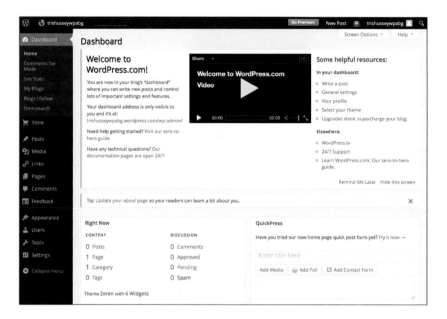

FIGURE 14.11

The WordPress.com Dashboard for your site.

At this point, your WordPress.com site is ready, the same as if you got to Chapter 6, "Setting Up Your WordPress Site Right the First Time." Because there are no themes or plugins to install, now you can go through settings. Yes, some of them are different, and settings like Permalinks aren't there, but I'll cover those in just a minute. If you follow along with Chapters 6 and 7 (skipping SEO and caching settings), you'll be all set. Even though it's WordPress.com we're talking about here, you still need to set the tagline, time zone, and a few other details.

What if you already have a WordPress.com account? That's next up.

Creating More Sites on WordPress.com

If you already have a WordPress.com account (smart!), you can always add scads of new blogs all connected to a single login, which is handy. From "that other Dashboard," choose My Blogs or from the "real Dashboard," click Manage My Blogs from the account menu (Figure 14.12). You'll get to a page with all the blogs—even if you only have one right now—tied to your account (Figure 14.13).

FIGURE 14.12

Manage My Blogs from the account menu.

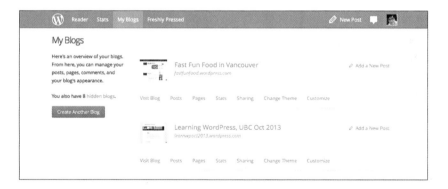

FIGURE 14.13

My Blogs screen.

If you click Create Blog, you'll see a screen much like Figure 14.2, except without the pesky email, username, and password fields. Go ahead, create another blog! Just for kicks! I'll talk about how to deal with deleting, hiding, archiving, or even transferring blogs within WordPress.com later in the chapter.

What's the Same

Let's start off easy using WordPress.com—what's the same between WordPress.com sites and WordPress.org/self-hosted sites? Just about everything, at least for the *most* crucial parts of a site. Creating content: same. Uploading and using images: same. Switching between themes, using widgets, using menus, custom headers, custom backgrounds, and how things just generally *work*—same. This is one of the true strengths of WordPress and the WordPress ecosystem— the guts are the same wherever and however you use it. A lot of this has to do with the great code unification that brought WordPress MultiUser (aka WordPress MU, aka what powers WordPress.com, aka Network Mode in WordPress.org) and WordPress together. With a single codebase, both "versions" of WordPress were pretty identical. This makes learning WordPress easy for most people. If you're wondering, "Gee, I read through all these chapters using WordPress.org and now I've decided WordPress.com is right for me"—have I wasted my time? No. Knowing the strengths and weaknesses of *both* systems helps you pick which way to create a site or blog is right for you.

What's Different

As I explained in Chapter 2, WordPress.com is like living in a dorm (maybe without the keg parties). For everyone to live together, there has to be some rules. What Automattic did with WordPress.com is to decide that if they couldn't have a feature or theme that is 100% rock solid *and* easy to use, they didn't want it in WordPress.com. There can't be features or themes that cause failures. Think about it, with *millions* of websites running on WordPress.com, if even a fraction of a percentage of sites crashed using a feature, or if a theme caused even a *slightly* higher than average amount of server resources to be consumed, the results could be disastrous for the entire system. A true cascading failure of sites around the world. Yes, WordPress.com has had a few (very, very few, around five that I recall) major outages, and the reason they have had so few outages is because they take care adding new stuff.

So what's different? No plugins to install. The features you see on the Dashboard are the features that you have. If you want to have a featured post slider and none of the different ways various themes do it for you—sorry. Want a different way to do contact forms, polls, or sharing to social media sites? You can find ways around some of these with other services (like sending your posts to Twitter and Facebook through RSS), but not all. Don't like any of the 200 themes? Or want to change how the theme works (I'll talk about cosmetic changes in a minute) or add new Page templates? Sorry. On the other hand, you don't need to worry about SEO settings or setting your Permalinks. Those are done for you and managed. You also don't have to worry about upgrades to WordPress or server issues. Those are handled for you as well. You give a little (customization, being able to load any feature under the sun) to get a lot (a site that is stable, upgradable, and doesn't lock you in—you can always and easily move from WordPress.com to your own server). Looking through the Settings section, you'll see a few new options (Polls, Ratings, AdControl, Email Post Changes, OpenID, and Webhooks), and under some "familiar" options, such as Reading, you see new settings—Related Posts and Enhanced Feeds. Do you need to worry about these right now? Nope, the defaults that are set for you are fine. They are always worth exploring, though.

The last important thing that is different about WordPress.com is that to embed media into posts or pages (videos, slides, sound clips), the embed code needs to either be a WordPress.com embed code or use oEmbed (like YouTube and many others). You can't embed iframes or JavaScript from just anywhere on WordPress.com. To ensure the security and stability of the entire system, those kinds of embeds aren't allowed. If you try to use an unsupported embed, it will be stripped out when you publish. It's that simple. Using iframes and JavaScript embeds, malicious sites can compromise the security and stability of a host. Even if sites *aren't* malicious, iframes and JavaScript codes can cause errors, problems with page loads, and a myriad of other woes that WordPress.com doesn't need. It's a case of the needs of the many outweigh the needs of the few (or the one).

Key Built-in Features

In addition to everything WordPress has to offer, WordPress.com does have some magic of its own that's pretty spiffy. I'm going to talk about just a few of the features here—Omnisearch, Polls, Feedbacks, and Ratings—but one thing to remember is that the Jetpack plugin is designed to bring WordPress.com features to WordPress.org/self-hosted users. So if it's in Jetpack, it's in WordPress.com. Photon? Built-in, automatic, just there. Super cool galleries? You bet. Social media sharing, publishing, and subscribe by email? Triple yep. One of the best things about WordPress.com is that often, new features hit there *before* the self-hosted worlds. The new theme Twenty Fourteen was available to WordPress.com users *weeks* before self-hosted WordPress users saw it (unless they were testing the early betas—like me). So, if you read through Chapter 8, "All About Jetpack Settings," you might learn a thing or two about WordPress.com—by learning about Jetpack. Let's move on to some of these key features.

Omnisearch

After a while, sites start collecting a lot of content. Posts, pages, comments, feedbacks (the contact form), and often *great stuff* gets lost there because you can't remember where you saw or read it. Previously, searching—even from within the Dashboard—would only return posts. Omnisearch searches *everything*. Posts, pages, every kind of content you have on your site. So if you remember a great comment, but don't remember which post it was on, use Omnisearch and some keywords you remember and—ta da! Well, hopefully. Omnisearch is such a powerful feature, it will likely be included in the core of WordPress for self-hosted users in the near future.

Polls

PollDaddy is a service/company owned by Automattic (it was one of the first of many WordPress tools that Automattic acquired) that does one thing and one thing well: polls, surveys, quizzes, and ratings (for individual pieces of content). PollDaddy powers the polls function on WordPress.com, and you can manage them through your admin Dashboard. After you sign up for a free PollDaddy account (there are paid levels for more features and options) at PollDaddy.com (you are guided there through your Dashboard), you can create polls from within WordPress.com under the Feedbacks section (Figure 14.14). For surveys and quizzes, you create those on PollDaddy.com and use shortcodes to embed them in your site (or email them or have them on your iPad).

Creating polls is almost like creating a new post or page. When you click Add New, you see the screen shown in Figure 14.14. Choose the options you'd like, and finish. You can even have the poll embedded in a new post right there. Polls are a simple and easy way to ask a quick question and get a quick answer. Polls can be in posts, pages, and even your sidebar using the text widget. Self-hosted WordPress users can either embed codes from PollDaddy.com or use the PollDaddy plugin to get the same features.

There are general settings for Polls under Settings, but most of your poll management (and reviewing results) will be under the Feedbacks section of the Dashboard.

FIGURE 14.14

Create new poll screen.

Ratings

Ratings are related to polls, because they come from PollDaddy, but these ratings are independent of the ratings you see if you go to PollDaddy.com. First, set your Rating Settings. By default, ratings are off for all content—you have to enable them yourself. This makes sure that people don't suddenly start getting star ratings on content that they really didn't want rated (Figure 14.15).

FIGURE 14.15

Ratings Settings.

NOTE   Okay, I'll fess up. The whole "what ratings do you see where" is actually a little more complicated than what I described earlier. Through Jetpack and having a WordPress.com account/site connected to PollDaddy, things can get pulled together in one place. However, if you look at the Ratings section for a WordPress.com site, you'll see only the ratings *for that site*. If you go to PollDaddy.com, you can see ratings for *all* connected sites. Oh, the joy of cross-site-connected accounts!

There are separate settings for Posts, Pages, and Comments. Yes, even comments. You can let people rate a comment, too! After your site has been around for a while—and assuming that you enabled ratings in the first place—you can look at all your ratings under the Feedback section (Figure 14.16).

FIGURE 14.16

Screen to review all your ratings.

The question that is on your mind right now is probably, "Should I turn ratings on?" Personally, I don't care for them. Like not getting comments on what you think is a great post, you might wonder why people don't rate your posts (not to mention not rating them all as high as you'd like). I had ratings turned on for a while on my personal site, and I eventually turned them off. I decided that the ratings area cluttered up the post too much *and* didn't offer my readers value *and* wasn't giving me useful information, either. It's up to you to decide; depending on what *your audience* is like, you'll determine whether or not ratings are worth it for you.

Feedbacks/Contact Forms

The contact form/feedback function works the same as the Jetpack-powered function that I talked about in Chapter 8, so I don't need to repeat that here. One little reminder on Feedbacks and Contact forms is not to limit yourself to just one contact form. You can have several forms for different reasons and different parts of your site: a general contact form, a get more information contact form, a submit an idea form. There are lots of ways to use "forms." The best part is that regardless of how many forms you have, you can review them all in one place under Feedback (Figure 14.17).

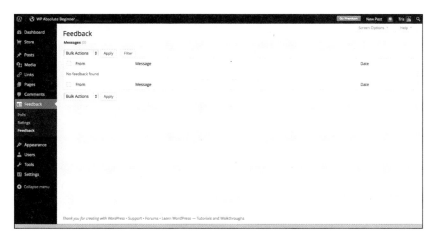

FIGURE 14.17

Feedback section and screen with all the Feedbacks.

These have just been four key, useful features on WordPress.com, but there are so many subtle and wonderful touches that it's worth exploring *and* keeping your eyes peeled for the new features that always pop up.

Users and Making a Private Site

One of the handier built-in functions of WordPress.com is the capability to make a site totally private—a site where if you aren't invited to see it, you can't. This setting is found under Reading (if you haven't discovered it already, Figure 14.18 points you in the right direction) and is an additional option to the standard "let search engines in" and "don't let search engines in" options.

FIGURE 14.18

Making a WordPress.com site private.

For self-hosted WordPress users, you can pull this off with a couple plugins (one to block the content, the other to make sure that uploaded files aren't accidentally exposed). I'll cover how to make a site private for self-hosted users in Chapter 17, "Advanced WordPress Settings and Uses." Here the first step is that check box and saving the settings. After that, it's inviting users to the site. You do that through the Users settings and inviting a new user (Figure 14.19).

FIGURE 14.19

Inviting users.

The user roles here work like the user roles I talked about in Chapter 6, "Setting Up Your WordPress Site Right the First Time." If you have a private site and you just want people to read the content, the Follower level is fine (like Subscriber in the self-hosted world). If you'd like someone to be able to post as well, Contributor or higher is what you need. Be careful doling out privileges to people. Don't give people more privileges than they need to do what you need them do to. Even Followers can leave comments, so you don't need to give them Contributor or Author privileges to do that. And most of all, give out Editor or Administrator privileges only to people you really trust.

Managing Blogs

At some point, you might have so many sites and blogs on WordPress.com that you need to wrangle or manage them. Right now there is no limit to the number of sites or blogs you start on WordPress.com, so if you're someone like me who creates a lot of sites for classes, demos, and so on, they can start getting out of hand. There are several ways of handling this problem—from "out of sight, out of mind" to "gone, gone, forever gone"—each with pros, cons, and considerations. Let's start with the easiest: hiding a blog.

Hiding Blogs

The first step is to find a listing of all your blogs and sites. Remember the My Blogs screen I showed you early on? Yeah, that's not it. What you want is the My Blogs screen that you reach under the Dashboard menu in the admin area/dashboard. Figure 14.20 shows you a portion of my listing, and I want to hide the site on the top. So I pass my mouse pointer over the word Visible and I see Hide and click it. That's it. The blog is hidden. What does this *really* do? It just cleans up the My Blogs menu. The site is still there, and still active. You can post on it and people can find it, it's just not taking up space in your menu when you're trying to jump from site to site.

FIGURE 14.20

Hiding a blog from the menu and screens.

Now what if you have a great site and you want to change the part *in front* of wordpress.com, but keep the rest? That's what changing a blog's address does.

Changing a Blog's Address

You might have noticed in Figure 14.20 the Change Blog Address link below the name. That's the link you click. You can see the same menu if you pass your mouse pointer over the name of the blog/site as well (Figure 14.21). There is a great article that walks you through the process (and will be updated if things change)—http://en.support.wordpress.com/changing-blog-address/—but here's the gist:

- Click the link.

- Get to the screen to request the change.

- Enter the new address for the site.

- Decide if you want to create a new account, keep the account you have, or change your username, too (I'd pick the No option myself).

- Decide if the old name is gone forever (and they really mean forever).

- Review.

- Finalize.

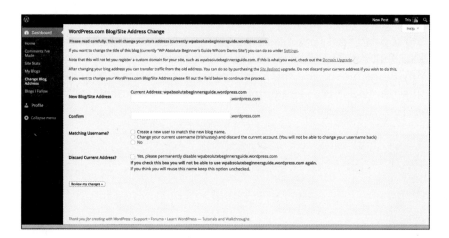

FIGURE 14.21

Change blog/site address screen.

That's it. This option *isn't* for deciding you want to use your own domain name with your WordPress.com site (I'll cover that option later in the chapter) or if you decide to switch to self-hosted WordPress and want to make sure the visitors to your old site find their way (again, later in the chapter). Use this when maybe you made a typo in the name or you decide the first name doesn't suit you anymore, for instance.

Transferring a Blog to Another User

What if you start a site, but you want someone to take it over for you? You could make them an admin of the site, but if the person wanted to add a domain name to the site or make other changes to the site (like other upgrades)—you as the site owner would need to do that. So, here's how to transfer the *ownership* of a blog/site to another WordPress.com user.

First, make sure you know the person's WordPress.com username or email address—you'll need this in a minute. From the same screen as Figure 14.20, you mouse over and click Transfer Blog. You'll get to a pretty dire-looking screen (Figure 14.22), and after you check the check box (like I did), you'll see the place to enter the username or email of the person you're transferring the site to. As the box says, you'll receive an email to confirm this change *and* make sure that if you still want to be allowed to publish on that site, you're added as a user, too.

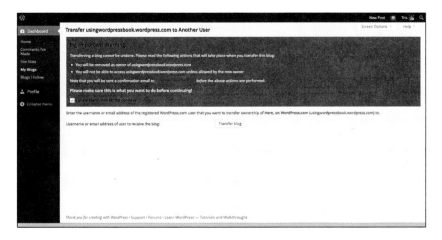

FIGURE 14.22

Transferring a blog to another user.

Deleting Blogs

This is the nuclear option. This option, found under the Tools menu, lets you choose to make the blog not just gone, but so gone that no one can ever use that name again.

When you pick the option, you first choose the Delete Site option from the pull-down menu. Yes, there are many other options there, but they don't *do* anything except point you to more information. After you select to delete the site, you'll see Figure 14.23.

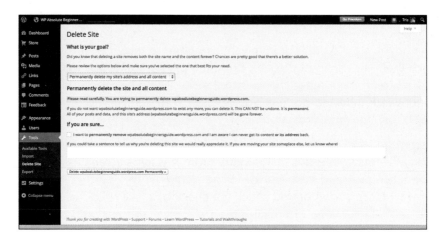

FIGURE 14.23

Deleting a site. Danger, Will Robinson!

 CAUTION   When they say it's gone, it's gone. I had trishussey.wordpress.com in the early days of WordPress.com and chose the option to delete, and now I can't get it back, never ever. Back then, we didn't have the option to delete the blog but allow the name to be available for other users. If I could do it over again, I would have left the blog and let it be stagnant, or make it private, or something. Deleting it was a stupid thing to do.

It's a simple form that will do *exactly* what it says. This is making the site gone baby gone. If you want to delete all your posts and start with a clean slate, you can use the All Posts screen to delete all the content. No kidding around—this is a nuclear option. There is no turning back. No mulligan. A site that is gone is gone.

You've been warned.

Premium Add-ons

There is a lot that WordPress.com has to offer for free, but it is a *freemium* service, which means there are additional features you can have that you can pay for. These features range from the simple (using your own domain name on your site, more space to upload media, and premium themes) to the more complex (Custom Designs, Site Redirects, and Guided Transfer). These options and features can be purchased on their own or in bundles (a relatively new option). Are they a good value? Yes. I absolutely think that some of the offerings are a *great* value. Others, maybe not so much; however, all of them make sense when you look at the big picture.

When you click the Shop link from within the admin Dashboard, you see all the options available to you (Figure 14.24). New options are always popping up, so what you see might have even more features and options when you look at it.

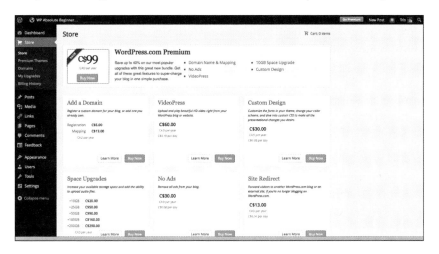

FIGURE 14.24

Premium upgrade options.

Domains

The first, and I think probably the most popular, option is to use your own domain name on your WordPress.com site. I could if I wish (and believe me I've thought about it) move my main website—trishussey.com—to WordPress.com and use trishussey.com there. The reality is that I often need my own hosting and server for other things, so it's not practical for me. That doesn't mean it isn't *really* tempting.

If you already have a domain name registered somewhere, you just need the Mapping option. You'll be given instructions for how to use your domain name with WordPress.com (it works very much like what I talked about for using your domain name with a web host in Chapter 1, "How Websites Work"). If you don't have a domain name, you can register the name through WordPress.com and the rest will be taken care of for you. At the time I'm writing this, domains at WordPress.com cost about half what they do at registrars like GoDaddy or Namecheap ($5 versus $10). The domain upgrade is a yearly fee to cover registration and mapping.

Premium Themes

One of the new features on WordPress.com is that in addition to having free themes in the theme browser, some of the themes cost money to use. Often these are versions of premium themes you could buy if you are using self-hosted WordPress (like many StudioPress themes), or they are ones that WordPress.com has found and asked to be included. The prices range from about $20 to more than $100. Like all premium themes, there are good and great ones. If you buy a premium theme it's a one-time cost forever, which is great as the theme designers add more features and refinements to the theme. You get those for free. The only gripe I have with premium themes is that although you can get your money back if you ask for a refund in 30 days, I would like to see a "try free for 14 days" system. Just try the theme and if you don't like it, don't buy it. If you do like it, then buy it. You can buy premium themes one at a time or pay to have access to all the themes whenever you want. Because I don't know many people who change themes *that* often, I don't think on its own it's a great deal.

I've found recently that although more and more free themes are available to WordPress.com users, the *coolest* themes are often the premium ones. This might sway you to buying a premium theme, because the designs and features tend to be more polished and cutting edge.

Custom Design

Custom design is kind of a misnomer. When you purchase this option (right now $30 per year), you're able to edit the CSS or style of a theme. This means you can change some of the colors of text, change the fonts that are used, change how text looks, and a few other touches. You *can't* do things like create a custom Page template or alter how content is laid out. Also, you'll need some expertise with CSS to *really* take advantage of this feature. Is CSS hard? Not really. It takes some practice, but it does involve learning a little about code and how that works. I'll talk more about this in Chapter 16, "Customizations Without (Much) Coding."

If you do go for this option, one of the most fun things is to use different fonts for your text. This is one of the easiest things to do and one of the main lessons in Chapter 16.

More Space

All WordPress.com sites are given 3GB (3,072MB) of space to upload images and other files. If you start filling up that space, you can upgrade with more space, starting with 10GB more all the way up to 200GB. That's a lot of space. If you're a photographer, however, it's pretty easy to use up a lot of space with high-resolution versions of your photos. Videos are a different matter. For videos, you need the VideoPress option *as well as* more space. All the more-space options are billed yearly.

VideoPress

Even if you have the space upgrade, you still can't upload videos to your WordPress.com site without adding the VideoPress option as well. Right now this is running $60 per year. Why pay for space *and* this option when YouTube is free? That's a good question—and a question you need to ask yourself. The primary reason I've seen this done is if you want to control access to the videos (say if you're selling subscriptions to have access to the video content) or if you want more control over how the videos are presented.

Although WordPress.com does have a substantial network of servers that can handle videos, I think the extra boost you get from having your content on YouTube makes the "cost" of being there worth it. VideoPress is a compelling option only for those who don't think YouTube is professional enough.

Site Redirect

If you decide at some point to move to a self-hosted WordPress site, and you didn't buy a domain name on WordPress.com, you can pay to redirect mycoolsite.wordpress.com to mycoolsite.com. This is a small yearly fee (right now $13) that makes sure that not only your visitors find your new home, but search engines find it as well. If you're making the move from WordPress.com to a self-hosted WordPress site, this is a must buy. It's a small amount of money for a lot of benefit.

Why don't you need this if you bought the domain package? Because when you move to the new site, you'll tell the new host to use your domain and your visitors (and search engines) will be none the wiser.

Guided Transfer

If you're making the move from WordPress.com to WordPress.org and hosting yourself, you might think about the guided transfer option. What you're paying for is a WordPress expert to move your site from WordPress.com to one of the WordPress recommended hosts (like Dreamhost or Blue Host) for you. At $130, it's not cheap, but you're guaranteed that the process will be done right. The process for moving from WordPress.com to self-hosting is just as simple as exporting your content from WordPress.com and importing it into the new site, but you know if this isn't your cup of tea. Letting an expert handle it isn't such a bad idea. You can learn more about importing and exporting content in Chapter 11, "Using WordPress: Content," and backing up your site (if you're self-hosted) in Chapter 15, "Maintaining WordPress Sites."

No Ads

If you're not logged in to WordPress.com, you might see an ad from Google or elsewhere on your site or other WordPress.com sites. Running ads with your content is one of the ways Automattic can afford to offer so much of WordPress.com for free. If you don't want your visitors to ever see an ad on your site, you can pay for that privilege. Myself, and maybe because I'm nearly always logged in to WordPress.com in some fashion, I've never seen an ad on a WordPress.com site. Maybe they are really unobtrusive or I've learned to ignore them, but I still don't remember seeing ads. WordPress.com is including the No Ads option in all the professional bundles that I'll talk about in a moment. So is this one worth it? I don't think so, but if your visitors say something about seeing an ad and it bothers you, then by all means paying to have them gone is worth it.

Professional Package Bundles

WordPress.com and Automattic figured out some time ago that people often bought a bunch of options together. To make that process easier, and be able to offer a bundle discount, they put together some bundles of services and options that users might like.

Pro

At the basic level is the Pro or Premium package for $99 (as I'm writing this) that gives you the following:

- Domain name and mapping
- No ads
- Custom design
- 10GB more of space
- VideoPress

Because on their own, VideoPress and Custom designs cost $90, this is a good deal. Even if you weren't thinking about using VideoPress, the rest together is like getting VideoPress for free. If you want to have a very professional site, this is pretty fair. Most hosting costs about $120 a year, plus the cost of a domain name (about $10), so you're coming out ahead of the game. Throw in a premium theme? If you buy themes outside of WordPress.com, they cost just as much if not *more*, so again you're ahead of the game. You still have the restrictions of WordPress.com, but you do have more freedom with uploads, the capability to tweak themes (free and premium) a bit, a domain name, and no ads shown to visitors.

Business

The Business bundle is the next step up, and it's a big step up. You get everything in the Pro/Premium bundle, plus all the premium themes and unlimited space. This is a package for people who want a business-class site, but are also okay with the features on WordPress.com *and* the choices of themes *and* the limitations of Custom Design. This is $300 a year right now. If you figure the cost of hosting, domain, a premium theme, *and* having someone make changes for you, this could be a good idea. I see and understand the level of service that WordPress.com is going for here, but it could be a hard sell to a penny-pinching business. If you're upgrading, I would try Premium/Pro first and then see if you need the other features to make it worth the additional cost.

Enterprise

The Enterprise level is a whole other kettle of fish. It's $500 a *month* (at time of writing) and is aimed at big companies who need a very stable environment that can take heavy traffic, *and* they don't have internal resources to manage that for themselves. If you're looking at this level of service and you pick it, you've probably been shopping around for other options as well. The Enterprise option gives you much more control, including adding from a choice of 100 plugins, to make your site custom. This isn't just fooling around website stuff; this is critical to your business, and you expect a lot of traffic (like millions of visits a day) website stuff.

As WordPress.com grows, they will, I know, be adding more premium features for users to buy and try. The freemium model works well, especially when the prices make sense and the steps up the ladder of complexity are pretty clear. WordPress.com is getting there with these offerings, and I can't wait to see more.

Conclusion

This chapter has been a different take on the whole WordPress experience. WordPress.com grew out of the self-hosted WordPress world with a vision of offering free websites using WordPress that were secure, fast, and powerful. Automattic and WordPress.com have done a great job at this. They are one of the leading hosted website services around. Only Blogger and Tumblr are around to challenge them, and only Tumblr has shown any innovation in the past few years. I use WordPress.com to teach my Introduction to WordPress/Making a Website with WordPress class because students can come in, sit down at a computer, start learning WordPress, and make a website. If they want to move to self-hosted WordPress, they have all the basic tools they need to get going with creating content.

WordPress.com is a great, solid platform to build your first or 101st website. And it's only getting better.

IN THIS CHAPTER

- How to update WordPress, plugins, and themes
- Backing up and maintaining your database
- Backing up the rest of your WordPress files

15

MAINTAINING WORDPRESS SITES

Remember in Chapter 2, "What WordPress Is and How It Works," that one of the main differences between WordPress.com and self-hosted WordPress.org sites is that when you self-host, you need to keep WordPress, your plugins, and your themes updated. If you got this far with easy installs of WordPress, plugins, and themes, you're in good shape. There isn't, believe it or not, anything new to learn, really. Just watch for the indicators that you have updates waiting, run the update, and you're done. Updates, though, are only part of the responsibility of self-hosting a WordPress site. You also need to make sure you maintain your database and back up essential WordPress files. Just like making sure your computer is backed up, making sure these basic maintenance tasks are done will help ensure that if disaster strikes, you'll be able to recover quickly and cleanly.

For updates, everything can be done under the Dashboard menu and Updates. That's where we'll be for the first half of this chapter.

Updating WordPress

There are two kinds of WordPress updates you need to think about: point updates and new versions. A point update is something like updating from WordPress 3.7 to 3.7.1. It's a small, incremental update that usually fixes bugs and (most importantly) closes security holes in WordPress. Starting with WordPress 3.7, chances are you won't have to worry about installing point updates ever again. From now on, point updates can be installed automatically for you, without your having to do a thing. How do you know if your site can do automatic updates? In the Dashboard, click Updates, and if you see on the page "Future security updates will be applied automatically," you're all set (Figure 15.1).

FIGURE 15.1

Ready for automatic updates!

How will you know if an update has been applied to your site? You'll get an email. Simple as that! Figure 15.2 shows the email I received when the 3.7.1 update was applied to the demo site.

FIGURE 15.2

Automatic update applied!

Automatic updates will work with most hosts; if yours doesn't support automatic updates, you can use the regular update process for WordPress. First, you'll see a notification throughout the admin area that a new update is available. You won't be able to miss it. Then when you go to the Updates screen, you'll see something like Figure 15.3, but with a lot less beta stuff and more "There is an update of WordPress ready." When you click the Update button (don't worry; if you follow my suggestions in this chapter, you'll be backed up), the process will run and you'll get to a screen like Figure 15.4 (because the figure came from the prerelease time for WordPress 3.8, there are mentions of WordPress 3.7, too). That's it! Really. If you get to that screen, WordPress is updated, and you're good to go.

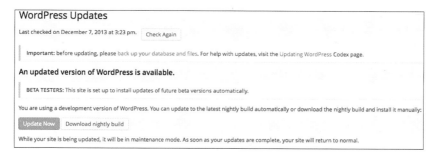

FIGURE 15.3

Oooh! Updates are available!

FIGURE 15.4

Done like dinner and updated.

As you might have gathered, if there is a version update to WordPress (like 3.7 to 3.8 or 3.8 to 3.9), the updating process *isn't* automatic, but works the same as if you couldn't have point updates installed automatically. That's really all there is to keeping WordPress updated. When there is an update to WordPress, click

Update; you're done, enjoy. If you're wondering if it's safe to jump from 3.7 to 3.7.1, the answer is yes. In fact, one of the main reasons that automatic updates were created was to make sure that people *did* update WordPress between major versions. These point updates are essential for keeping your WordPress site secure. *Essential.* Major updates are a little trickier to answer whether you should just click Update. Recently, the changes even between major versions of WordPress (3.5, 3.6, and 3.7) weren't really huge. A lot of behind-the-scenes changes aimed to make WordPress run faster. WordPress 3.8 brought in major changes to how the admin dashboard looks (it brought it in sync with WordPress. com, actually), but *functional* changes? Not really. If you remember from the Introduction, I started this book with WordPress 3.6 and finished with WordPress 3.8 (this is between September and December of 2013). All I've needed to update are the screenshots from pre-3.8 admin dashboard, how the Themes area looks and works, and some polish on the Widgets area. *How* WordPress works— writing, publishing, menus, widgets, settings—hasn't changed much.

If you have been running your own site and haven't messed around with how WordPress does things, updating to the next new version shouldn't be a problem for you. If you have questions, there are always posts on WordPress.org about the upcoming versions and what it means for people. If you're still a little skittish, ask your friendly neighborhood geek. He or she will know.

Updating Plugins

In the great scheme of things, you're going to be updating plugins more than anything else. You might see a few point updates to WordPress a year and maybe one or two version updates to WordPress a year (2013 was very unusual with three big updates). Themes? You might see one or two updates a year, period. Plugins? You'll see those all the time. How do you know when you have updates? Look for the red numbers in your menu bars. Figure 15.5 shows that I have two updates available. When I clicked through to the Updates screen, I had one plugin and one theme to update. The plugin section looks like Figure 15.6.

FIGURE 15.5

Updates! Woo hoo!

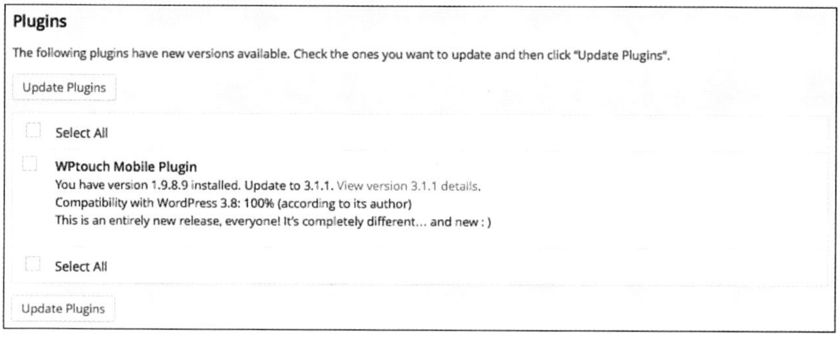

FIGURE 15.6

One plugin to update.

Click the check box next to the plugin(s) to update (or the box at the top to check them all), and click Update. WordPress will go through the update process and you'll eventually come to a screen like Figure 15.7. All done, all updated. From here, you can continue on your merry posting way or, as in my case, I have more updates to do. A theme needs an update!

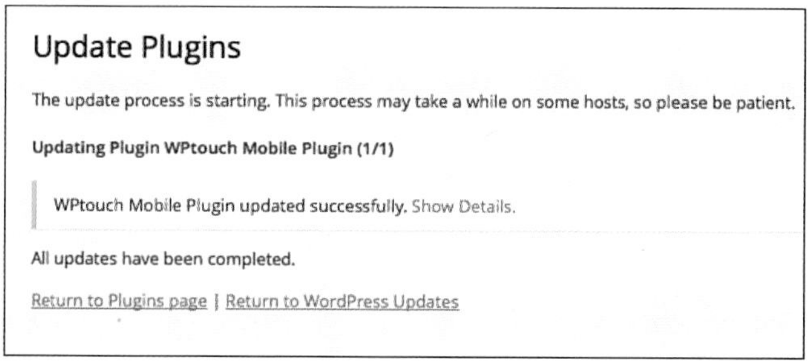

FIGURE 15.7

Plugin updated.

Updating Themes

Theme updates are so rare that I thought I was going to have to wait until WordPress 3.8 came out to have a theme update to show (Figure 15.8). Lucky for me, one came up before then to take a screenshot of! Updating themes works exactly like updating plugins. You *can* just click and update, but....

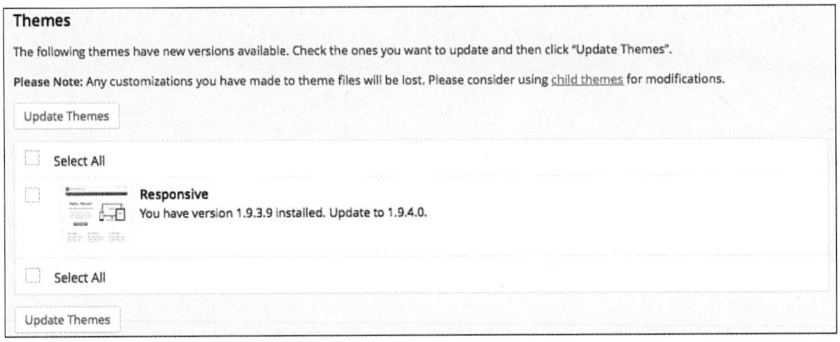

Themes

The following themes have new versions available. Check the ones you want to update and then click "Update Themes".

Please Note: Any customizations you have made to theme files will be lost. Please consider using child themes for modifications.

Update Themes

☐ Select All

☐ **Responsive**
You have version 1.9.3.9 installed. Update to 1.9.4.0.

☐ Select All

Update Themes

FIGURE 15.8

One theme to update.

This is where things get tricky. If you have customized your theme and edited the theme files, and that theme requires an update—updating a theme will cause you to lose all those changes. Headers, backgrounds, widgets, and Custom CSS that we will talk about in Chapter 16, "Customizations Without (Much) Coding," are safe; those changes would be overwritten. If you know what you're doing enough to be editing themes, you should know this hazard already. If you had a theme customized *for you*, ask your theme designer/developer before updating. If you're not using a theme that needs an update (like the core WordPress themes), don't worry about updating those themes as they come up (the core themes 2010–2014 will update for most new versions of WordPress).

Those are the three things you need to keep updated: WordPress (semi-frequently), plugins (often), and themes (rarely). If you keep those things updated, you're going to avoid a lot of problems and potential security woes that site owners sometimes face. Maintenance doesn't end there, though. We have a couple other things to manage: the database and the rest of the files.

Managing Your WordPress Database

In Chapter 2 and Chapter 3, "Installing WordPress," I touched on the WordPress database. The database that powers your WordPress website is, without a doubt, the heart of your site. It holds all your content, all your settings, all the comments, where the images are, all the categories and tags, *everything important to your site is in the database*. If your database gets corrupted or your site hacked, you're hooped. Well, unless you have backups. And that's what this section is all about.

As far as I'm concerned, there is only one plugin you need to look at for keeping your database in shape: WP-DBManager. It's simple, effective, and it works (Figure 15.9).

FIGURE 15.9

WP-DBManager on WordPress.org.

After you install and activate the plugin, you'll see a dire warning in red at the top of your screen (Figure 15.10).

FIGURE 15.10

Yikes! This sounds serious!

First, don't panic. This isn't earth-shattering, and you haven't just opened up a huge security hole in your site. WP-DBManager creates a new directory in wp-content to store your backups, and the plugin must make sure that if the directory isn't hidden already, it will be. You're going to need to fire up your FTP program for this step. Don't worry; it's simple stuff here. Just navigate to wp-content/plugins/wp-dbmanager and you'll see a file called htaccess.txt. The easiest thing is to copy that down to your local machine (it's tiny, and it will take just a moment). Still in your FTP program, go back up to wp-content and then into backup-db. Drag htaccess.txt into that folder (Figure 15.11). Now you need to rename it. Different programs handle this differently; in my program, I just right-click to get to rename the file. If you're not sure how to do it, check your program's help file. You'll need to rename the file to .htaccess (so lop off .txt and put a period in the front) (Figure 15.12). That's it. It's simple, and now that directory can't be browsed by interlopers trying to get a sneak peek into your database.

FIGURE 15.11

Before renaming.

FIGURE 15.12

After renaming.

As for settings, I've found that WP-DBManager *generally* can figure things out on its own, so the only options I check are under DB Options and at the bottom of the screen (Figure 15.13).

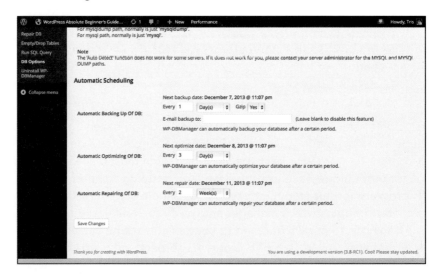

FIGURE 15.13

Just three options to set.

I like my database to be backed up every day and compressed (that's what Gzip does, so pick the Yes option). Every three days, my database is optimized, and every two weeks, it's repaired. If you have a very active site, you might need to back up more often and optimize more often. Repairing once a week is probably enough for almost anyone. If you'd like a copy of the database emailed to you, put your email address in the email address spot (actually it's there by default). I leave it out because I found it a little much. However, it's a nice safety net. If you set up a Gmail account just for these backups, your regular email isn't cluttered, and if you ever need to go back and find an old database, you know where to go.

If you've gotten this far, keeping your site updated and backing up your database on a regular basis, you're in really, really good shape. This will keep your butt out of a sling 99% of the time. There is one more step you can take to protect yourself: back up the rest of the files.

Backing Up Your Site

As far as WordPress is concerned, if you have a copy of your database, a copy of wp-config.php (and you can even do without that at worst), and the contents of wp-content/uploads, you can get your site back up and running. It's also helpful to have your plugins and themes, too (especially if you have customized themes), but those are the *core* things you need. So, if you want to back up your site manually, use your FTP program and download a copy of wp-config.php from the root of your site, your uploads folder, the database backup folder, and maybe your themes folder. Plugins I'd just leave, because you'll most likely want to download new copies of them. It will take a few minutes to a few hours to download all that (depending on how many files we're talking about). If you keep this on an external hard drive or other media that is also backed up, you're in good shape. But what if you don't want to have to *remember* to do that all the time? Then you can use tools to do it automatically for you!

The gold standard for backing up WordPress sites is VaultPress from Automattic. This is a paid service that can make sure you're protected (Figure 15.14).

FIGURE 15.14

VaultPress.com.

Depending on the level of service you choose, you can have more (and more rapid) backups and restore points for your site. It's a solid option that can bring a site back from the dead if disaster (or hackers) strikes. You don't have access to those backups; Automattic makes sure they stay nice, safe, and secure for you. What if you'd like to have the backups handy? Then WordPress to Dropbox (WP2DB) (Figure 15.15) might be what you're looking for. This plugin (basic levels are free) lets you back up your website to your Dropbox account. Dropbox is a storage in the cloud company, and I have a preponderance of storage there (it's where I keep 99% of my files), so having my site backup there made a lot of sense to me. I paid for the extras to have my backup compressed before copying to Dropbox (I have *a lot* of files in my uploads directory) and to email me when the process is complete, but for a site just starting out, the free options are great. In fact, when you sign up for Dropbox, you get enough free storage to back up a decent-sized website—if you pick the right files to back up. In the settings, I *excluded* everything except wp-content and wp-config. Even within wp-content, I didn't back up plugins and the cache folders. Those don't need to be backed up (especially the cache, which just adds a lot of extra space you don't need) (Figure 15.16).

FIGURE 15.15

WordPress to Dropbox.

FIGURE 15.16

My exclusions (partial look).

Then I have the plugin run the backup every day at midnight. Simple and done.

The final way to make a backup of sorts is to use a plugin like WordPress Duplicator (free) http://wordpress.org/plugins/duplicator/, which makes a copy of your site that you can then use to either move your site to a new host (we'll talk more about this in Chapter 17, "Advanced WordPress Settings and Uses"), use as a backup, or use to make a copy of your site for development. It's a very handy plugin, but if you have a very large site, you *could* run into issues with it timing out trying to copy and compress all the files. When I've used it to set up a mirror of a site so I could work on it, it was simple and easy for me to use. However, I'm also familiar with all the geeky parts of getting sites together and moving them. It might not be your cup of tea.

What About the Rest of the WordPress Files?

I know you're wondering that. Don't worry about them. If you have to restore a site from the dead, the best thing is to download a fresh copy of WordPress to work with. You'll most likely be going for a full manual install and might want some help with it, too.

Conclusion

You know the adage "An ounce of prevention is worth a pound of cure." That's where we've been this entire chapter. Updates and backups are the prevention. If your host's servers crash, if you're hacked, if a plugin or theme goes sideways and does something bad, or even if a WordPress update/upgrade fails spectacularly, you'll have the files you need to fall back on.

That's what it's all about. Preparing for disaster and hoping it doesn't happen. It's okay to be a little paranoid; it is your website, after all.

IN THIS CHAPTER

- Using Widget Locations for interactive sidebars
- Editing your site's stylesheet
- Changing your site's fonts with Google Fonts
- Using Font Awesome for menus
- Introduction to Custom Post Types

16

CUSTOMIZATIONS WITHOUT (MUCH) CODING

There are times when all the widgets, headers, menus, theme options, and everything else can't pull off what you need WordPress to do. This is when you think to yourself, "If I could only just change how the theme handled this…or I wish I could work with Posts like that." (We'll get more into this later.) Some of these tasks are beyond the scope of this book, but there are some things that you can do to customize your site without too much coding (or any at all). Some of the parts of this chapter crank the geek-o-meter up to a nine or ten, so if this isn't your cup of tea, don't worry. This chapter isn't going anywhere, and you can always come back to it when you'd like. However, as WordPress matures, more and more of these customizations become easier and easier (with less coding and registering lower on the geek-o-meter), so you might come back and realize that there's a *much* easier way to do some of these customizations. That's progress.

This chapter is going to cover three customizations that many WordPress users ask about: changing how text and images look, using different fonts (especially the fonts from Google), and using Posts in a more flexible way. And I'm going to throw in some bonus things, too, just to keep things interesting.

Easy WordPress Theme Customizations Without Much Coding

For these customizations, there are a few programs and things you'll need to have before you get going. All the resources are free, but they are essential for you to make heads or tails of what we're doing. You will also be doing a lot of copying and pasting in this chapter, so having a blank text editor window open to paste code into (for multistep tasks) is a good idea (I often use Stickies on my Mac for this). I'll be using Chrome or Safari on the Mac as my browser and the free text editor TextWrangler (http://www.barebones.com/products/textwrangler/ or the Mac App Store) for some (but not all) text-related things. We're also going to rely on Jetpack to power some of the key functions, so it's best to have that turned on, as well.

Tools you'll need:

- Recommended browser: Chrome (Mac/Windows) or Safari (Mac).

- Add-on: Firebug Lite for Chrome or Safari (https://getfirebug.com).

- Basic text editor: Notepad on Windows or TextEdit on Mac will suffice. Notepad++ for Windows (http://notepad-plus-plus.org) or TextWrangler for Mac recommended.

Before you continue on with the chapter, make sure you have all these installed and ready. And Jetpack, don't forget Jetpack.

Widget Locations

The first thing isn't a customization, *per se*, but it's rather cool. One of the features of Jetpack is being able to set where a widget is or *isn't* visible when you add it to a sidebar. Why is this handy? Suppose you're in one section of your site and you want to have a menu or maybe special offers or a video *just for that section*. Let me show you.

On the demo site home page, I have *a lot* of widgets (Figure 16.1). Yeah, we've been goofing around, so that's okay. It's cluttered, though. What if I wanted only search, the video, recent posts, and recent comments on the home page? Fine, just put only those widgets there. Right, but I want the menus, pages, and other stuff on interior pages. Actually, maybe I only want the Category archive list to show on other archive pages. Here's how you do it.

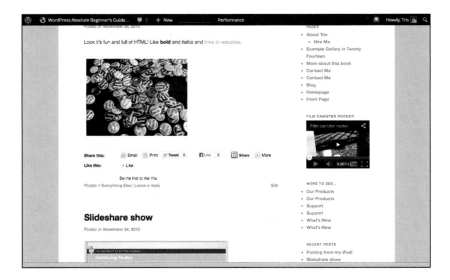

FIGURE 16.1

Gee, that's a mess!

First, on the Widgets screen in the Dashboard, pick the first widget you'd like to play around with. I'm going to pick Pages as the example for how to hide something from the front page/home page. Click the Visibility button in the widget. From the first menu, choose Hide; then if Page (from the menu) is Front page and click Save (Figure 16.2). I'm going to repeat this for all the widgets I don't want on the home page. When I'm done, it looks like Figure 16.3.

FIGURE 16.2

Hiding a widget from the front page/home page.

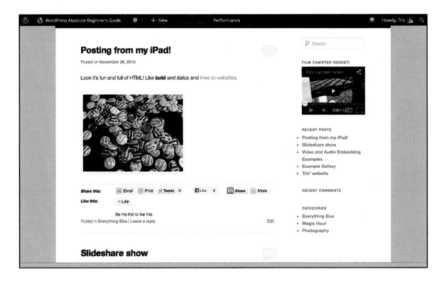

FIGURE 16.3

Much tidier!

You saw from the menu there are *lots* of permutations there, and you can combine them with more options. Here's the thing about combining showing/hiding: You have to pick your show or hide as the first rule. For my archives example, I want it to show in a particular place, so I'm switching to Show If Category Is All Category Pages (Figure 16.4). The result, looking at ones of the category pages, is in Figure 16.5.

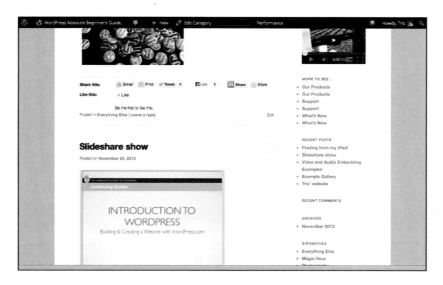

FIGURE 16.4

Showing for category pages.

FIGURE 16.5

And there it is.

For Twenty Eleven, this is an odd exercise because on individual Posts or Pages, there are no sidebars, but there are sidebars in archive pages, search results, and such. But imagine having archive and category listings only on pages where someone doesn't find the right page (a 404 page), or archives show a calendar of posts. Or whatever. Right now, widget visibility is just getting good. You can't, for example, have "hide here but show there" kinds of combinations. That's coming, I'm sure.

Okay, that was a pretty easy one. Not very high on the geek-o-meter. That's fine; we're just getting warmed up. Now for some of the fun stuff. Changing how text and things appear on the page by adding custom CSS through Jetpack.

Editing Your Theme's Style with CSS

The colors, fonts, size of the text, and the general layout of your theme (and site) is defined by your theme's stylesheet, which is written in a format called CSS (Cascading Style Sheet). To do something like change the size, color, or font of your post titles, you need to know how your theme's stylesheet is structured and what each of the objects you want to change are called in the stylesheet. You can't just guess these, either; you need to *know* before you start off changing things. We're going to find this out by looking at the underlying code for the site using Firebug in our browser.

Before we get to that part, we need to make sure we *can* easily edit the stylesheet for our theme. Or, in our case, we're going to tell WordPress to override parts of what is in the stylesheet with our changes. We're going to do this with Jetpack. One of the handy modules (activated by default) is Custom CSS, which allows you to override as much of your theme's stylesheet as you want *without actually changing the theme's files*. This means that if you make a mistake (or change your mind), you don't have to worry that you've "damaged" your theme. You can just delete the changes you made in Custom CSS and you're back to where you started.

WHY NOT EDIT THE THEME FILES DIRECTLY?

If you talk to a designer or developer, they would suggest that you edit the theme files directly. Oh, and make a child theme first, or use the custom.css file for that theme, or.... The issue here is simplicity. Yes, you could certainly edit your theme's style.css file (what the stylesheet is called), but that opens up a whole can of worms around doing it right. Is the theme a parent-child theme, a theme framework, or a "normal" theme? How do you back up the original theme? What do you do when the original theme is updated? How do you make sure that your changes aren't lost? For all intents and purposes, I'd need to write another book on that (I am, in fact, doing just that). So we're playing it safe. We're using Jetpack's Custom CSS module, and you're not *really* changing the theme or its style; you're just telling WordPress to override some of the theme's original style with your updates.

With Jetpack on, you will find under the Appearance menu an item called Edit CSS. This is where we'll be doing a lot of our changes in this chapter (Figure 16.6). We'll come back to this screen in a moment, but first we need to learn a little more about our theme and how it's structured. As in Chapter 10, "Tweaking, Tuning, and Customizing Your WordPress Site," I'll be using Twenty Eleven as the example. What you see in your theme might be a little (or a lot) different, but the steps and process are going to be the same for all themes.

FIGURE 16.6

Edit CSS screen.

First, we need to visit the home page of our site and see what we'd like to change. I'd like to change the fonts around in this theme. I'd like a different font for the headers, posts, menus—well, everything. I'd also like to change the color of the links on the pages. Minor stuff.

NOTE More About CSS

I'm not going to get too deeply into how CSS works, but this is a beginner tutorial that the folks at WordPress.org recommend: http://www.htmldog.com/guides/css/beginner/.

Here's the thing about CSS—you can't just write in something like header: bold, blue or links: red, underlined. Not only are there rules, syntax, and terms that have to be used, the person who created the theme gave the different elements of the page names. In order to change how something looks, you first have to know what it's called. There are a lot of ways to go about figuring this out. One way is to look at the CSS as it is and find what you're looking for. Sound crazy? Actually it isn't. Under Appearance, if you click Editor, you can see the stylesheet for your current theme. Figure 16.7 gives you an idea of what it looks like for Twenty Eleven. Can't make heads or tails of it? Step back and scroll a bit. There are parts that will start to make sense. Like seeing "body" and a list of fonts and a font size and color! That's promising. Copy that and paste it into Notepad or TextEdit; we'll need it later. What you copied should look like this (for 2011):

```
body, input, textarea {
        color: #373737;
        font: 15px "Helvetica Neue", Helvetica, Arial, sans-serif;
        font-weight: 300;
        line-height: 1.625;
}
```

A quick look at the stylesheet will give you an idea of how things might be structured later on. In this case, if you get all the way to the bottom, you might have noticed not very many places that mention any font names. This means that changing fonts is going to be pretty easy. Change in one place and we'll take care of it all! Well, sort of. We're going to be cooler than that.

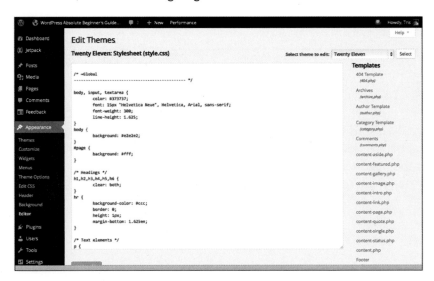

FIGURE 16.7

Yep, this is a stylesheet. Notice the font names.

The next way to check things out is to use Firebug to figure out exactly what is what.

NOTE Firebug in Safari is…odd. It works, but some of the ways it displays things are strange. The built-in developer tools are good, so if you want to skip Firebug in Safari and use the built-in tools, I can't blame you.

After installing Firebug in your browser, right-click the part of the page you want to know about and choose Inspect with Firebug Lite. In the example, I've picked the title of the post (Figure 16.8), and we know now that it's called "entry-title." Excellent. I'm not planning to do anything more than change the font for it, so that's all we need for now. Since we're here, I've also clicked and inspected a link and learned that all the links are a blue shade. Now we have all the information we need to get started. First, let's look for some cooler fonts.

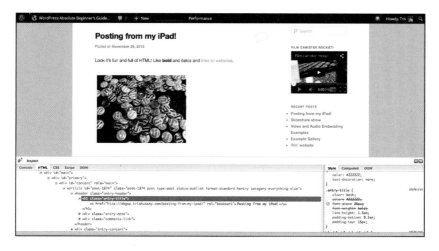

FIGURE 16.8

Whoa. More code. See the patterns, though?

Using Google Fonts

Google developed a free set of fonts that you can use on any website. The full project and list is here: http://www.google.com/fonts/, and you'll figure out that, wow, there are a lot of fonts. Don't worry, there are lots of resources to help you pick font sets that look good together. I like some of the combinations that the folks at StudioPress came up with (http://www.studiopress.com/design/google-font-combinations.htm), and if you Google for "Google font combinations," you'll get plenty more. For our exercise, I'm going to use Quattrocento fonts: http://www.google.com/fonts#UsePlace:use/Collection:Quattrocento%7CQuattroc ento+Sans. One of the pluses of using Google fonts is that you get access to lots and lots of fonts. The downside is that the more fonts you load, the slower your page will load. That's why as you pick fonts to use, Google gives you that gauge to show the impact on load time (Figure 16.9).

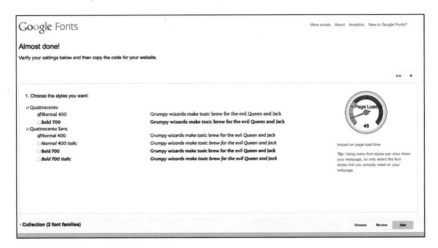

FIGURE 16.9

Picking the two fonts to use. Notice the page load. Not bad.

Lower in the page we get to how to use these fonts. We're going to tell our Custom CSS to load these fonts from Google using the @import line:

```
@import url(http://fonts.googleapis.com/css?family=Quattrocento|
Quattrocento+Sans);
```

This is going to be the first thing we paste into the Custom CSS. Copy your import code from the Google page; then head back to your Dashboard and under Appearance, click Edit CSS. Paste the @import code like you see in Figure 16.10.

FIGURE 16.10

Adding the @import line.

Now we need to change that body text and then the entry-title text.

Remember that code I said we'd need later? It's later. Copy and paste that code into the Custom CSS window.

We're only going to change this line:

```
font: 15px "Helvetica Neue", Helvetica, Arial, sans-serif;
```

So you can delete all the rest of the lines. What! Right. This is the beauty of CSS, to change something you only need to define in the Custom CSS the things that are *different*. If you're not changing it, you don't need to tell the theme, it will use the original style. For this first change, we're going to make all the body text Quattrocento Sans. Although I really like Helvetica Neue, we'll just replace that text with Quattrocento Sans, so the line looks like this:

```
font: 15px "Quattrocento Sans", Helvetica, Arial, sans-serif;
```

This means that if for some reason the Google fonts don't load, the site will load Helvetica; if that isn't available, Arial, and so on. If we had added Quattrocento Sans to the front and kept Helvetica Neue in there, that would have worked in the same way. This changed all the fonts in the entire site to use Quattrocento Sans in one fell swoop. This worked out nicely because of how 2011 was written; the fonts were defined in the HTML body element, not through later CSS classes and IDs. For the entry title, we will do something very similar, but the code looks like this:

```
.entry-title {
        font-family: Quattrocento, Helvetica, Arial, sans-serif;
}
```

Notice the "." in front of "entry-title"; that's because it's a CSS class, it defines a larger group of text elements on the page. If it were trying to define a very specific instance of something on a page, you would use an ID (and we would see in the stylesheet using a "#"). When you're looking at your stylesheet, note what things are classes (.) and IDs (#); there can be .entry-title and #entry-title ("can", but it isn't a good idea because it gets confusing), and you need to make sure you're calling it by the right name. All that line does is tell the theme that everything defined as class entry-title should use Quattrocento as the font. I'm falling back to our friends Helvetica and Arial if it doesn't.

NOTE   Font purists might get miffed at this choice. Quattrocento is a serif font, like Times New Roman, so one *should* stick to other serif fallbacks, but I'm a rebel so I'm picking sans-serif fonts.

The last thing I wanted to do is change the color of the blue in the links. Using my image editor, I found the color blue that I wanted. There are lots of places to do it online. ColorPicker.com is probably one of the easiest to just find the right shade of a color for what you are looking for. To change the color of all links, I used this line of code:

```
a {
    color: #246ba3;
}
```

That changes all lines all at once. The result? Here you go (Figure 16.11).

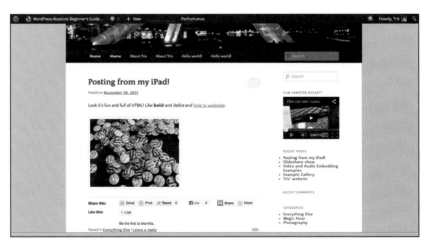

FIGURE 16.11

All done—for now.

And the final edits to the stylesheet? Very simple (Figure 16.12).

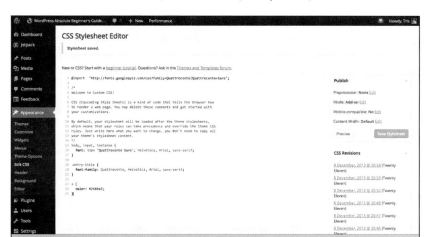

FIGURE 16.12

That's it, really!

There is much, much more that can be done using stylesheets. You can change the width of text areas and sidebars, the height of headers and footers, how images look, how blockquotes look—really, almost anything, as long as it has already been defined in the stylesheet. Playing with Google Fonts, and using them in your site is a great way to make your site your own. It's probably the most fun and easiest thing to do to give your site a little punch. Well, except for adding cool icons to your menus.

Icon Menus with Font Awesome

Let's get even trickier. Not tricky as in hard, though; tricky as in cool looking and having people wondering how you did it. Let's start adding icons to menus and other things using the scalable font set from Font Awesome (http://fortawesome. github.io/Font-Awesome/). Cruising around the site (and checking out the cheat sheet: http://fortawesome.github.io/Font-Awesome/cheatsheet/), you'll see a lot of icons that you might recognize. What Font Awesome did was to make a font that *has* all the icons in it. Why? Because well-made fonts *scale up and down beautifully*. If you want to make sure your site looks great on everything from mobile devices to desktop, your icons have to scale. Making graphics to do that is a royal pain; using a font is painless. To use Font Awesome in our site, we're going to use the plugin Font Awesome 4 Menus (http://wordpress.org/plugins/font-awesome-4-menus/). You can use the fonts in other places, but we're going to do Menus for right now.

After downloading and installing the plugin, head over to Menus under Appearance. Before we start, we need to hit the Screen Options and make sure we can see the CSS Classes option (Figure 16.13). Make sure that box is checked, and we're ready to continue.

FIGURE 16.13

You have to be able to see the CSS Classes for this trick.

All I need to do now is know what Font Awesome classes to use. The cheat sheet, the icons list (http://fortawesome.github.io/Font-Awesome/icons/), and examples (http://fortawesome.github.io/Font-Awesome/examples/) have everything you need to find the right icon for what you want to do. For me, I wanted a house for Home (fa-home), a coffee cup for About Me (fa-coffee), and an envelope for Contact Me (fa-envelope). In the properties of each of the menu items I put in the class (Figure 16.14), and with a click of the Save button, look at my spiffy menus (Figure 16.15)!

FIGURE 16.14

Adding the right classes.

FIGURE 16.15

Check out those icons!

There is a lot more that can be done with Font Awesome, but this is pretty awesome I think. The last thing we're going to do is work with content that *behaves* like a blog post, but doesn't mix in with posts: the custom post type.

Custom Post Types

I introduced you to the *idea* of custom post types in Chapter 11, "Using WordPress: Content." Now it's time to add them. As a quick refresher, custom post types *behave* like blog posts, but they aren't in your stream of posts. Custom post types are great for things like testimonials, featured items, even galleries of images. Custom posts types are for times when you'd like all the content to be grouped together, but not intermingle with the rest of your posts.

When WordPress first came out, Custom Post Types were hard to work with. Lots of people put them into their themes. We thought it was a great idea, but it turns out that the better way to go (for many cases) is to use a plugin to manage your custom post types so if you change your theme, you don't lose all that content. Asking around with the folks I know who use a lot of custom post types, they tell me Custom Post Type UI (http://wordpress.org/plugins/custom-post-type-ui/) is the plugin to use.

After installing and activating the plugin, you'll see a new CPT UI menu item on the sidebar (Figure 16.16). I want to add a new post type called Essays. These would be longer pieces of content that I don't want cluttering up my blog, but I'd like visitors to be able to look at an archive page for them. Creating a new post type (Figure 16.17) is easy, but I because I want an archive page for this type, I need to open the advanced options and switch Has Archive from False to True (Figure 16.18).

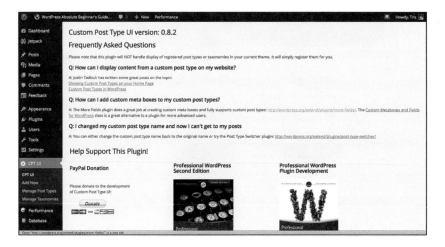

FIGURE 16.16

CPT UI main screen.

FIGURE 16.17

Adding the Essays CPT.

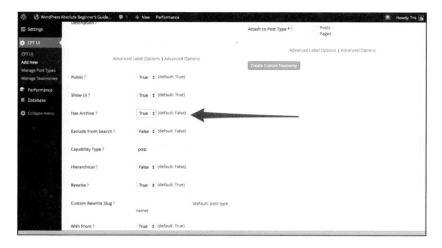

FIGURE 16.18

Making sure there is an archive page.

After I click Create Custom Post Type, I now have an Essay menu item (Figure 16.19)!

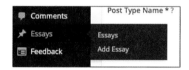

FIGURE 16.19

I can create new essays!

Essays are great, but I'd like to group them together, like with categories, for instance. That's easy enough. First, we have to create a *container* for those things—a taxonomy. Categories and tags are types of taxonomies, so we're going to create another called "topics" and attach it to Essays (Figure 16.20). If you open the Advanced Options, you'll see an option for hierarchy. If you keep it False, "topics" would behave like tags (all tags are equal); if you switch it to True, then "topics" would behave like categories. I chose to have a hierarchy, so in Figure 16.21, you can see my Add New Essay window with the topic Internet and Society in place.

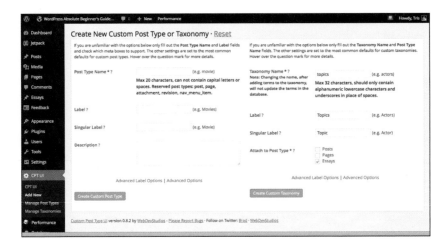

FIGURE 16.20

Creating a container—a taxonomy—for types of essays.

FIGURE 16.21

And here we go!

I created a new essay (all lorem ipsum), and you can see that I can roll up to "/essays/" and be able to see all the essays (when there is more than one) (Figure 16.22).

FIGURE 16.22

One essay done!

Is this a perfectly finished use of custom post types? No. I would want to make sure I edited template files so my new custom taxonomies (also known as categories) were visible with the content. I'd probably tweak how the layout looked too for long-form content.

However, if you stopped where I did, you'd still be able to have Essays and the Topics on Menus and included in other parts of your site (Figure 16.23) and read the content. This is amazing and powerful stuff. One plugin and a little experimenting and you have more than just simple posts and pages—you have all sorts of kinds of content that you can create and that doesn't interfere with each other! It might take a few tries to get things right. That's okay, though. This is why if you want to get into custom post types, or really any of the tricks in this chapter, you will want to have a "safe" place to goof around. In Chapter 17, "Advanced WordPress Settings and Uses," I'll show you how to do that. Then you can play around with all these things *before* you put them all online.

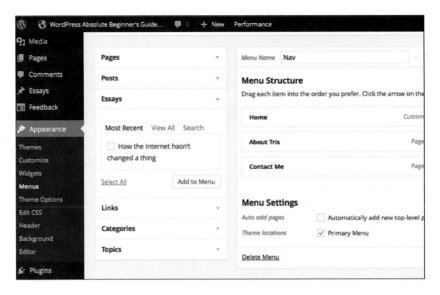

FIGURE 16.23

See! You can add custom post types to menus!

Conclusion

This chapter only scratches the surface of all the customizations and cool tricks you can do with WordPress. We'll get into a few more interesting uses of WordPress in Chapter 17, but I hope these little extras whet your appetite for more. After you start playing with all these ideas, you might get hooked on them. I wholeheartedly encourage playing around with CSS, widgets, icons, and custom post types. There is so much more that can be done that it's impossible to put it all in one chapter of one book.

Lots to do. Lots to explore. Lots of fun.

17

ADVANCED WORDPRESS SETTINGS AND USES

At this point, if you've been reading through the entire book, you're a pretty savvy WordPress user. However, there is still *a lot* more that can be done with WordPress. We've touched on one already—using WordPress to make a "regular" website—but there are things like using WordPress to power forums, make private sites, and even run WordPress on your computer. Then there are the tasks like how to move a WordPress site from one host to another (or from your computer to a host), which can be a lot harder to do right than it seems. These topics are what this chapter is all about—using WordPress in new and different ways.

Using WordPress as a Website

Long before I was writing books about WordPress and blogging, I was helping people create "regular" websites using WordPress. The idea was pretty simple at first, set a Page as the home page with nice graphics and text, use lots of other pages to cover the rest of the content, and then reserve posts for a blog for the site. Back in 2006, this was pretty cutting-edge stuff. For a while, it took a little behind the scenes tweaking, a couple plugins, and more than a little coding to make WordPress a "website." Now in 2013–2014, *not* using WordPress to build your website seems a little silly. There are hundreds of themes available designed not for WordPress as *blog*, but WordPress as *website*. And we've moved on from only using a page as the home page. Now you can keep your front page your "latest Posts"—at least as far as the Reading Settings go—and have a mix of content from posts, pages, widgets, sliders, and galleries all together in one place. And still have a blog, too. So *technically* it's a lot easier to use WordPress to build a website; now the complicated part is picking the theme and content that you want to put there.

In general, there are two ways to use WordPress for a website. First is the home page as static Page model. It works great for many situations and it's very simple to do. In fact, I'll show you how Twenty Twelve was *designed* especially to do that very job beautifully. The other way is to leave the default setting the way it is (the home page is the set of the latest posts), but the *actual* homepage is anything but default. From magazine style themes with widgetized content areas to themes that focus on key pieces of featured content (parts of posts or pages, or both) to one-page themes with several areas that use static content, sliders, Custom Post Types, *and* posts to make an engaging layout, the world of WordPress as a website is pretty amazing. In this section, we'll go through the two main ways and use two different free themes to do it: first the static Page model using Twenty Twelve and then the Customizr theme for the posts as home page layout.

In Chapter 16, "Customizations Without (Much) Coding," I used Twenty Eleven as the example theme, and in this chapter, I'll be using Twenty Twelve because Twenty Twelve has a unique and powerful Page template (remember those from Chapter 11, "Using WordPress: Content") that allows you to combine static content on the front page with a couple handy widget areas. The example page on WordPress.com (http://theme.wordpress.com/themes/twentytwelve/) gives a taste of what you can do with this theme. It has a nice concise landing page with a call to action. Do you want intro text and some space for your latest posts? The sky is the limit, so let's get going on the why and how—and there are lots of "hows" for making WordPress a website—of using WordPress to create a "traditional" website with the static Page model.

For this to work, you need *at least* one page to use as the home page. You can also have a page that will be used as a container for all your blog posts. It serves as a way to have all your posts in one place without having to put *all* the posts in a single category (that you also have to remember to use). For this example, we're going to go with the two-Page setup: a front page and a blog page. The first step is to create the front page.

According to the instructions (the link from earlier), we just need to activate Twenty Twelve, create a page, and make sure to use the Front Page template. To get the look in the example (Figure 17.1), we also need to use a featured image that is 624 pixels wide (any height, but I'm going to go for square). I'm going to cheat a little and use a paragraph of lorem ipsum for the text. Figure 17.2 shows the completed page we'll use for the front page.

FIGURE 17.1

The Twenty Twelve demo page.

FIGURE 17.2

Home page ready.

The title for this page matters; it's displayed above the introductory content of the site. So I used a name I'd be able to pick out from a mass of pages but one that also made sense—Welcome. For the blog page, we just make a new page with whatever title (I usually use Blog) and save it. No content is needed in the content area (Figure 17.3). Now to take the first step to making this site into a website. Go to the Reading Settings and under the Front Page Displays, click A Static Page option and pick the two pages we just created from the menus (now you understand why you need to name them something recognizable). Then click to Save Changes (Figure 17.4).

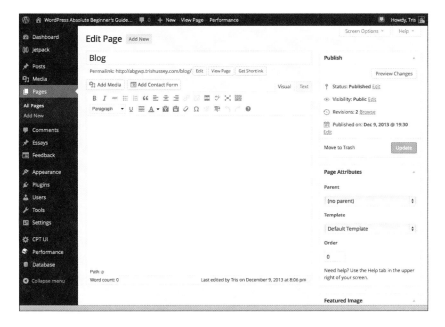

FIGURE 17.3

Creating the blog page.

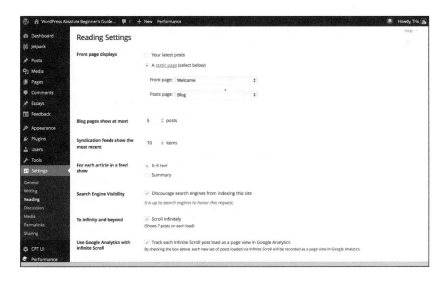

FIGURE 17.4

Reading Settings, set.

You can switch tabs to look at the site and, after refreshing, there it is! The content of the page is there (I added a header to make things look nice) and below are a couple widget areas (Figure 17.5). The example theme page from WordPress. com uses a text block for About the Team and then recent posts. I've done the same using a text widget and a couple handy Jetpack widgets (Figure 17.6). I also added the Blog Page to our menu (and used the Font Awesome pencil icon, which you learned about in Chapter 16), so when you click that menu item, you see all the blog posts published thus far (Figure 17.7). As far as making a "site," that's about it. There isn't a heck of a lot more to do. As you create more content, you decide if the content should be pages or posts or even Custom Post Types. Since we're using a page as a container for all your posts, if you want to have content that is easily connected, like posts, the Custom Post Type route is a good one to take. You might wind up having to look up a little advanced theme editing (maybe) to add the custom taxonomies to the layouts, but at this point this is the start of a great site. Next is taking a step back, resetting the Reading Settings to the default settings (Front Page shows the latest posts) and switching to Customizr so we can use a magazine theme for the website.

FIGURE 17.5

The new layout.

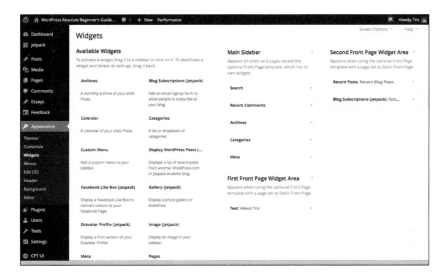

FIGURE 17.6

Twenty Twelve widget settings with two front page widget areas.

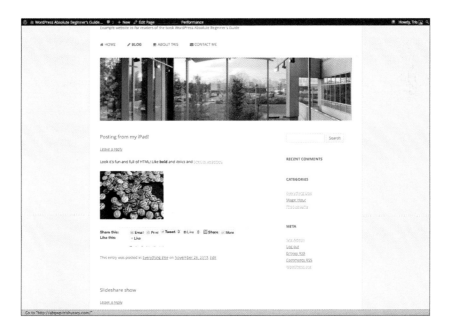

FIGURE 17.7

Blog posts.

Customizr is an interesting option for a theme that has several components to the home page. Just turning it on, you can see the site has a whole new look and feel. It's impressive and dynamic (Figure 17.8) with a slider (which is defined through clever use of Media settings) and the capability to set featured pages to highlight as key content. For posts, you can display as many as you want on the home page, but I think one or two is good for this layout. Customizr, like many other themes of its kind, has a set of menus and options you can use to set the various aspects of the theme and the layout. Customizr happens to use a clever application of the live theme preview so you don't have to hop from settings to site to settings to site to see what looks good (Figure 17.9). For example, here I'm setting what the featured pages are on the home page; before saving the settings, I can see what they look like (Figure 17.10). Customizr is just one example of a theme designed to adapt to different kinds and uses of WordPress. If Customizr looks like the theme for your project, I encourage you to read more about it on its site: http://www.themesandco.com. There are so many different options out there to pull off a website with WordPress. Many themes use the same approach as Customizr, with settings and options to go through and customize for yourself. When you're picking a theme—free or paid—that you want to use for a website, make sure there is good documentation on how to use it. Customizr (which is free), StudioPress (paid), and WooThemes (paid and free) all have examples, sample code, and great user forums (the StudioPress forum is even powered by WordPress) to help you learn how to tap into the power of these themes.

FIGURE 17.8

Using just the default settings, it's pretty cool already.

FIGURE 17.9

The settings screen and preview.

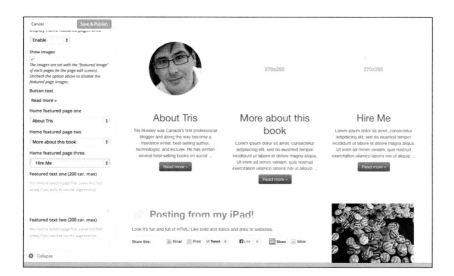

FIGURE 17.10

The Featured Page settings, with preview.

While you're developing your next great online masterpiece, you might want to keep it hidden from the world—probably doing more than just telling search engines not to index it. Welcome to the world of private sites, and the good news is that it takes only a couple plugins.

Making a Private WordPress Site

Whether it's for a site that's in progress and not ready for the whole world or—as we'll cover in a minute—a private site for team communication and collaboration, sometimes things just need to be on a need-to-know basis. The fastest and easiest way to make a private site is with a plugin like Private Only (http://wordpress.org/plugins/private-only/). It does one thing really well: keep people out. The settings are very simple (Figure 17.11), you actually don't need to configure anything. After you install and activate the plugin, only users with Subscriber or higher privileges can see the site. Everyone else? Nope. If you go to the site's URL, you see this (Figure 17.12).

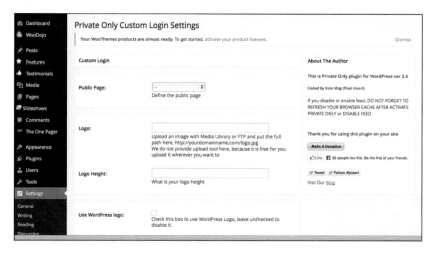

FIGURE 17.11

Private Only settings.

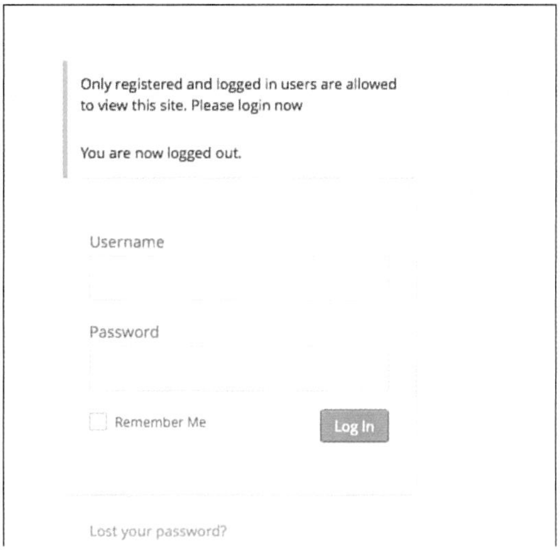

FIGURE 17.12

Sorry, this isn't the site you're looking for.

When you're ready for the site to be public, all you have to do is turn off the plugin. There are a couple of caveats here. First, the people who need access to the site need to remember their usernames and passwords. This can be a challenge for some folks to manage (Why do I have to keep logging into this site? Do you want the rest of the world to see it? No. Then…), but this is the cost of a little measure of security. Also some plugins (like Jetpack and some premium plugins and themes) like to "call home" once in a while. Most of the time, the plugin won't interfere with that process, but it could, so just keep an eye out if you're having issues getting something working. Now that you have a private site, how about using that bit of knowledge to make a new communication and collaboration site with WordPress? Not possible? Oh, yes it is.

WordPress for Communication and Collaboration with P2

In May 2009, the folks at Automattic unveiled P2 (http://wordpress.org/themes/p2), a new theme built especially for collaboration. In the announcement post—http://ma.tt/2009/05/how-p2-changed-automattic/—Matt Mullenweg talked about how P2 evolved from the theme Prologue, which was one of the first themes to let people create posts from the home page, and how Automattic (with its decentralized, mostly remote workforce) needed something to be able to communicate without getting bogged down with emails. P2 grew out of the need to stay in touch, converse, comment, see updates in real-time, and be able to follow specific conversations more closely. At the end of the post, Matt says this:

> It completely transformed how Automattic works internally and I think is one of the most valuable things we've adopted in the past year. I'm on the road a lot, and sometimes my only connection is checking the mobile-optimized P2 on my iPhone.

> I'm excited about P2 partly because blogs provide an incredibly robust infrastructure on which to build more advanced apps, and this is a good example of that. I'd love to see more themes that transform what WordPress can do top-to-bottom.

That was four years ago, and P2 has only gotten better. I've used it on a number of projects and although design-wise it's spartan, functionality-wise it's rich (Figure 17.13). You create posts from the top of the home page, tag with keywords to help people track conversations and topics, and post. Simple. When your team visits P2, all the new posts and comments won't just be at the top of the page; they will be highlighted with a subtle yellow color. As you read, the color fades away. P2 is great and works really well, but the folks at WooThemes took it a step further with a child theme called Houston (http://www.woothemes.com/2013/11/houston-we-have-lift-off/ ; http://wordpress.org/themes/houston). Like Automattic, WooThemes needed to keep its folks in the loop, even when they couldn't be in the same space (or even if they were in the same space). They loved P2, and because P2 can work as a parent theme for other themes, they started work on their own version—Houston (Figure 17.14). Combining P2 or Houston with plugins like P2 by Email (http://wordpress.org/plugins/p2-by-email/) and Markdown for P2 (http://wordpress.org/plugins/markdown-for-p2/) and many others (http://wordpress.org/plugins/tags/p2) can enhance your P2 or Houston-powered site with additional functions and settings. In the end, if you can get more communication, more collaboration, and less email, you're going to come out ahead of the game.

FIGURE 17.13

P2 in action.

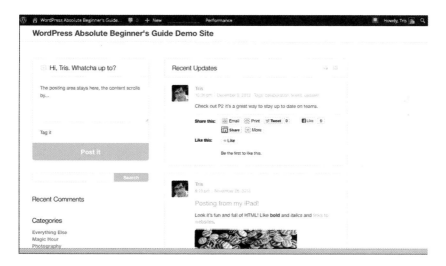

FIGURE 17.14

Houston, with its similar take on the P2 design.

Setting Up Forums in WordPress

Maybe a private site or collaboration site isn't what you need. How about a forum? How about a place where people can post, discuss, and answer things? Forums are some of the oldest tools on the Internet, except that many of the ones that are web-based are a royal pain to set up, use, and maintain. Between a raft of settings and keeping spammers at bay, forums can be more hassle than they are worth. That is why Matt Mullenweg created bbPress, a forum system that is built as a WordPress plugin so you can run it either as a portion of an existing site or run it on its own separate site (using WordPress) (Figure 17.15).

FIGURE 17.15

bbPress home page.

After you download and install the bbPress plugin, getting a forum set up takes just a few minutes (Figure 17.16). The bbPress Codex is a good starting place— http://codex.bbpress.org/step-by-step-guide-to-setting-up-a-bbpress-forum/—but here is the real gist (and how I got a little confused in the first place). When you think of a "forum," you need to think a little more broadly than just "a place for discussion"; think "a container for discussions," and these containers can have parent-child relationships (to define the topics for discussion). For example, on one of my sites, I have a parent forum for beta testers and then child forums for release notes, bug reports, feedback, and feature requests. Topics, in the bbPress world, aren't groups of conversations; they are the first post in a discussion, within a forum. In the old forum parlance, they are posts, threads, or discussions. Topics were the idea of what bbPress uses for child forums. After you get your head wrapped around that, bbPress is a breeze. You can create new topics and replies from the admin Dashboard or from the site. You have control over users and what they can do. You can make your forum as locked down or open as you want. One of the big problems with managing forums is keeping spammers and spam out of the equation. Thankfully, bbPress is fully integrated with Akismet, so you're covered there, too.

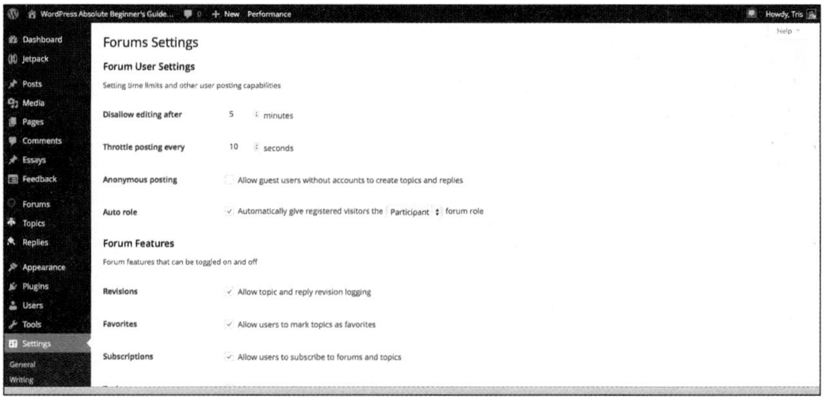

FIGURE 17.16

bbPress settings.

I created a couple forums on the demo site along with a primary parent (WordPress Questions) and a child (Writing and Creating Content). On the site (using the new default theme Twenty Fourteen), it looks like Figure 17.17, and in the admin Dashboard, the forums look like Figure 17.18. If topics (the threads of discussion) have been started and replied to on the site, it looks like Figure 17.19. Now on the Dashboard, the Topics are in one place (Figure 17.20) and the Replies are in another (Figure 17.21). I find that a little disjointed, but this isn't what your visitors see; it's what you, as the admin, see in the back end. So users just think they are seeing a forum that works.

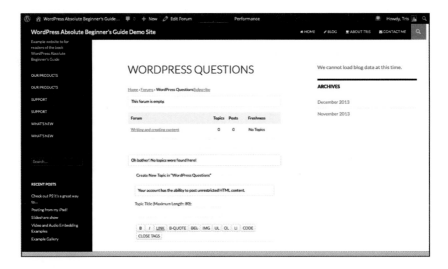

FIGURE 17.17

The forum is open!

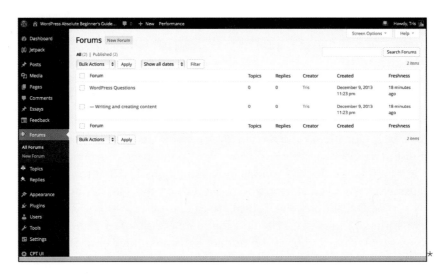

FIGURE 17.18

Forums in the Dashboard.

FIGURE 17.19

Topic and reply.

FIGURE 17.20

Topics in the Dashboard.

FIGURE 17.21

Replies in the Dashboard.

As far as making your forum look cool, like StudioPress has done (Figure 17.22), it's just a matter of using a theme for your forum. For a starter forum, you can stick with your current theme and grow from there.

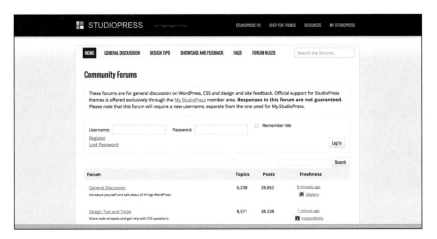

FIGURE 17.22

StudioPress.com forums, powered by bbPress.

Because your site can't *really* run two themes at once, if you want a completely different look and feel for a forum, you either run the forum as a separate install of WordPress *or* learn more about making custom WordPress themes. The former you have covered through this book; the other is a book for another day.

What if you want to experiment on your own, without even a host or domain or anything but a computer? Can you "try out" WordPress on your own computer without anyone on the Internet being able to get to it? Absolutely. Having a local install of WordPress is how most of us develop our new WordPress themes and sites, not to mention how we learn and experiment. So how do you pull this off? It just takes a little downloading.

Running WordPress on Your Computer

Yes, I know I said that WordPress isn't like a program you run and install on your computer. So how can you run WordPress on your computer if it isn't designed to run on a computer? Simple, we install all the extra programs that servers have running, and then we can run WordPress. Yep, I'm saying we make your computer a little server.

NOTE   Just because we're making your computer a server, that doesn't mean that people can get to your computer through the Internet and start browsing around. We're putting the software in place that servers run and have, but *not* opening your computer up to the world. Your computer will stay nicely hidden on your network at home behind your router and everything. Yes, if you know what you're doing, you *can* take what I'm showing you here and make your computer available on the Internet. But most, okay all, Internet service providers frown upon this. So don't. Not unless you really know what you're doing and know the risks. For now we're going to keep things safe and locked away.

The first step is to get the right components. In the server world, the generic term for what is needed for WordPress to run is called a LAMP stack. LAMP stands for Linux Apache MySQL PHP. Linux is the operating system, Apache the web server, MySQL the database program, and PHP is the scripting language. Now most of us aren't running Linux—we're running Macs or Windows, so do you have to switch to Linux? Not at all, because there are MAMP and WAMP stacks too (Mac and Windows, respectively)! Here's the gotcha, though; using a generic MAMP or WAMP stack is going to mean doing a lot of manual things to install WordPress. Hard? Nope. More than many folks want to deal with to experiment? Yes. On the other side, if you are thinking about getting into WordPress development and this book is your first foray into that world, then learning to use a generic MAMP or WAMP stack is a really good idea. For everyone else, I have something better: a prepackaged stack that installs WordPress, all the other components, and does all the configuring for you. It *is* like being able to run WordPress on your computer like any other program!

If you want to check out a generic MAMP stack, MAMP from MAMP.info (Figure 17.23) is the choice of every programmer and developer I know (on a Mac). For Windows, XAMPP (http://www.apachefriends.org/en/xampp.html) (Figure 17.24) is the leading choice. Those aren't the only choices out there, just the *most flexible* ones. For something prepackaged to just run apps WordPress (and many others), I love BitNami and its stack bundles (Figure 17.25), and the one for WordPress is especially awesome (Figure 17.26). After you download the application, just run the installer and go through the steps. The installer will ask you for your name, email, username, password, and what you'd like to call your site. Remember, these are standard things WordPress needs regardless of where it's installed, so don't worry. The rest of the install process takes just a couple minutes more, and when it's done you can click to visit your new site and log in (Figure 17.27), and there will be a little controller program running that lets you relaunch your new WordPress site (and shut it down) when you need to work on it again (Figure 17.28). Beyond that, WordPress works just the same. There might be a few plugins (like Jetpack) that don't behave quite right because your local install of WordPress isn't accessible on the Internet, but that's about it. Remember, because this local install isn't available on the Internet, you can't send someone the link that you see in your browser (http://127.0.0.1:8080) and have them arrive at your computer. That URL is also referred to as localhost and references the machine you're on. Your localhost is your computer, your friend's localhost is your friend's computer. Adding more WordPress instances requires downloading an additional WordPress module and running the installer for it. The module assumes that you already have a stack installed on your machine. I use BitNami over MAMP because I can install WordPress quickly and just as quickly *uninstall* it if I don't need the demo server around anymore.

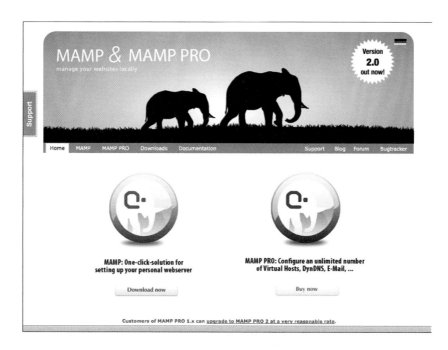

FIGURE 17.23

MAMP.info.

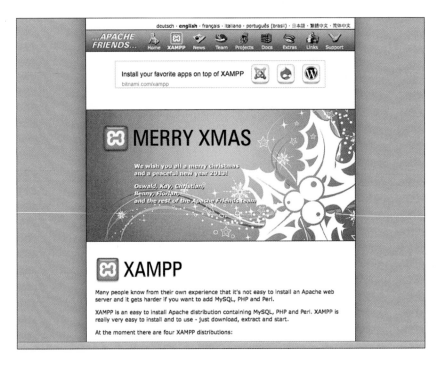

FIGURE 17.24

XAMPP.

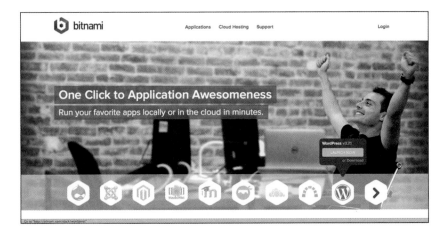

FIGURE 17.25

BitNami.com.

FIGURE 17.26

BitNami WordPress stack.

FIGURE 17.27

Local launch page for WordPress.

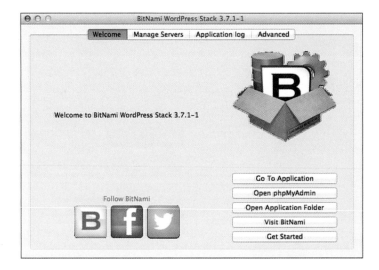

FIGURE 17.28

BitNami controller program.

So what if you have made an awesome site locally and you want to move it to a host (or WordPress.com if you're just making content)? Possible or problematic? Possible—in fact, with the right tools, it's pretty easy.

Moving a WordPress Site

There are a few ways to move a site from one host to another or from your machine up to a host. Before we get into the mechanics of it, let's talk about what actually needs to be moved. First, is your content. If you've written content you want to keep, you'll want to move that. Next are the images with that content and with your theme (headers, backgrounds, and the like). Next is the theme *if* you've customized it. If you haven't done anything special to it, you don't actually need to move the theme, you just need to install it. Plugins are a toss-up for moving. It's handy to move them, but unless you're moving the database, too, you'll just have to reenter the settings anyway. WordPress itself? You also don't need to move it. You can just do a nice, clean install of that on your new host.

Here's the easy way to move a WordPress site. Set up your new WordPress site on the new host. If you are going to be switching your domain to that host, too, ask them for help to make the switch and moving as painless as possible:

- Export the content from your local install or old host.

- Import into your new site (we covered this in Chapter 11) with the images.

- Install the plugins and theme you need.
- Reconfigure everything.

Yes, this involves redoing settings and widgets and all the rest. However, all your content should be there, and by reinstalling plugins and themes, you make sure that the settings are correct and not pointing to the wrong places. This method doesn't, however, also involve exporting your database, importing your database, and making sure all the references to the old site are removed from the database. Messing around with databases is not something to be taken lightly. If you mess up your database, you're in a world of hurt—a world where I hope you took the backup advice from Chapter 15, "Maintaining WordPress Sites," seriously. Still, if you're a little braver, I suggest the Duplicator plugin I mentioned in Chapter 15, which makes the process of moving your site, all the files, *and* the database about as painless as I can imagine.

Duplicator doesn't just package up and make a copy of your site, it also creates an installer script to put everything right where you expect it to be. After download-ing and installing the plugin, you open the Duplicator page to create a package. There is a link to make sure your server where the site is can handle the plugin. Click that to be sure everything will work, then create your package (Figure 17.29). When it's done, you'll download two files: the installer and the package (Figure 17.30). The installer is just a little PHP file, and the package is a compressed copy of your site (with everything in it). So a giant site will be a giant download. The demo site isn't too big, but still a few megabytes.

FIGURE 17.29

Creating the Duplicator package.

FIGURE 17.30

Package complete.

To use the installer and package, you need to drop them into an empty directory on your host (or local MAMP or WAMP install), create an empty database, and go to installer.php in your browser (Figure 17.31). Yes, the wording is dire and it needs to be. If you don't pay attention, you can very easily take out a live site. When it's all said and done, you should have a perfect mirror of your site, but in a new home. So what is Duplicator doing? The big thing it's doing is moving your database *and* changing all the references from the old location to the new one (Figure 17.32). This is no mean feat. If you manually export your database using a tool like phpMyAdmin and then *import* the database to the new location (also using phpMyAdmin), you're not even close to done yet. Before you kick off the new WordPress site, you have to make sure the database is pointing to the new home or you might accidentally change something on the *original* site, not the *new* one (believe me, I've done it more than once).

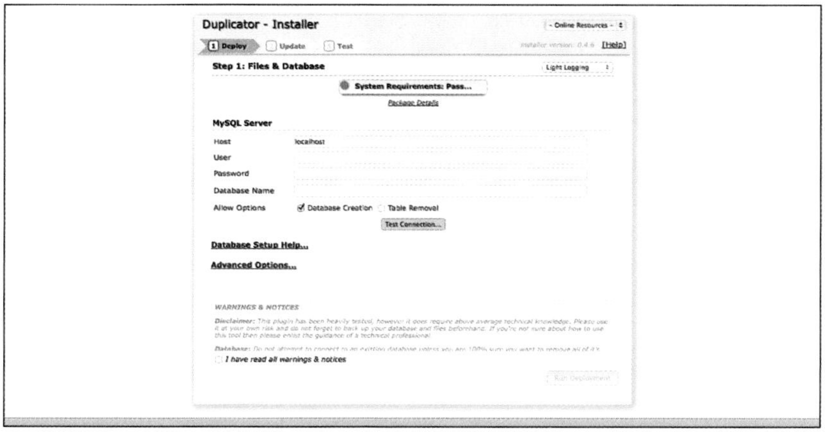

FIGURE 17.31

Ready to redeploy the site in a new home.

FIGURE 17.32

Old settings to new settings. Changes made for you!

After Duplicator is finished, you can log in to your site with the same username and password you had before. It's pretty amazing how well it works. Sure, some plugins might not take kindly to the move; however, in my tests, I've been very pleased with the results of the moves and haven't had any show-stopper issues. After years of moving sites either the "easy" way (which might be easy, but is also time consuming to reset everything) and the hard way before finding Duplicator (which has led to a lot of swearing and finding the right database queries to run to fix things), I'm glad I'm using Duplicator now. I have found hosts where it doesn't work, where it looks like it runs out of memory or something before it finishes. However, if you are moving a site, you might think about not just using Duplicator, but also having a geek friend in your back pocket to call in for help.

Conclusion

This chapter has, I hope, opened your eyes to lots of possibilities for using WordPress. Not long ago, building a website with WordPress was a chore; now it's an accepted best practice in web development (because of the time it saves and the results you can get). So a website now might be old hat, but forums, collaboration platforms, and private sites are pretty cool options that are only getting more sophisticated.

I have one last piece of advice for you when trying things in this chapter: read up on the latest updates and be patient. Lots of these tasks (like moving your WordPress site to a new host) have steps that you need to follow closely. Forums, even bbPress, can still be complicated if you don't take some time and read a bit more on their ins and outs. Patience. Reading. More patience. Those are the keys to these advanced topics.

18

TROUBLESHOOTING COMMON WORDPRESS PROBLEMS

I hope you don't ever have to use this chapter. Really. It's no fun when your website breaks. However, given all its complexity, WordPress doesn't actually break all that often for most people. Not that WordPress, or any of its pieces and parts, is perfect—it's just that WordPress seems to be rather *forgiving* when things go wrong. This chapter won't, in fact, be very long or very complicated. For the scope of this book, if the easy fixes I can offer don't work, you're going to need to call in an expert. The sage advice I can offer here is the equivalent of if you emailed me that your site was having an issue, gave me some basics details, and I email back with suggestions. These are the "my best guess without seeing it" kinds of fixes. It's a good thing that most of the time that's all you need.

Fixing Problem Plugins

There is a BBC show called *The IT Crowd* where the intrepid IT support team answers most calls with, "Have you tried turning it off and back on again?" Yeah, this isn't just an IT cliché, it really does fix a lot of issues—especially with plugins. It's mostly the turning off part. If your site is not behaving or is behaving strangely, try disabling the last plugin you installed. If that doesn't help, disable *all* the plugins and see how the site works then. Better? Good, then turn your plugins back on one at a time, checking to make sure that things are still working all along the way (go to the home page of your site, refresh, click around). Hopefully, this will narrow down the list of suspects that are causing issues. If you install a plugin and it immediately breaks your site *and* you can't get back to the Dashboard to disable it, don't panic. Just launch your handy FTP program, connect to your site, and navigate to wp-content/plugins/. Find the plugin you just loaded and delete it. You should be able to reload the Dashboard now. When you visit the plugins page within the Dashboard, you'll see a nasty warning that such and such plugin can't be found so it has been deactivated, and so on. This is *exactly* what you want. WordPress might grumble when a plugin disappears, but it usually doesn't *break*.

If you have a plugin that was working but has gotten messed up, there are two ways to approach the problem. One, if the plugin has an option or button to reset to default settings, do that. Starting from scratch often helps set things straight. If that doesn't work, go into the plugins list and delete the plugin. First deactivate the plugin; then click the Delete link. WordPress asks you on the next screen if you really want to delete the files or just go back (Figure 18.1). After you delete the plugin, try reinstalling a new copy from the plugin repository and starting over. It happens; maybe the last update hiccupped at the wrong moment, maybe something else caused the plugin to break. Often, just deleting and reinstalling a plugin fixes a lot of issues.

FIGURE 18.1

Deleting a plugin.

Still not working? Then you are looking at one of several issues that could be going on: two plugins conflicting with each other (like two social sharing plugins, two caching plugins, two SEO plugins) or the plugin isn't compatible with that version of WordPress. You can maybe find out the latter by looking at the plugin details on the WordPress plugin repository, but often there isn't enough data to know. In these cases, your best bet is to call in someone who can troubleshoot the issue with you. Good thing the chances of it getting to that point are pretty low.

Untangling WordPress Theme Issues

Themes are a whole other place where things can go sideways (or pear shaped or just plain broken). Unlike plugins, themes are a little trickier to fix. The first step, if your site is looking just wrong (and you're sure it's not a plugin issue), is to switch to another theme like Twenty Ten, Eleven, Twelve, or the like. Choose one of the basic, default, works-all-the-time themes. If it's a new post that looks like it's causing the issue (sometimes post issues *look* like theme issues), push it back to draft. After you get your site looking okay in a default theme, switch back to your regular theme and try resetting the settings. Check and disable new widgets. Just start looking at the different theme functions and try setting them back to defaults. Custom CSS? Get rid of it (copy your changes and paste into a text file first so you don't lose them). If you're still having problems, delete the theme. You'll have to switch to another theme before deleting, but after you do that, you can reinstall a fresh copy and try again. While working on this book, I was trying early builds of Twenty Fourteen and I just couldn't get it to work right. Finally, deleting and reinstalling it fixed everything. Often that's the simplest way to go.

That brings me to customized themes. If you start customizing a theme—that is, editing the files of the theme and not making a child theme or using Custom CSS, you need to keep a clean, unedited, untouched version of that original theme handy for just these occasions. More than a few times I've edited a theme and gotten things so messed up, I had to start over. It happens, so you want to have clean copies handy of themes you work on, just in case.

Fixing a Damaged Database

If you're having database issues or your database has been corrupted by a hacker, the only thing to tell you is I hope you have backups of the database. Really, I'm sorry that's the only real option. Most of the time when a database has gone south, the only way to fix it is to find the last good, uncorrupted copy and replace the database with that one. Yes, you might lose posts. Yes, you might have to redo some settings or plugins. But often that's the only hope. Also, this might not be something you want to take on yourself. Database stuff can be tricky. I'm okay with erasing my database and bringing up an old one from a backup, but really digging in and fixing tables and other problems? Nope, I'd call in favors for that.

Don't worry if you have to call in an expert to fix your database; sometimes all of us do.

When WordPress Doesn't Work

What if the site won't come up at all? You get something like a 500 configuration error. Panic? A little panicking is understandable, but don't worry, there are ways to start working through the causes and solutions. Here's a checklist of things to start with:

- Check whether you can get to the Dashboard. If yes, then it's probably a theme or plugin issue that can be fixed easily (see the section earlier in this chapter).

- Ask a friend to check your site. Sometimes it might be just you.

- Contact your host. Ask them if something is up. Sometimes it's not even your site that's having a problem—it's your host.

So if you can't get to the Dashboard, your friend says your site is toast, and your host says that it isn't them, it's time to step things up.

- FTP into your site and go to wp-content/plugins/. Take a screenshot or write down all your plugins; then delete them all. Yes, all of them.

- Try your site and Dashboard again. Sometimes a single plugin or too many plugins has caused the site to flip out. Usually this is just the kick in the pants it needs to reset itself.

- If you're using a caching plugin, delete the cache files from wp-content. Try again.

- If that didn't do it, copy/download your theme down to your computer and delete that, too. WordPress will switch to one of the other themes automatically.

If your site still isn't working, the next thing to try is a bit of a nuclear option, but it's nearly the last step before calling in your local WordPress geek to help: deleting WordPress and reloading.

Here's what you do. First, go to WordPress.org and download the latest version of WordPress. Unzip the file so you can see all the files. Through FTP, delete all the WordPress files *except* wp-config.php and wp-content. Then upload the files from your computer, making sure you do *not* upload wp-content; you want to keep that directory. Remember, the only irreplaceable things in WordPress are the things you've uploaded and changed. Pretty much that's what's in wp-content. Keeping wp-config.php is more of a convenience so you don't have to reenter your database information. After all that uploading, see if your site is back. Yes, sometimes even WordPress gets corrupted (rarely, but I've seen it happen a few times), and deleting all the files and starting fresh can fix things.

At this point, if WordPress and your site aren't working, you've got a bigger problem, something that you're going to need help fixing.

Help! I've Been Hacked!

It happens, even to the best of us. Unfortunately, when people get hacked, they don't know for a while because the hacks are typically very clever. The common WordPress hacks insert spammy code into your posts and pages for, well, the stuff you see in your spam folder. After doing the obvious thing of changing your WordPress password and all the passwords of the users of the site, you're going to need to call in an expert. If you've been hacked, the fixes are complicated, and you need people who have fixed these problems before to help. If you have the situation where someone has gotten into your site and is publishing and changing things, that's different. If you're not locked out of your site, change all the passwords. If you *are* locked out of your site, ask your host or a geeky friend about resetting passwords right in the database, and then get help locking your site back down again.

What are the best ways to keep from getting hacked? First, keep WordPress, your plugins, and themes updated, and then use good, strong passwords for your site. Don't use an admin account with the username "admin". Don't use the same password you use for other sites. Don't share your account with other people. One person, one account, and insist on strong passwords for all users who have administrator privileges. Most of keeping from getting hacked is prevention: updates and good passwords.

Conclusion

I hope if you needed to use this chapter that your site is back and working. Just remember, if something goes wrong, don't panic. If you have backups, you're probably going to be okay. Even if you don't have backups, you'll probably be okay. As long as your WordPress database is intact, you'll be able to get your site and content back. You might have to redownload a lot of plugins and your themes, but your words will be there. You might lose images, but....

Just remember, don't panic. Don't do anything you're unsure of doing because you think it looks like the right thing. And if you get stuck, call in a friend who is a WordPress expert. There are lots of us around, and sometimes all it will take is some pizza and beer to get things straight.

Index

X-Y-Z

FULL COLOR

WordPress®

ABSOLUTE BEGINNER'S GUIDE

No experience necessary!

que

Tris Hussey

Safari
Books Online

FREE
Online Edition

Your purchase of *WordPress Absolute Beginner's Guide* includes access to a free online edition for 45 days through the **Safari Books Online** subscription service. Nearly every Que book is available online through **Safari Books Online**, along with thousands of books and videos from publishers such as Addison-Wesley Professional, Cisco Press, Exam Cram, IBM Press, O'Reilly Media, Prentice Hall, Sams, and VMware Press.

Safari Books Online is a digital library providing searchable, on-demand access to thousands of technology, digital media, and professional development books and videos from leading publishers. With one monthly or yearly subscription price, you get unlimited access to learning tools and information on topics including mobile app and software development, tips and tricks on using your favorite gadgets, networking, project management, graphic design, and much more.

Activate your FREE Online Edition at
informit.com/safarifree

STEP 1: Enter the coupon code: KDJNJFH.

STEP 2: New Safari users, complete the brief registration form.
Safari subscribers, just log in.

If you have difficulty registering on Safari or accessing the online edition,
please e-mail customer-service@safaribooksonline.com